Integrating CATS

SAP® Essentials

Expert SAP knowledge for your day-to-day work

Whether you wish to expand your SAP knowledge, deepen it, or master a use case, SAP Essentials provide you with targeted expert knowledge that helps support you in your day-to-day work. To the point, detailed, and ready to use.

SAP PRESS is a joint initiative of SAP and Galileo Press. The know-how offered by SAP specialists combined with the expertise of the Galileo Press publishing house offers the reader expert books in the field. SAP PRESS features first-hand information and expert advice, and provides useful skills for professional decision-making.

SAP PRESS offers a variety of books on technical and business related topics for the SAP user. For further information, please visit our website: *www.sap-press.com*.

Manuel Gallardo
Configuring and Using CATS
2008, 159 pp.
978-1-59229-232-5

Brian Schaer
Time Management with SAP ERP HCM
2008, app. 500 pp.
978-1-59229-229-5

Jeremy Masters and Christos Kotsakis
Implementing Employee and Manager Self-Services in SAP ERP HCM
2008, 432 pp.
978-1-59229-188-5

Martin Gillet

Integrating CATS

Bonn • Boston

Contents

1 Introduction 11

- 1.1 About the Content 11
- 1.2 Functionalities Update with ERP 5.0 12
- 1.3 Functionalities Update with ERP 6.0 12
- 1.4 Introduction to the Cross Application Time Sheet 13
- 1.5 Brief Technical Overview 15
- 1.6 Integration Overview 16
- 1.7 What You Will Learn in this Essentials Guide 19
  - 1.7.1 Acknowledgments 19

2 Customizing and Enhancing CATS 21

- 2.1 Customizing the CATS Data-Entry Profiles 23
  - 2.1.1 General Settings 25
  - 2.1.2 Time Settings 27
  - 2.1.3 Person Selection 28
  - 2.1.4 Organizational Unit 30
  - 2.1.5 Cost Center 30
  - 2.1.6 Selection Report 30
  - 2.1.7 Accounting Variant 30
  - 2.1.8 Default Values 31
  - 2.1.9 Worklist 32
  - 2.1.10 General Data-Entry Checks 33
  - 2.1.11 Print Entry Data Sheet 35
  - 2.1.12 Integrating CATS with Workflow 35
  - 2.1.13 Determine Variant of Approval Report for Workflow 40
- 2.2 Customizing the CATS Fields 42
  - 2.2.1 Screen Grouping—Settings 43
  - 2.2.2 Screen Grouping—Worklist 43
  - 2.2.3 Screen Grouping—Data-Entry Section 43
  - 2.2.4 Hiding New Fields According to SAP Release 43
- 2.3 Customizing CATS for Web-Enabling 44

5

Contents

	2.3.1	Create Data-Entry Profile for Employee Self-Services (ESS)	44
	2.3.2	Record Working Time	45
	2.3.3	Release Working Times	48
	2.3.4	Create Data-Entry Profile for ESS	51
	2.3.5	Specify Additional Information for ESS Profile	51
	2.3.6	Define Field Selection for ESS	54
	2.3.7	Edit Possible Entries in the Search Help	55
	2.3.8	Select Allowed Absence Types	56
2.4	Additional CATS Customizing	59
	2.4.1	Define Print Report	59
	2.4.2	Define Authorization Groups	59
	2.4.3	Specify Task Types, Components, and Levels	59
	2.4.4	Define Rejection Reasons for the Approval Process	61
	2.4.5	Determine How to Fill CO Documents during Transfer to Controlling	63
2.5	Enhancing CATS	65
	2.5.1	Determine the Target Hours	66
	2.5.2	Compile the Worklist	67
	2.5.3	Supplement Recorded Data	67
	2.5.4	Validate Recorded Data	68
	2.5.5	Deactivate Functions in the User Interface	70
	2.5.6	Customer Fields Enhancements	72
	2.5.7	Validate Entire Time Sheet	73
	2.5.8	Subscreen on the Initial Screen	73
	2.5.9	Determine Workflow Recipient for Approval	74
	2.5.10	Customer-Specific Text Fields in Data-Entry Profile	75
	2.5.11	Customer-Specific Text Fields in Worklist	76
	2.5.12	Customer Functions	76
	2.5.13	Subscreen on Data-Entry Screen	77
	2.5.14	Exit for Time Sheet Transfer to BW	77
2.6	Lessons Learned	80

3 Integration with Human Resources 83

3.1	Background Information for the Human Resources Module	83
	3.1.1 Enterprise Structure	85
	3.1.2 Personnel Structure	86

3.2	Human Resources Mini-Master Data		87
	3.2.1	0000—Actions (Must Have)	87
	3.2.2	0302—Additional Actions in Infotype 0000—Actions (Nice to Have)	88
	3.2.3	0001—Organizational Assignment (Must Have)	88
	3.2.4	0002—Personal Data (Must Have)	89
	3.2.5	0315—CATS Time Sheet Defaults (Nice to Have)	90
3.3	Time Management Infotypes		92
	3.3.1	0007—Personal Work Schedule (Nice to Have Even Without Time Management)	92
	3.3.2	2006—Absence Quotas (to be Set Up with Time Management)	93
	3.3.3	2001—Absences (to be Set Up with Time Management)	96
	3.3.4	2002—Attendances (to be Set Up with Time Management)	97
	3.3.5	2010—Employee's Remuneration Statement (to be Set Up with Time Management)	98
3.4	Human Resources Personnel Development		99
3.5	Practical Applications		102
	3.5.1	Option Required to Record Times in Time Sheet Enabled	103
3.6	Lessons Learned		105

4 Integration with Finance and Controlling ... 107

4.1	Background Information for Financial Accounting		107
	4.1.1	Key Elements for Integrating CATS with Financial Accounting	107
	4.1.2	CATS Integration in Financial Accounting	109
	4.1.3	Integration between Human Resources and Financial Accounting	109
	4.1.4	Basic Information about Financial Accounting	112
4.2	CATS Customizing Integration with Financial Accounting		118
	4.2.1	Focusing on the Available Fields for Controlling	121
	4.2.2	Focusing on Document Generation	122
	4.2.3	Available User-Exit to Enhance CATS Flexibility in Controlling	124
	4.2.4	CATS and Controlling Transfer	124
4.3	Lessons Learned		126

5 Integration with Plant Maintenance and Customer Service 127

- 5.1 Background Information for Plant Maintenance 127
  - 5.1.1 Key Elements for Integrating CATS with PM and CS 127
  - 5.1.2 Basic Information about PM 128
- 5.2 CATS Integration for PM 136
  - 5.2.1 Focusing on Available Fields for PM 136
  - 5.2.2 Available User-Exit to Enhance CATS Flexibility 137
  - 5.2.3 CATS and Plant Maintenance Transfer 137
- 5.3 Lessons Learned 138

6 Integration with Project System 139

- 6.1 Background Information for Project System 139
- 6.2 Setting Up CATS Integration with the Project System Module 140
  - 6.2.1 Basic Information About PS Transactions to Be Integrated ... 140
- 6.3 CATS Integration for Project System 145
  - 6.3.1 Focusing on the Available Fields for PS 145
  - 6.3.2 Available User-Exit to Enhance CATS Flexibility 146
  - 6.3.3 CATS and PS Transfer 146
- 6.4 Lessons Learned 148

7 Integration with External Services Management 149

- 7.1 Background Information for External Services Management 149
  - 7.1.1 Basic Information for MM 150
  - 7.1.2 Integration with Human Resources 152
- 7.2 CATS Integration Aspects for Materials Management 158
  - 7.2.1 Focusing on the Available Fields for Materials Management 158
  - 7.2.2 CATS and Materials Management Transfer 158
- 7.3 Lessons Learned 160

8 Authorizations for CATS 161

- 8.1 Setting Up the Authorization Group 161
- 8.2 Assigning the Authorization Group to the Data-Entry Profile 162

8.3	Restricting Access to a Determined Data-Entry Profile and/or for Own Personnel		163
8.4	Authorization for Reporting in CATS		164
8.5	Lessons Learned		165

9 Reporting for CATS 167

9.1	Employee Listing		167
9.2	Master Data Export		168
9.3	Display Working Times		170
	9.3.1	Data Sources	171
	9.3.2	Document Flow Analysis	172
	9.3.3	Display Work Times, Tasks, and Activities	172
9.4	Time Levelling CATC		174
9.5	Display Single Document		177
9.6	Approve Working Times from R/3 backend		177
	9.6.1	Approve Working Times (Selection by Master Data)	177
	9.6.2	Approve Working Times	179
	9.6.3	Approve Working Times and Travel Expenses	181
9.7	Approve Working Times from the Portal		183
	9.7.1	Introducing a New Functionality	183
	9.7.2	Customizing the New Web Dynpro Approval Screen	185
	9.7.3	Working with the New Approval Screen	190
	9.7.4	Collective Approval	191
	9.7.5	Individual Approval	192
	9.7.6	Review and Save	193
9.8	CATS General Reporting		194
9.9	Archiving		198
9.10	Reorganizing the Time Sheet		199
9.11	User-Linking to Employees		200
9.12	Common Authorization Reporting		202
9.13	Reporting per Target Component		203
	9.13.1	Human Resources	203
	9.13.2	Finance & Controlling	203
	9.13.3	Plant Maintenance & Customer Service	203
	9.13.4	Project System	203
	9.13.5	Materials Management	204
9.14	Lessons Learned		204

Appendices 205

- **A Resource Guide** 207
  - A.1 List of Transaction Codes 207
  - A.2 Message Class HRTIM00CATS 207
  - A.3 List Tables and Structures 208
  - A.4 Summary of Fields Used in CATS and Target Components 209
  - A.5 CATS Configuration Assistant 212
  - A.6 CATS BAPIs 215
  - A.7 CATS BAdIS 217
  - A.8 Some Useful OSS Notes 217
  - A.9 Websites 218
  - A.10 Recommended Readings 219
    - A.10.1 Recommended Articles 219
    - A.10.2 Recommended Books 220
- **B Frequently Asked Questions** 221
- **C Bibliography** 227

Index 229

1 Introduction

1.1 About the Content

This Essentials guide will provide a broad overview of the Cross Application Time Sheet, also known as CATS. Although there are several ways to collect times in SAP, we will focus on the CATS classic and CATS regular versions, which enable employees to collect times in the R/3 back-end or through the company's intranet (or via the Internet) if the security protocol allows it.

We will cover the basics of CATS, from understanding its concept to setting up and configuring the time sheet according to the business requirements. Through practical examples, we will guide you in using and working with CATS, including times collection, the releasing process, the approval step, the transfer to the respective receiving modules, and their integration with CATS.

We will introduce the required master data (among the target SAP components), the reporting, the printed Time Sheet form, the cost determination, the integration with surrounding SAP modules, and authorization.

For the advanced user and the quick learner, we will cover the different user-exits provided, to address particular cases and to stay as close as possible to the SAP standard.

CATS classic and regular being extremely flexible, we will briefly describe additional ways to use the time-collection Time Sheet, such as CATS mobile, CATS mini-app, and CATS for service providers.

The user reference in Appendix A will cover the main tables and transactions, for the quick deployment of CATS. The content of this Essentials guide is based on working with SAP Release 4.7 (R/3 Enterprise). With regard to the SAP Enterprise Portal, we assume that Release 6.0 is in use.

I'd also to take the opportunity to introduce the new SAP CATS functionalities delivered through SAP releases ERP 5.0 and ERP 6.0.

1 | Introduction

1.2 Functionalities Update with ERP 5.0

As of release ERP 5.0 (formerly SAP ERP 2004 or ECC 5.0), SAP made a significant turn into technology. Indeed, they have converted most Internet Transaction Server (ITS) based services into a new screen, known as 'Web Dynpro'. For the Time Sheet, we are migrating from the web based service **CATW** into a new Web Dynpro screen. I have updated and illustrated this new screen in Chapter 2, where you can see the new layout as well as the new Calendar functionality now made available to the end users. This functionality is delivered through the Employee Self-Services (ESS) Business Package. The same functionality is provided throughout ERP 5.0 and 6.0.

Depending on the SAP backend release you are using, this business package (BP) is named:

- As of ERP 5.0 this business package (BP) is named "Business Package for Employee Self-Service (mySAP ERP 2004)" – Release 60.2
- As of ERP 6.0 this business package (BP) is named "Business Package for Employee Self-Service (mySAP ERP) " – Release 1.0

The business packages for Employee Self Services (ESS), which includes the CATS time collection screen, can be downloaded at the following address:

https://www.sdn.sap.com/irj/sdn/contentportfolio -- > Section Business Package for Every User

1.3 Functionalities Update with ERP 6.0

In these challenging times, SAP has finally listened to us. As of release ERP 6.0, SAP provides two main new functionalities for CATS and an important update regarding workflow tasks:

- The possibility to add an approval process in order to avoid sending all time entries to the manager. This functionality is available through the new feature (decision tree) CATEX and the settings in the CATS Data Entry Profile.
- New web enabled screens for Time Entries approval through the SAP Enterprise Portal. These screens, known as Web Dynpros, are providing different views such as the Line Manager and the Project Manager. These views can eas-

ily be adjusted, or you can simply create new ones. This is a major step forward as now the whole time collection and the approval process are now fully web enabled.

- As of ERP 6.0, you can also forget the good 'old' CATS standard workflow tasks delivered by SAP. All CATS workflow tasks have been renewed. These new tasks are effective right away. Former Workflow tasks must be discarded.

In Chapter 9, I'd like to illustrates theses changes and provide you with the latest information regarding these functionalities.

As of ERP 6.0, the business package (BP) for Manager Self-Services (MSS) is named:

- "Business Package for Manager Self-Service (mySAP ERP)" – Release 1.0

The business packages for Employee Self-Services (ESS), which includes the CATS time collection screen, can be downloaded from the following address:

https://www.sdn.sap.com/irj/sdn/contentportfolio -- > Section Business Package for Managers

1.4 Introduction to the Cross Application Time Sheet

Daily information flow is becoming of increasing importance; particularly when it comes to collecting times and activities spent on different projects, purchase orders, or simply attendance at events.

What business entity or company hasn't dreamed of being able in real time to collect the time entries of each employee through a tool that could be used by employees, administrative assistants, project leaders, and managers? This tool would have checked online the accuracy of the time entries, such as the validity period, the budget status, and the quotas available. This useful tool would be accessible online through the intranet or even the Internet thanks to its security features.

Since the early release of R/3, SAP has provided a simple and efficient tool, formally named the Cross Application Time Sheet, better known as CATS. While lacking some functionality, the tool fulfilled its main purpose: to provide a quick, simple, efficient, and user-friendly interface for employees to report on their daily, weekly, or monthly activities. As SAP was evolving through its release cycles, CATS

1 | Introduction

was enriched with more and more functionalities, sometimes in response to questions from user groups.

Today, CATS is a standard tool provided by SAP, to collect employees' working times towards each target component that receives and processes labor time. CATS is provided as standard functionality with R/3, and requires very little customizing to be quickly deployed. Thanks to its flexibility and its means of access, it can closely match each business requirement provided by a company, market, or process.

CATS' major asset is that it provides a single central point of entry for collecting all time entries. Its optional two-step process (release and approval) makes the time-collection loop more clearly visible, allowing each individual to monitor his activities, release the time entries when they are ready to be approved, and to approve or reject the time entries.

These release and approval steps are valuable because they are not available as such in the time confirmation within each module. Furthermore, the approval process is provided in standard form with different workflow tasks, allowing a smooth circulation of the information between the employee, the time administrator, and the manager.

Basically, the system allows two types of entries: individual-entry process or multiple-entry process. An additional nice to have feature is Web-enabling, which allows each individual to collect or book his time entries around the clock, even if he is outside of the company's premises.

SAP has recently enlarged the functionalities by adding an offline solution for its CATS solution and an add-on for PDA use, as well as a solution tailored to service providers.

The CATS family is well equipped to meet every business requirement and makes life easier for every participant in the time-collection process. It is not surprising that sales of CATS through the Internet are among the highest for SAP products.

Figure 1.1 depicts the four-step operation of CATS among related modules. In a nutshell, the key benefits of using CATS are:

- Single point of entry for all working time processes (less administrative paper work)
- Release and approval process to enforce the CATS process-efficiency

- Large panel of interfaces provided for each type of employee (sales representatives, managers, super users, end users, etc.)
- Real-time access to the information, making reporting more accurate
- Information provided to the employee can be defaulted
- Time Sheet can be Web-enabled
- Quicker follow-up on critical projects activities; enhanced billing process thanks to weekly time collection
- Full integration with SAP products: SAP Enterprise Portal, Internet Transaction Server, Business Information Warehouse, etc.

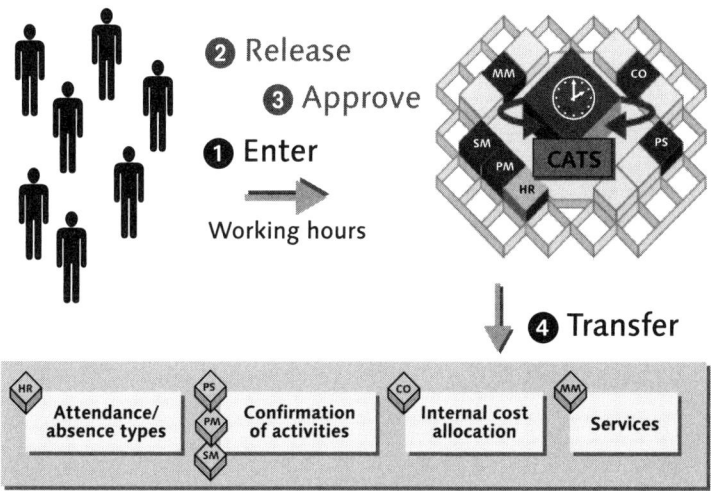

Figure 1.1 CATS and the Surrounding Target Modules

1.5 Brief Technical Overview

To better understand the core structure of CATS, let us look at the main technical information. CATS is built on its own database, the CATSDB, which allows each time-collection step to be safely stored.

Each time entry is sealed with a status that identifies each event in the time collection process:

- Status 10: in process (= time entry saved)

- Status 20: released by the employee (= ready to get through the approval process)
- Status 30: approved data (= document number is issued)
- Status 40: rejected data (= data is returned to the employee for correction)
- Status 50: data has been changed after approval
- Status 60: time entry has been cancelled

Please note that the release and approval steps are optional. Therefore they can be disregarded if not applicable in your time-collection process. Only the time entries marked with the status 30 (approved) are taken into consideration for transfer to the target components. Once the data is approved by the manager or simply upon saving—depending on the customizing settings—the data is inserted and written into the interface tables.

The interface tables are meant to support a clean and smooth relationship between CATS and the target modules. They should never be changed or used for reporting. CATSDB remains the only central database to check, view, or report the time entries.

Hint

Since CATS can process several thousands of records per month, it might be useful, from time to time, to ask the CATS owner within your team to run the transaction code CATR, to check the potential inconsistencies in these tables.

Please execute this transaction code carefully because it can lead to severe inconsistencies if misused. We would strongly advise using the option **Test mode** prior to any real action in a production environment.

1.6 Integration Overview

CATS allows time-entries collection for further processing in SAP target modules. Therefore, one of the components listed below must be installed prior to using CATS. The time entries either can be provided individually or in combination with the target components. Inside SAP core components, nearly all modules can be filled with information through CATS. These include:

- Human Resources (HR): attendance, absences, and remuneration information

- External Services (MM-SRV): entry of services performed by external providers
- Controlling (CO): internal activity allocation, statistical key Figures
- Plant Maintenance (PM): confirmation for orders
- Customer Service (CS, formerly Service Management): confirmation for orders
- Project System (PS): confirmation for networks

As an example look at Figure 1.2 for an understanding of how CATS works in an HR allocation scenario.

Please be aware that the working times are only relevant for labor time spent, not machine time. The Production Planning (PP) module is therefore neither included nor supported in CATS.

CATS is also integrated with the surrounding SAP products, such as:

- Business Intelligence—Business Information Warehouse (BW)
- Enterprise Portal (EP)
- Internet Transaction Server (ITS)
- CATS for Service Provider
- CATS Offline thanks to the Mobile Engine

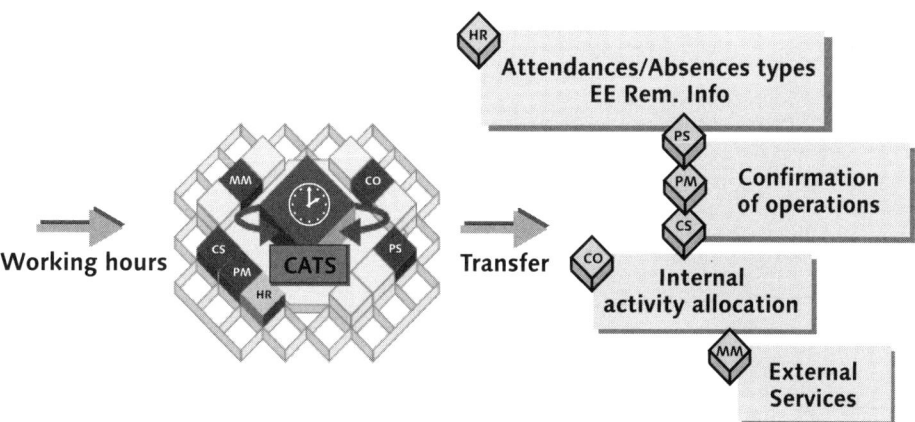

Figure 1.2 CATS and HR Allocation

1 | Introduction

Table 1.1 highlights the requirements vs. the components in SAP. For instance, if you want to book expenses you have to know that the travel and expenses component is required.

Required function	Required component
Decentralized recording of employee attendances and absences	SAP HR Time Management (PT)
Decentralized recording of employee remuneration information	SAP HR Payroll (PY)
Internal activity allocation and entry of statistical key figures	SAP Controlling (CO)
Confirmations	SAP Logistics
	Plant Maintenance (PM)
	Project System (PS)
	Customer Service (CS) formerly Service Management (SM)
Recording external services	External Services Management (PT-IN-ES)
Recording travel expenses with activity reports	SAP Travel Management (FI-TV)
Recording activities for services provider	SAP Service provider

Table 1.1 Business Functions and SAP Components

Given that the R/3 system is used to its full advantage, data duplication is not enforced. Therefore, to avoid double cost allocation, the combinations in the following table are available when collecting working times through CATS.

CO	HR	MM-SRV	PM/S	PS
X	X			
	X	X		
	X		X	
	X			X
	X	X	X	
	X	X		X
		X	X	
		X		X

Table 1.2 Working Hours Allocation to the Target Modules

1.7 What You Will Learn in this Essentials Guide

You will learn how managers and end users can derive maximum value from CATS through integration with a variety of SAP modules: Financials and Accounting, Human Resources, Materials Management, Plant Maintenance, Project System, and Customer Service. We'll highlight the flexibility of CATS as it is used to centralize all time-related activities through these four steps:

- Time collection (mandatory)
- Release process (optional)
- Approval process (optional)
- Transfer to target modules (mandatory)

1.7.1 Acknowledgments

I have spent a great deal of time trying to piece together the different parts for the Cross Application Time Sheet integration, also known as CATS. One of the conclusions I've come to over the years, is that even though we know the basics of the SAP and CATS settings and their impacts, each implementation is a new challenge. This is because each customer has specific requirements, but it is mostly due to the great flexibility provided by CATS, which can be set up in several ways.

Although this Essentials guide is built on the knowledge acquired since my first acquaintance with SAP in 1997, it is also a product of indirect influences from the people met through my assignments and due to the business experiences we had together. This list is long and distinguished, but I would like to particularly thank my first two mentors in the SAP world: Jean-François Jennes and Marc Rondia. A special thanks goes to all the delegates met while teaching the CA500 courses. They have provided additional feedback and ideas about how this tool can be enhanced or used. I trust the sharing of these experiences and expertise can enhance the foundation of your knowledge. I would also like to thank Dieter Flack for providing me with the CATS Configuration Assistant tool.

Ever since the first edition of this CATS SAP PRESS Essential has been published, I have received positive feedback through multiple different channels (HR Expert, SAP HR Conferences, Support platforms, etc.). I would like to thank you all for your support and your kindness, and for providing all SAP users with the latest information and bug fixing. Keep up the good work, and keep sharing the information.

I also would like to thank Manuel Gallardo for taking the time to provide us with more detailed information through the new SAP PRESS book *Configuring and Using CATS*. This book will develop our knowledge of this great functionality.

Last but not least, I also would like to thank the SAP PRESS editorial team, for their dedication, their commitment, and most of all for their patience.

Regarding the update process for this book, I'd like to thank Jenifer Niles and Justin Lowry for their support and patience while updating this book.

2 Customizing and Enhancing CATS

As SAP is a standard product meant to be adapted to each organization's needs, the customizing guide, also known as the implementation guide (IMG), is the backbone of the R/3 settings. Advanced users can access the customizing nodes directly through transaction codes or via the tables.

While CATS is extensively documented, this chapter aims to provide an executive summary of the customizing steps for CATS. Through these customizing steps, we will point out the integration switches for setting CATS with specific target modules.

Customizing can be found in the IMG (transaction SPRO), under the path SAP CUSTOMIZING IMPLEMENTATION GUIDE • CROSS APPLICATION COMPONENTS • TIME SHEET. Most of the transactions are not listed in the system, as SAP refers to them as SPRO.

Figure 2.1 shows the common access to the SAP R/3 customizing backbone. This Figure is based on the standard implementation tree; local restrictions may apply if the company manages implementation projects.

In Appendix A there is a list of the transaction codes to be used for customizing. Using the list will allow quicker access when setting up and tuning CATS for the system. We suggest using the CATS configuration checklist in Appendix A to gather the business requirements into customizing specifications. This checklist will also help document the customizing steps at a later stage.

2 | Customizing and Enhancing CATS

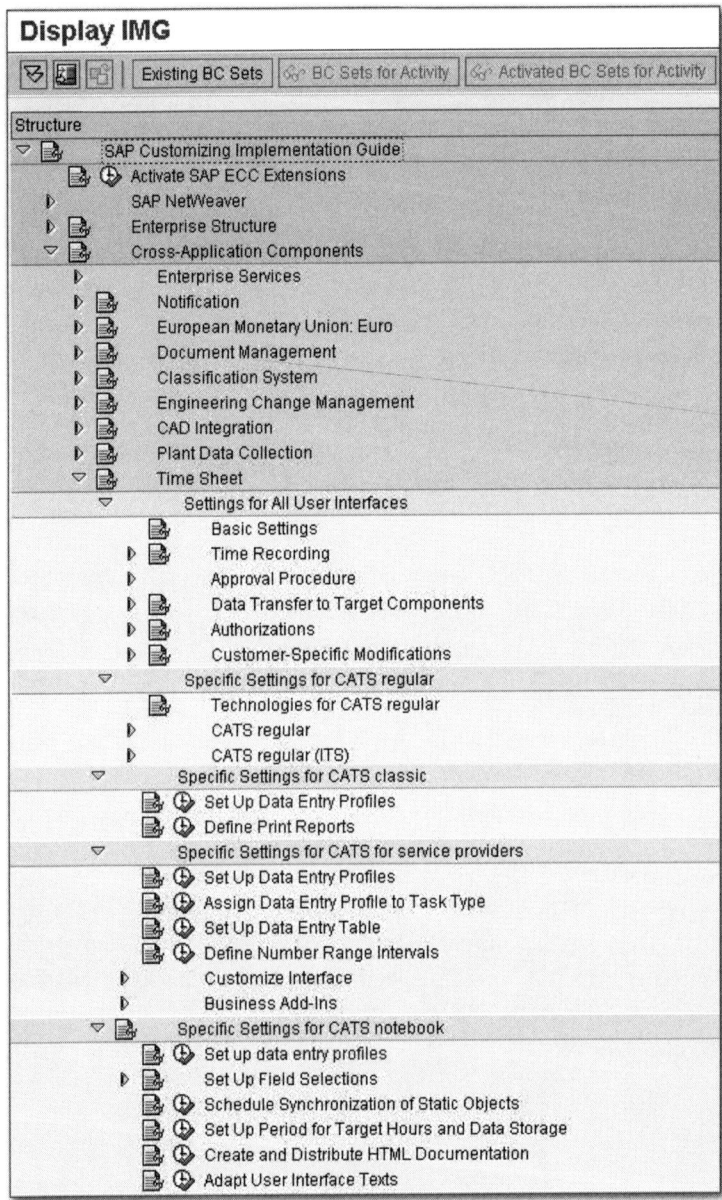

Figure 2.1 Standard IMG for Configuring CATS

The next section will help you to understand each possibility and to set it up, as your technical specifications require.

2.1 Customizing the CATS Data-Entry Profiles

This section aims to provide the basic necessary steps required to set up CATS and then to enable its integration with target modules. The CATS data-entry profile provides an identity card when accessing the Time Sheet. It gathers all the options that can be enabled so that the user can follow a clear and simple process.

The data-entry profile will summarize the different settings enabled by the CATS configuration and point out which target modules are to be used. The data-entry profile will also play an important role in setting up the screen layout, because it will act as a container for the fields to be shown, frozen, mandatory, or hidden.

Figure 2.2 illustrates the first important step in CATS configuration: customizing access for configuring the CATS data-entry profile. This step is important as it provides the key elements for entering the Cross Application Time Sheet.

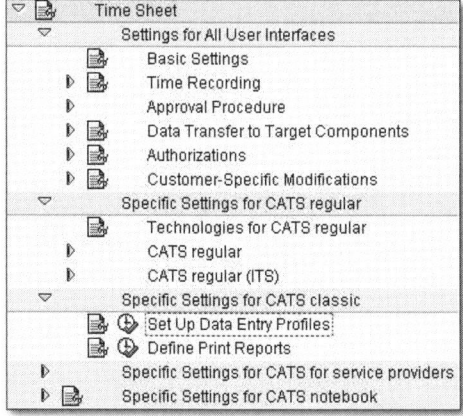

Figure 2.2 Access to Data-Entry Profile Configuration

> **Hint**
>
> To directly access the CATS data-entry profiles customizing options, call transaction code CAC1.

It is important to set a clear naming convention when setting up the names of the CATS data-entry profiles. Each profile can be up to eight characters long, and should start with a letter. Although much of the CATS data-entry profile can be created based upon end user demand, we would advise you to restrict, as much as possible, the creation of data-entry profiles.

> **Hint**
> When starting to customize CATS, basic requirements normally include three CATS profiles in the back-end system: a profile for the employees, a profile for the time administrators, and a profile for the managers.

The following is an example of a naming convention:

- US-EMPL (USA Employee's profile)
- US-ADMIN (USA Administrator profile)
- US-MGR (USA Manager's profile)

Look at Figure 2.3 for an example of an added entry with the required naming convention enforced.

| Data Entry Profile | US-EMPL | USA - Employee's CATS Profile |

Figure 2.3 Data-Entry Profile with Naming Convention Enforced

Please bear in mind that these profiles will have to be included in authorization management. Chapter 8 of this Essentials guide will cover this important setup.

> **Hint**
> The CATS data-entry profile can be defaulted in the user's parameter, thanks to the parameter CVR. In the return-value fields, carefully set the CATS profile to be used by default.

Figure 2.4 illustrates the assignment of the CVR parameter, as it is managed by the user or by the system administrator in the transaction code SU3.

Parameter ID	Parameter value	Short Description
CVR	US-EMPL	CATS: Variant for time recording
PER	1000	Personnel Number (HR)
SAZ	1300	Time Data Administrator
SGR	MGI	Administrator Group (HR)
VSR	DEFAULT	Selection Report Variant

Figure 2.4 Assigning CVR Parameters in SU3

2.1.1 General Settings

The general settings for the CATS data consist of the basic settings for each CATS profile. Where applicable, a simple YES or NO will provide the answer to the customizing step. To enable the customizing setting, please flag it where appropriate.

Figure 2.5 displays the sub-section GENERAL SETTINGS from the CATS customizing screen. It allows a focus on each customizing step.

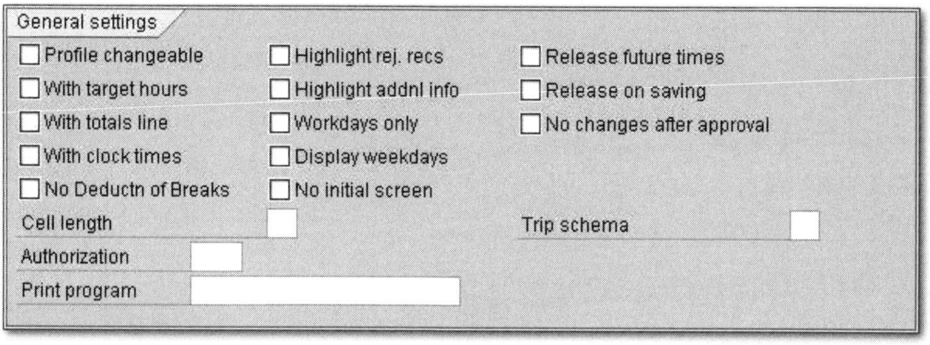

Figure 2.5 General Settings in the CATS Customizing Screen

We will briefly describe the questions addressed by these settings.

- **Profile changeable**
  Will the user be allowed to make non-essential setting to the CATS profile?

- **With target hours**
  Will this profile display the employee's daily work schedule as seen in his Infotype 0007—*Work Schedule*?

- **With total lines**
  Will this profile display a row with a sum of all hours entered for each day?

- **With clock times**
  Will this profile display clock-in and clock-out time?

- **No deduction of breaks**
  Should unpaid breaks be taken into account when calculating?

- **Highlight rejected records**
  Should the rejected records be highlighted?

- **Highlight additional information**
  Should fields containing additional information such as short and/or long text be highlighted?
- **Workdays only**
  Should end users be allowed to enter times on non working days?
- **Display weekdays**
  Should weekdays (Monday through Friday) be displayed in addition to the date?
- **No initial screen**
  Should the system skip the initial screen? This option is only possible in the R/3 backend system.

In addition to this customizing step, you must default the personnel number via the parameter PER in the employee's profile and / or in the employee's *Communication* Infotype (0105 — subtype 0001).

The default CATS profile also must be defaulted in the employee's parameters thanks to the parameter CVR.

The end user will always have the ability to come back to the initial screen when using the standard menu within the functional screen.

> **Hint**
> The user parameter can either be managed directly by the end user through the transaction code SU3, or by the system administrator using the transaction code SU01.

- **Release futures times**
  Can the data entered for future dates be released?
- **Release on saving**
  Should the data be released on saving?

This customizing option will disable the optional release step in the CATS process.

- **Approval required**
  Is an approval step required? This customizing option will enable the approval step in the CATS process.
- **No changes after approval**
  Will the end user be able to change time entries after approval?

> **Note**
> Normally, for obvious data accuracy reasons, the end user is not allowed to change any data (overtime bonuses and hours). This option is left to a time administrator data-entry profile. The time administrator will centralize the correction request and act as a data accuracy keeper.

- **Immediate transfer to Human Resources**
  Will data be transferred directly to the Human Resources module upon save?
- **Cell length**
  Specify here the cell length to be used. This will overwrite the standard setting.
- **Authorization**
  Specify here the authorization group to be assigned to the CATS data-entry profile.
- **Print program**
  CATS provides a fairly basic program for printing purposes. Since it is not tailor-made for each case, you can insert your own printing program name to overwrite the standard program call. The CATS standard screens will then call up your program instead of the standard.
- **Trip schema**
  You can specify here a trip schema if the end users are allowed to jump to the Travel Management sub-module from the CATS functional screen.

2.1.2 Time Settings

Figure 2.6 displays the sub-section TIME SETTINGS, allowing a fine-tuning of the time aspects in the time-collection process.

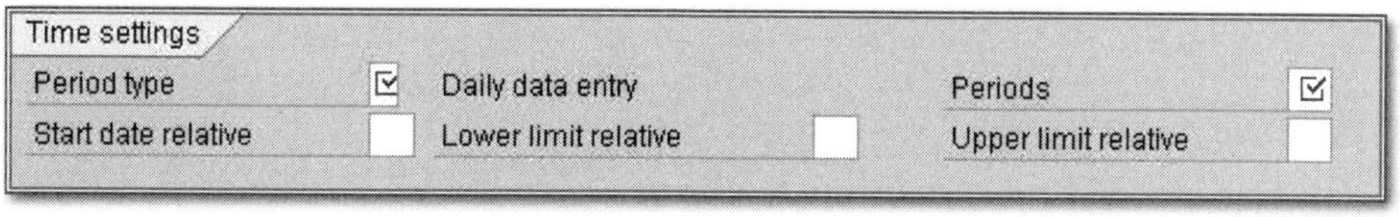

Figure 2.6 Time Settings Sub-Section with Period Information Defined

- **Period type**
  What data-entry period will the profile use?
- **First day of the week**
  What day of the week should be displayed first?
  Normally, Monday is displayed as the first day of the week but some shift crews could start their work during other parts of the week.

> **Caution**
> This customizing step only works with weekly and bi-weekly periods.

- **Key relative date**
  The initial entry screen should display the number of periods in relation to the present date.
  The symbol must be entered to the right of the number, e.g.: 1+
- **Periods**
  - **Lower-limit relative**
    How many screens can the end user scroll back?
  - **Upper-limit relative**
    How many screens can the end user scroll forward?

> **Note**
> The lower- and upper-limit relative could slow the system response time when submitting the data for display to the employee. We recommend allowing, e. g., two weeks in the past and 12 weeks in the future.

2.1.3 Person Selection

Let us look now at the settings for person selection, shown in Figure 2.7. These settings allow us to stick with the user requirements.

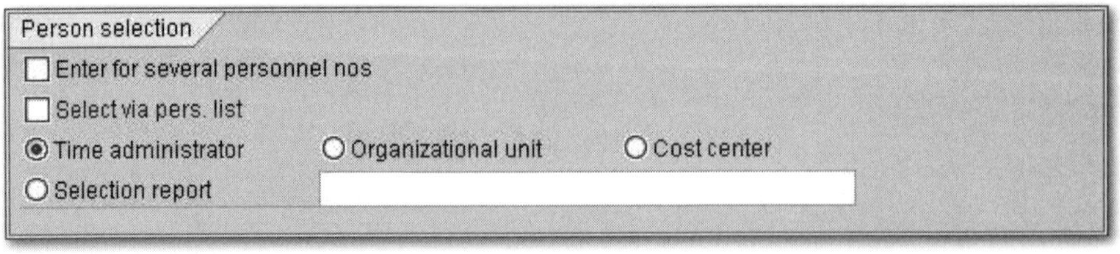

Figure 2.7 Sub-Section Person Selection

The person selection can be useful if you wish to make a mass time entry. Depending on your system's settings, you could use a standard list to retrieve the personnel by running a standard program.

Alternatively, you can use the features provided by SAP as shown below:

- Time Administrator as assigned in the *Organizational Assignment* Infotype
- The Organizational Unit among the company's structure
- A cost center

Enter for several personnel numbers

Will this profile be used for entering data for a single or multiple employees at a time?

Selection via personnel list

Under this choice, the following options are to be considered. This option requires the following prior steps:

- Time administrators have been defined in the table T526

> **Hint**
> To directly maintain this table, use the transaction code SM31.

- Feature PINCH has to be managed

> **Hint**
> To assign the administrator groups, use the transaction code PE03 to maintain it.

- Time administrators have been assigned to the relevant employees in their Infotype *Organizational Assignment* (0001).

> **Hint**
> To maintain the employee's Organizational Assignment, use the transaction code PA30.

2.1.4 Organizational Unit

This option assumes that you have set up the Organizational Management (OM) structure in the Personnel Development module.

> **Hint**
> To display the organizational structure, you can use the transaction code PPOME or PPOM_OLD.

2.1.5 Cost Center

This option assumes that cost centers have been defined by Controlling and assigned either directly in the Infotype OM (0001) or through the position as it is linked in the organizational structure.

> **Hint**
> To display the cost center, you can use the transaction code KS03.

2.1.6 Selection Report

Enter the name of your report here only if you wish to use your own program to build the list. Otherwise, the list will be built using SAP's standard report.

> **Tip**
> Your own ABAP query is considered an SAP report and can therefore be added here.
> When using the standard report, the parameter VSR (Selection report variant) can be used so that the end user does not have to go through the program-selection screen.

> **Hint**
> The sample program RPLFST01, provided by SAP, can be viewed using the transaction code SA38.

2.1.7 Accounting Variant

Figure 2.8 displays the sub-section COST ACCOUNTING VARIANT, which allows several options.

Customizing the CATS Data-Entry Profiles | 2.1

It is a flexible customizing process, allowing the system to respect the requirements from the financial department.

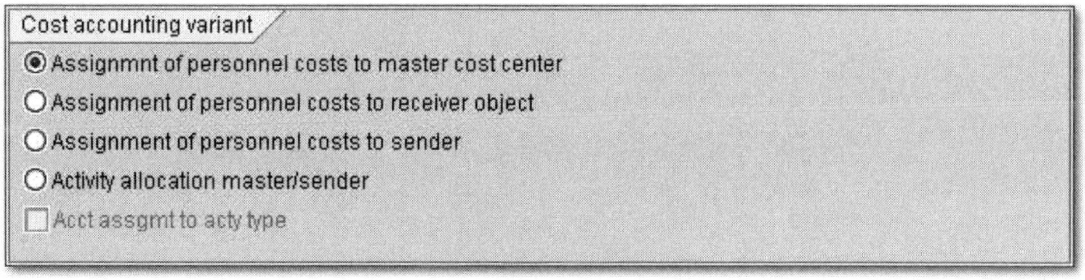

Figure 2.8 Assignment Options for Cost Accounting Variant

The following accounting variants are available:

- Assignment of personnel costs to the master cost center
- Assignment of personnel costs to the receiver object
- Assignment of personnel costs to the sender
- Activity allocation between master cost center and sender
- Account assignment to activity type

These options will be seen in more detail in Chapter 4.

2.1.8 Default Values

Figure 2.9 displays the sub-section DEFAULT VALUES, which allows different settings in order to get a smoother process for the end user while collecting time entries. This is achieved through the defaulting of different values.

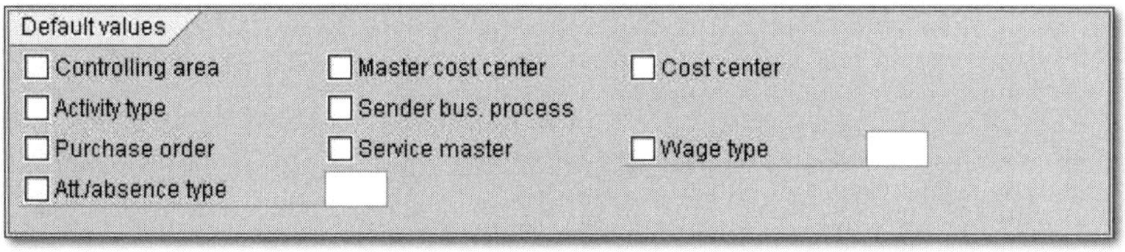

Figure 2.9 Default Values Which Allow Different Settings

31

2 | Customizing and Enhancing CATS

CATS simplifies time collection by providing a central point of entry. To ease time collection further, the system also provides a wide range of default values. Once activated, these values will assist the end user while collecting his or her time. These fields can be displayed only in the screen, overwritten by the end user, or can be hidden. The following fields are available:

- Controlling area
- Activity type
- Purchase order
- Attendance/absence type
- Master Cost Center
- Sender business process
- Service Master only
- Cost Center
- Wage type

This default values setup will allow the end user to just type the minimum data required.

2.1.9 Worklist

Figure 2.10 displays the sub-section WORKLIST, which enables the setting up of a worklist in the end user's screen. This is another way to simplify the time collection process, by providing the information to the end user.

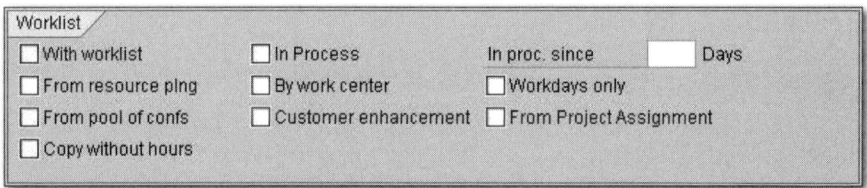

Figure 2.10 Worklist Sub-Section, with Options

Indeed, in addition to the default values to be set in the CATS data-entry profiles, the system can also provide a worklist that compiles all the relevant activities for the employees. This list saves precious time because employees do not have to chase down administrators or managers to get the right activity object. It also decreases the number of corrections in the system because the employees can only collect time entries against the activities allocated to them; they cannot pick a wrong entry from an endless list.

The worklist can be used in the backend system as well as in the Web CATS service. Because the worklist is only meant for single use (one employee versus one worklist), it cannot be set up along with a CATS data-entry profile for several persons. To enable the worklist, tick the box WITH WORKLIST, and then select the relevant options according to your SAP modules and requirements.

The data provided in the worklist can be retrieved from the following sources:

- Resource Planning
- Assigned to work center
- Pool of confirmations
- In process (work already begun)
- Further customizing options are made available:
- Customer enhancement (data retrieval from third-party software like Microsoft Excel)
- In process since (days): Allow the time line buffer.
- Workdays only
- Copy with hours

2.1.10 General Data-Entry Checks

Figure 2.11 displays the subsection DATA ENTRY CHECKS: GENERAL. It allows the system to set up the different checks and controls all along the time collection process.

The time-collection process is done through CATS with a direct-only check while entering the data. The system automatically checks several items such as the receiving object status (open/closed, etc.), the correctness of such master data as the cost center, and the controlling area. Since the main goal of CATS is to deliver accurate time collection, and to minimize the correction in the system, the customizing steps also allow additional checks.

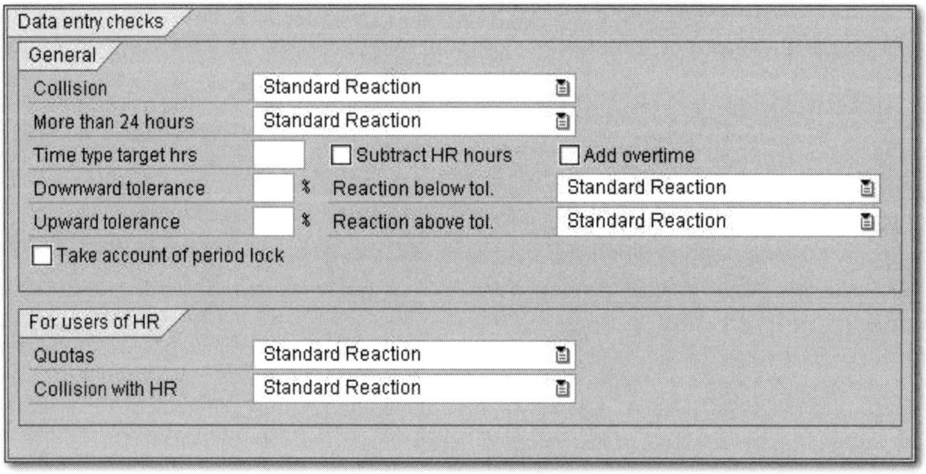

2 | Customizing and Enhancing CATS

Figure 2.11 Data-Entry Checks for General Use and for HR Users

> **Tip**
> We advise against setting the control check to the lower level, such as Error, as this will block the end user and will not allow saving the Time Sheet.
>
> Another goal of the CATS system is to empower employees, thus holding them responsible for data collection as well.

The following general checks can be enabled:

- Collision
- More than 24 hours
- Time type target hours
- Subtract Human Resources hours
- Add overtime
- Downward tolerance
- Reaction below tolerance
- Upward tolerance
- Reaction upward tolerance

For each of these options, a message type must be specified so that the system can return the appropriate message to the end user when the scenario is met.

With the SAP Human Resources module installed, these additional online checks can be enabled:

- Quotas
- Collision with Human Resources

2.1.11 Print Entry Data Sheet

A standard printing program (RCATSP01) is available for all printing purposes from the CATS GUI screen. As a start, the specialized printing program can be based on the standard or it can be developed from scratch.

Once the program has been developed, tested, and approved for production use, simply insert the name of the program in the field PRINT PROGRAM under the general settings of the data-entry profile.

Figure 2.12 displays the PRINT PROGRAM field, which enables the system to bypass the standard printing program and to instead use the company's own printing program.

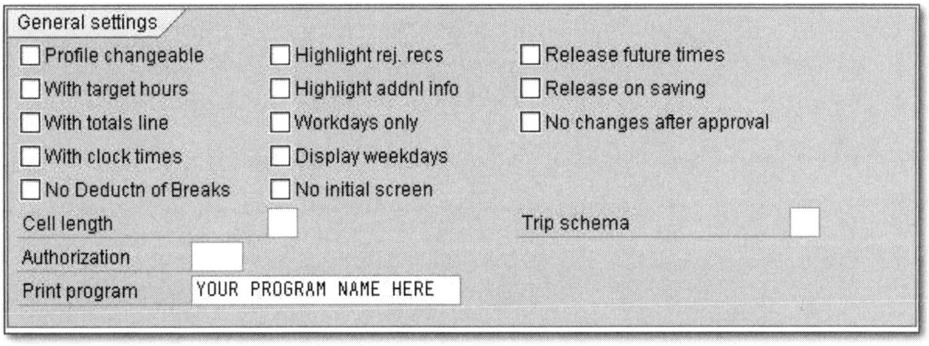

Figure 2.12 Print Program Field

2.1.12 Integrating CATS with Workflow

Prior to any workflow setup for time approval, make sure that the option Approval required is flagged in the first option box under General settings.

In order to enable the workflow, the option WORKFLOW APPROVAL must be enabled, as shown in Figure 2.13. The option AUTOMATIC RECIPIENT also can be enabled. It requires an automatic role resolution for the workflow task to be picked up.

2 | Customizing and Enhancing CATS

Figure 2.13 Required Settings in Subsection Workflow Settings up to Release ERP 5.0

Figure 2.14 Required Settings in Subsection Workflow Settings as of Release ERP 6.0

Several tasks are provided in the standard version, up to SAP release ERP 5.0, as shown in Figure 2.14. The most common approval task used for time approval is the approval by the superior (TS20000460), which requires the organizational structure and a chief position linked to the specific unit. Approval by the time administrator (TS20000459) is easier to maintain.

Figure 2.15 Standard Tasks-List Available Within the CATS Workflow up to SAP Release ERP 5.0

As of release ERP 6.0, SAP is replacing the former Workflow tasks illustrated by the following tasks:

Figure 2.16 Standard Tasks-List Available Within the CATS Workflow up to SAP Release ERP 6.0

> **Tip**
> When dealing with Workflow setup, do not forget to synchronize the Organizational Management Structure buffered by SAP, by running Transaction code SWU_OBUF.

AS of ERP 6.0, SAP also provides the possibility to determine which hours must undergo an approval process. This is achieved through a new feature CATEX — Rules for Special Approval in Cross-Application Time Sheet. This decision tree can be accessed through the transaction code PE03.

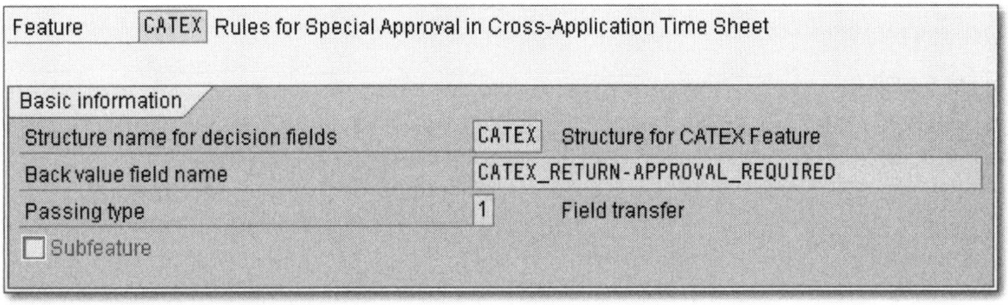

Figure 2.17 The New Feature CATEX

This feature contains in standard the following decision criteria when setting an approval rule:

RULES	Description
RULE_ID	Rule for Special Approval
BUKRS	Company Code
AWART	Attendance or Absence Type
LGART	Wage Type
VERSL	Overtime Compensation Type
AUFKZ	Extra Pay Indicator
TRFGR	Pay Scale Group
TRFST	Pay Scale Level
PRAKN	Premium Number
PRAKZ	Premium Indicator
OTYPE	Object Type
PLANS	Position
TASKTYPE	Activity Type

RULES	Description
TASKLEVEL	Task Level
TASKCOMPONENT	Task component
KOKRS	Controlling Area
ARBPL	Work center
WERKS	Plant
SKOSTL	Sender Cost Center
LSTAR	Activity Type
SEBELN	Sending purchase order
SEBELP	Sending purchase order item
SPRZNR	Sender Business Process
LSTNR	Activity Number
RKOSTL	Receiver Cost Center
POSID	Work Breakdown Structure Element (WBS Element)
RAUFNR	Receiver Order
RNPLNR	Network number
VORNR	Operation/Activity Number
UVORN	Suboperation
RKDAUF	Receiver sales order
RKDPOS	Item number in receiver sales order
RKSTR	Receiver cost object
RPRZNR	Receiver business process
STATKEYFIG	Statistical key figure
FUND	Receiver fund
FUNC_AREA	Receiving Functional Area
GRANT_NBR	Receiver Grant
S_FUND	Sender fund
S_FUNC_AREA	Sending Functional Area
S_GRANT_NBR	Sender Grant
CPR_EXTID	External Project ID
CPR_OBJGEXTID	External ID of Project Subobject
CPR_OBJTYPE	cProjects Object Type

Customizing the CATS Data-Entry Profiles | 2.1

By default, the SAP feature CATEX is provided empty, as illustrated in Figure 2.18.

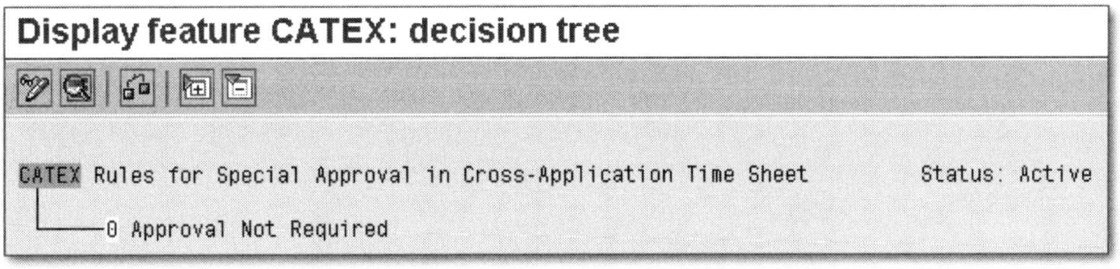

Display feature CATEX: decision tree

CATEX Rules for Special Approval in Cross-Application Time Sheet   Status: Active
 └─ 0 Approval Not Required

Figure 2.18 The Decision Tree of Feature CATEX

> **Tip**
> Should you have more complex rules, you can use the BAdI CATS_APPROVAL (CATS Genehmigung) with the method 'Check Approval by Exception.'

In order to enable the approval rule, you must switch on this functionality through the customizing. This new functionality is provided through the transaction code CAC1.

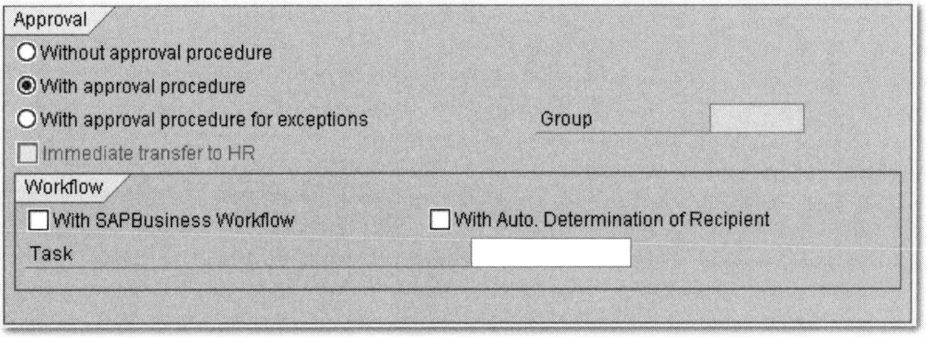

Approval
- ○ Without approval procedure
- ● With approval procedure
- ○ With approval procedure for exceptions   Group [ ]
- ☐ Immediate transfer to HR

Workflow
- ☐ With SAPBusiness Workflow   ☐ With Auto. Determination of Recipient
- Task [ ]

Figure 2.19 The New Configuration Options Provided in Customizing

Shall no approval rule be required, simply flag 'Without approval procedure' which will set all time entries directly to the status 'approved.'

In parallel to the setting up of the feature CATEX, additional customizing steps have been added in the customizing tree. It allows us to define the different rule.

2 | Customizing and Enhancing CATS

It can be found under the customizing tree, with the following path: TIME SHEET • SETTINGS FOR ALL USER INTERFACES • SPECIAL APPROVAL

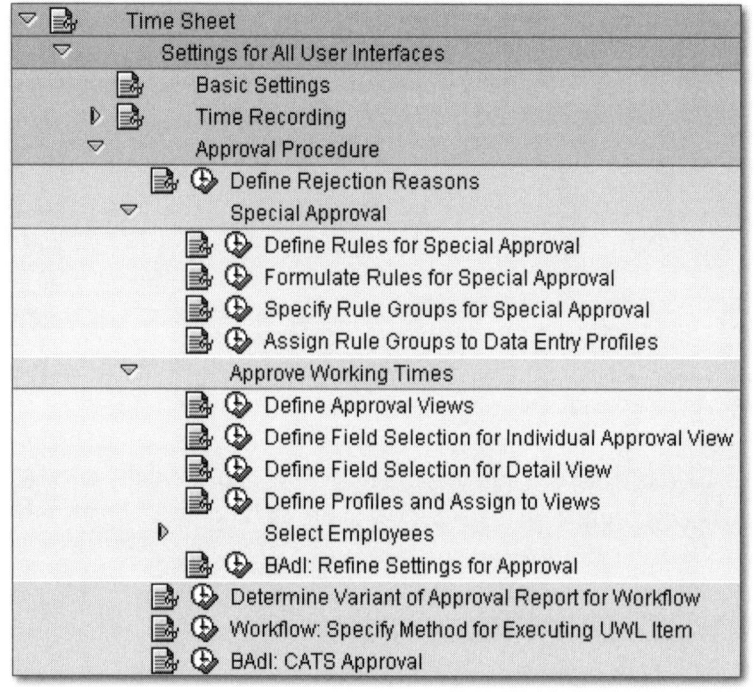

```
▽  Time Sheet
   ▽     Settings for All User Interfaces
            Basic Settings
         ▷  Time Recording
         ▽  Approval Procedure
               Define Rejection Reasons
            ▽  Special Approval
                  Define Rules for Special Approval
                  Formulate Rules for Special Approval
                  Specify Rule Groups for Special Approval
                  Assign Rule Groups to Data Entry Profiles
               ▽  Approve Working Times
                     Define Approval Views
                     Define Field Selection for Individual Approval View
                     Define Field Selection for Detail View
                     Define Profiles and Assign to Views
                  ▷  Select Employees
                     BAdI: Refine Settings for Approval
                  Determine Variant of Approval Report for Workflow
                  Workflow: Specify Method for Executing UWL Item
                  BAdI: CATS Approval
```

Figure 2.20 The New Configuration Options Provided in Customizing

> **Tip**
>
> If none of the standard tasks suit your needs, you can use the user-exit CATS0008—Determine Workflow Recipients for Approval.

2.1.13 Determine Variant of Approval Report for Workflow

Assuming that the workflow setup and agent assignment have been done, this last step will ensure that the CATS workflow is set to operational mode. To achieve this step, the selection variant WORKFLOW must be created for the program RCATSB01—Approval Report.

Figure 2.21 displays the customizing access for maintaining the report RCATSB01 and for creating the mandatory selection variant WORKFLOW.

Customizing the CATS Data-Entry Profiles | 2.1

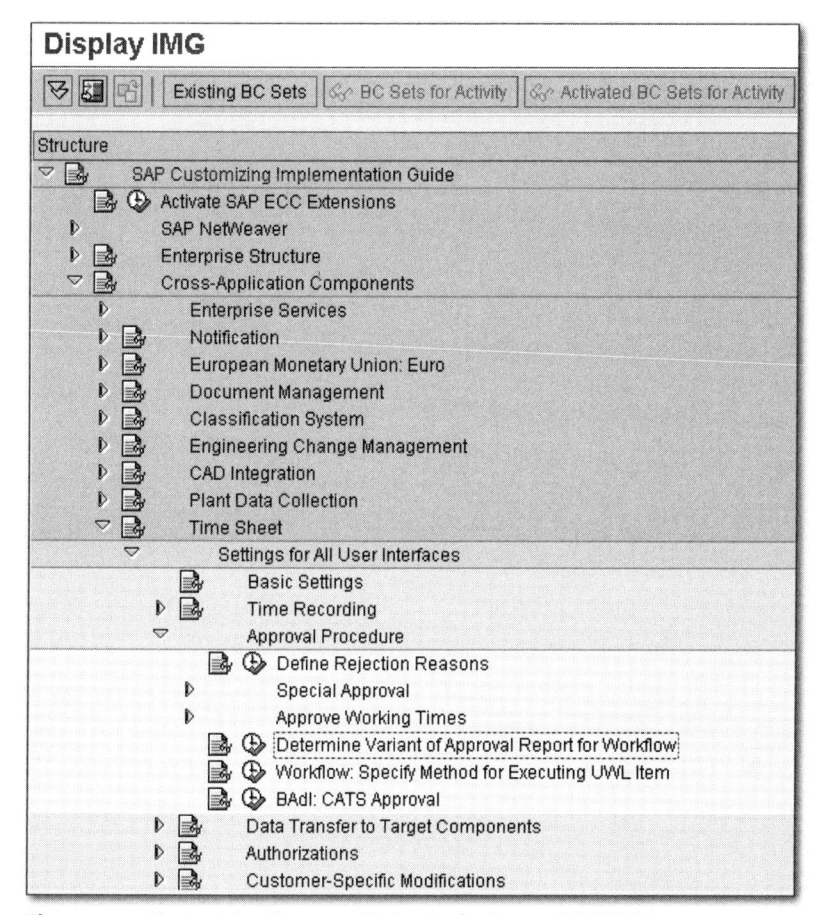

Figure 2.21 Customizing Access to Maintain the Report RCATSB01

Depending on your requirements, options IMMEDIATE TRANSFER TO HR and SEND NOTIFICATION OF REJECTION can be switched on, as shown in Figure 2.22.

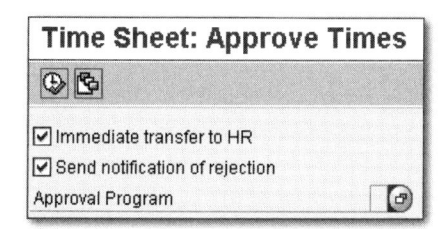

Figure 2.22 Options Within the Program RCATSB01

2 | Customizing and Enhancing CATS

> **Hint**
> The task chosen must be enabled in transaction SWDD, as a general task, in the agent-assignment determination step.

While testing the workflow settings and making changes in the organizational structure, you may not want to wait for the system to buffer the organizational structure, given that the standard program is set to run on a periodic basis.

> **Tip**
> If you prefer to work directly with the changes you can manually synchronize the buffering of the organizational structure by using transaction code SWU_OBUF. Workflow monitoring can be easily done using the Transaction code SWIA.

Further information about workflow settings can be found in the book *Practical Workflow for SAP* by SAP PRESS.

2.2 Customizing the CATS Fields

Since SAP CATS is a standard product, fields for the CATS screen have to be chosen in accordance with the integration requirements.

This section provides a quick reference guide for the different fields available in CATS.

You will find the complete list of the fields available in Appendix A. Each field is relevant for one or more integration module. These fields will be highlighted in the forthcoming sections introducing each module.

> **Warning**
> While setting up the CATS fields assignment, we strongly advise you not to change any field settings from the top entries. All entries should be enabled as Available. Failing to do so will result in inconsistencies in the different profiles already created.

For each step listed hereunder, carefully indicate the profile name that the field's setup will affect. Carefully press ENTER on the keyboard to ensure that the field's selection will affect the profile chosen.

Under the customizing steps, choose CROSS APPLICATION • TIME SHEET • SET UP ENTRY FIELDS. Once you reach the selection screen, the following options are available.

> **Hint**
> Rather than going through along the customizing, use the Transaction code CAC2.

While accessing the customizing screen, you can see three different sections:

2.2.1 Screen Grouping — Settings

This screen grouping gathers the fields relevant for the headers, the selection screens, and the basic information shown into the screens.

2.2.2 Screen Grouping — Worklist

This screen grouping gathers all the relevant fields for the worklist, providing this option has been enabled in the prior CATS basic customizing.

2.2.3 Screen Grouping — Data-Entry Section

This screen grouping, the most important of all, gathers the fields relevant for the data-entry section where the user inputs his data through CATS. This screen grouping allows a custom-made screen in order to be adequate for the target modules.

2.2.4 Hiding New Fields According to SAP Release

For each screen grouping, the following options are available:

- Field setup as input
- Field setup as required
- Field setup as displayed
- Field setup as hidden
- Field setup as highlighted

Please refer to Appendix A for a full list of the fields available within CATS. The relevant fields for each target module will be described in the forthcoming sections.

> **Hint**
>
> When upgrading CATS from any release below 4.6C: To hide the new fields in your existing data-entry profiles, use report RCATSFAW_2 (Time Sheet: Hide Fields New for 4.6C). The new fields for additional account assignment information are ready for input in all data-entry profiles in the standard system. Therefore, after you have upgraded the data-entry profiles that are implemented at your enterprise, the new fields are present.

> **Hint**
>
> When upgrading CATS to Release 4.7 (R/3 Enterprise): Program RCATSFAW_3 (Time Sheet: Hide New Fields for Release 4.7) enables you to hide these fields.

2.3 Customizing CATS for Web-Enabling

Until now we have worked on CATS as used in the R/3 backend system. Today, when most processes are Web-enabled, SAP has provided CATS with its own Web version as well.

While referring to the Web Time Sheet we don't differentiate between Internet (access from any location in the world) and intranet (access only within the company's private network). The difference mainly resides in the security settings.

Naturally, within SAP we don't duplicate customizing settings, except when an exception arises. All the customizing steps already undertaken are still in application. Nevertheless, while remaining faithful to its intentions, SAP provides the following additional steps to tune the Web-enabled Time Sheet.

2.3.1 Create Data-Entry Profile for Employee Self-Services (ESS)

To web enable CATS through the Web scenario CATW, which means that you are using an Internet Transaction Server (ITS), one or more dedicated profiles must be created in this table. This data-entry profile allows integration with the Employee Self-Services (ESS), as well as the Enterprise Portal (EP).

The Service CATW becomes obsolete once you upgrade to the Web Application Server (WAS), which provides a new screen based on the Web Dynpro technology.

Customizing CATS for Web-Enabling | 2.3

This new Web Dynpro, which is a screen, is provided by SAP as of release ERP 5.0. It is based on the Java technology. Every user agrees that the layout rendering to the end users has been greatly enhanced.

Runtime Technology	Java/Web Dynpro
Technical Name of iView	com.sap.pct.erp.ess.recordworktime com.sap.pct.erp.ess.releaseworktime
Technical Name of Web Dynpro Application	sap.com/ess~cat/CatDataRecord sap.com/ess~cat/CatDataRelease
Available as of	SAP NetWeaver 7.0
Data Source	SAP ECC 6.00 and higher RFC function modules called: ● HRXSS_CAT_WD*
Software Component	EA-HR 500 and higher
Support	CA-TS-IA-XS
Languages Available	All languages supported by SAP

Figure 2.23 The Web Dynpro Properties

The Web Dynpro consists of two screens:

- Record Working Times
- Release working time, shall a release procedure been setup

2.3.2 Record Working Time

The technical name of the iview is "com.sap.pct.erp.ess.recordworktime". The full access path in the portal content directory (PCD) is:

pcd:portal_content/com.sap.pct/every_user/com.sap.pct.erp.ess.bp_folder/com.sap.pct.erp.ess.iviews/com.sap.pct.erp.ess.working_time/com.sap.pct.erp.ess.recordworktime

This dynpro consists of 3 steps: edit, review & save, completed.

Besides the updated layout, users will greatly enjoy the calendar, which eases the browsing through the civil year as well as allowing them to see the status of their recorded time entries. The system displays a color for each recorded day. For example, green for approved and red for rejected.

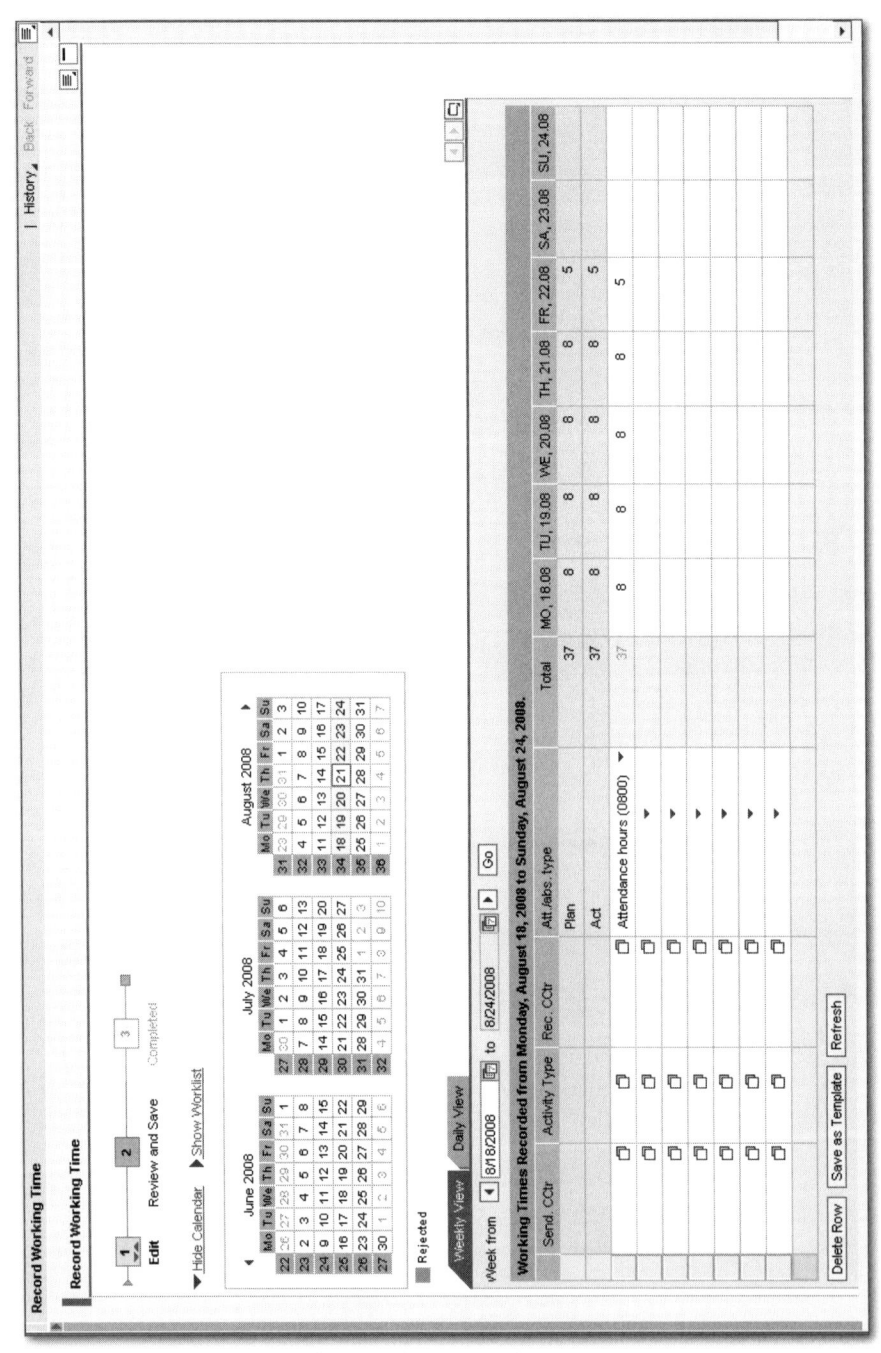

Figure 2.24 The Web Dynpro for Recording the Working Times

Customizing CATS for Web-Enabling | **2.3**

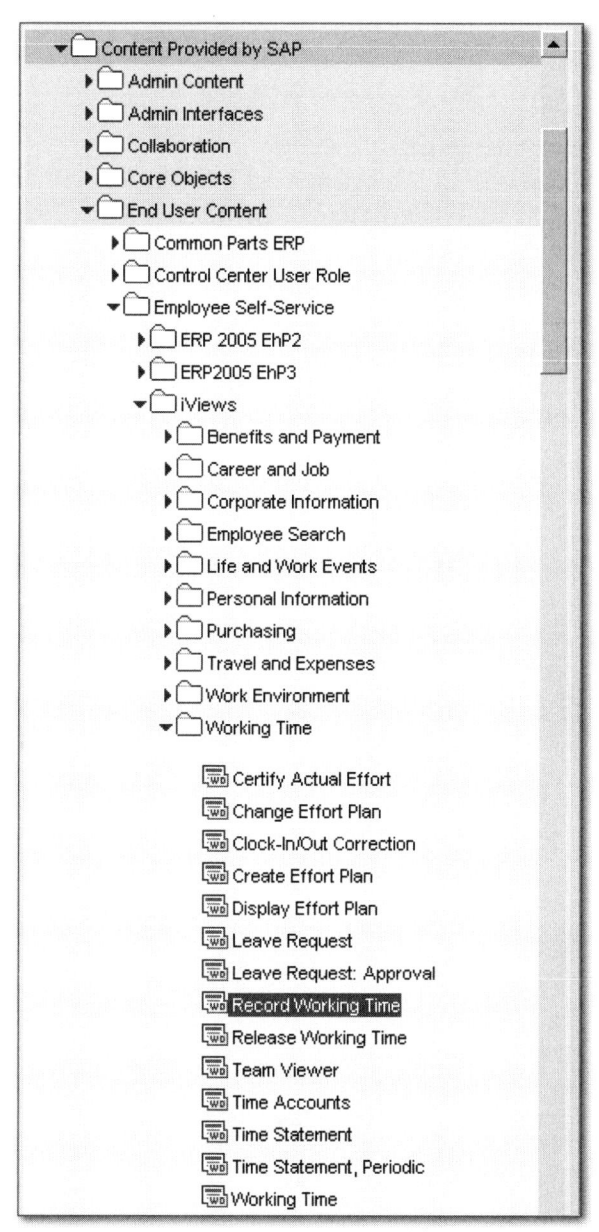

- ▼ Content Provided by SAP
  - ▶ Admin Content
  - ▶ Admin Interfaces
  - ▶ Collaboration
  - ▶ Core Objects
  - ▼ End User Content
    - ▶ Common Parts ERP
    - ▶ Control Center User Role
    - ▼ Employee Self-Service
      - ▶ ERP 2005 EhP2
      - ▶ ERP2005 EhP3
      - ▼ iViews
        - ▶ Benefits and Payment
        - ▶ Career and Job
        - ▶ Corporate Information
        - ▶ Employee Search
        - ▶ Life and Work Events
        - ▶ Personal Information
        - ▶ Purchasing
        - ▶ Travel and Expenses
        - ▶ Work Environment
        - ▼ Working Time
          - Certify Actual Effort
          - Change Effort Plan
          - Clock-In/Out Correction
          - Create Effort Plan
          - Display Effort Plan
          - Leave Request
          - Leave Request: Approval
          - **Record Working Time**
          - Release Working Time
          - Team Viewer
          - Time Accounts
          - Time Statement
          - Time Statement, Periodic
          - Working Time

Figure 2.25 Location of the Web Dynpro for Recording the Working Times in the Portal Content Directory (PCD)

47

2.3.3 Release Working Times

The technical name of the iview is "com.sap.pct.erp.ess.releaseworktime."

The full access path in the portal content directory (PCD) is:

pcd:portal_content/com.sap.pct/every_user/com.sap.pct.erp.ess.bp_folder/com.sap.pct.erp.ess.iviews/com.sap.pct.erp.ess.working_time/com.sap.pct.erp.ess.releaseworktime

This dynpro consists of 3 steps: edit, review & save, completed.

This step only applies shall you have chosen the option not to release the time entries upon saving, which will allow the user to manage the release process.

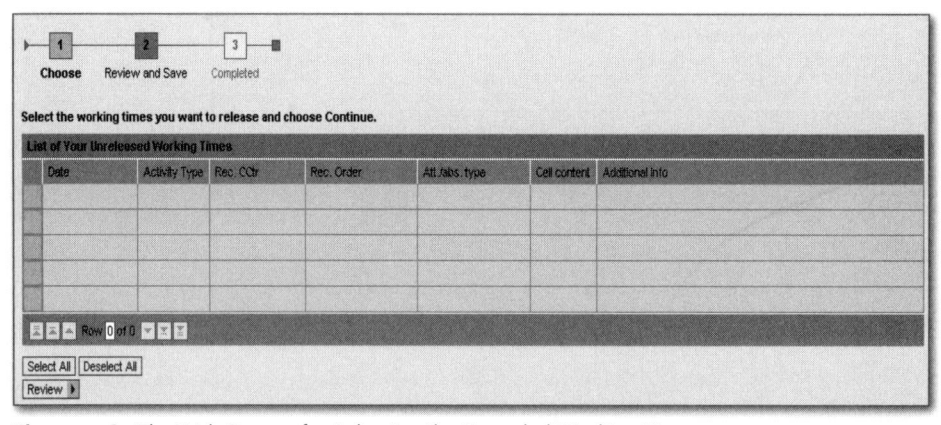

Figure 2.26 The Web Dynpro for Releasing the Recorded Working Times

The configuration provided hereunder only applies for the ITS based service CATW. When dealing with the new Web Dynpro for CATS, no configuration options exists from the customizing side. It is provided with two views: weekly and daily. This cannot be changed. Even if you set up a different period time setup in the customizing, it will not affect the Web Dynpro.

This step is not redundant regarding the profiles already created. It is available in the system so that you can provide different screens and functionalities based on the way the end user will connect. This can be through the R/3 backend access or it can be an online access. If the requirements are exactly the same, the profiles will be identical in each access mode.

Customizing CATS for Web-Enabling | 2.3

> **Hint**
>
> The profile ESS must always exist as it is used as a default while accessing the Web-enabled Time Sheet.

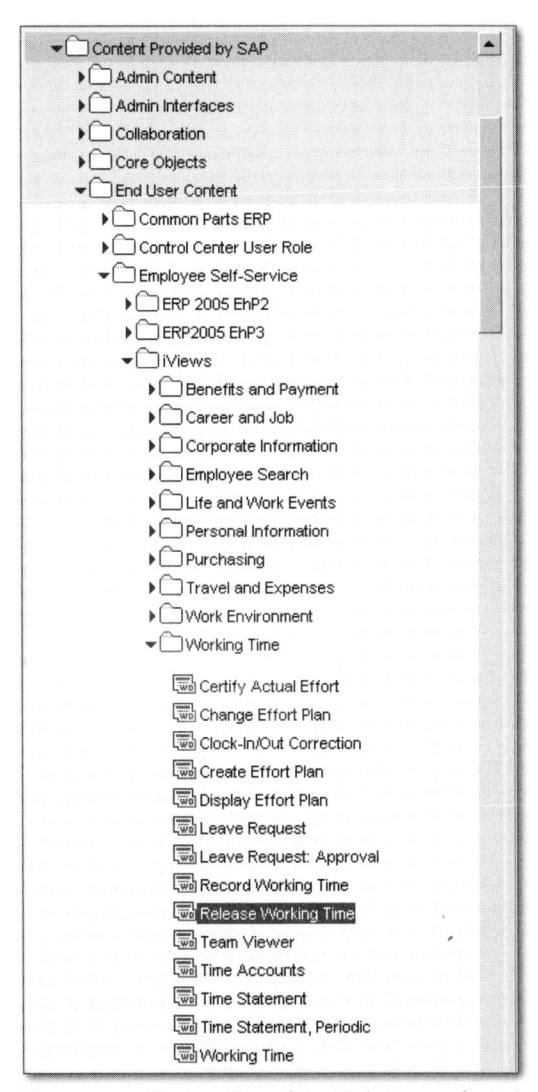

```
▼ Content Provided by SAP
  ▶ Admin Content
  ▶ Admin Interfaces
  ▶ Collaboration
  ▶ Core Objects
  ▼ End User Content
    ▶ Common Parts ERP
    ▶ Control Center User Role
    ▼ Employee Self-Service
      ▶ ERP 2005 EhP2
      ▶ ERP2005 EhP3
      ▼ iViews
        ▶ Benefits and Payment
        ▶ Career and Job
        ▶ Corporate Information
        ▶ Employee Search
        ▶ Life and Work Events
        ▶ Personal Information
        ▶ Purchasing
        ▶ Travel and Expenses
        ▶ Work Environment
        ▼ Working Time
            Certify Actual Effort
            Change Effort Plan
            Clock-In/Out Correction
            Create Effort Plan
            Display Effort Plan
            Leave Request
            Leave Request: Approval
            Record Working Time
            Release Working Time
            Team Viewer
            Time Accounts
            Time Statement
            Time Statement, Periodic
            Working Time
```

Figure 2.27 The Location of the Web Dynpro for Releasing the Recorded Working Times in the Portal Content Directory (PCD)

2 | Customizing and Enhancing CATS

Figure 2.28 illustrates the customizing access for the WEB enabling CATS through the Internet Transaction Server (ITS). Once you have launched this customizing step, a popup screen will appear, providing the guidelines for the different customizing steps.

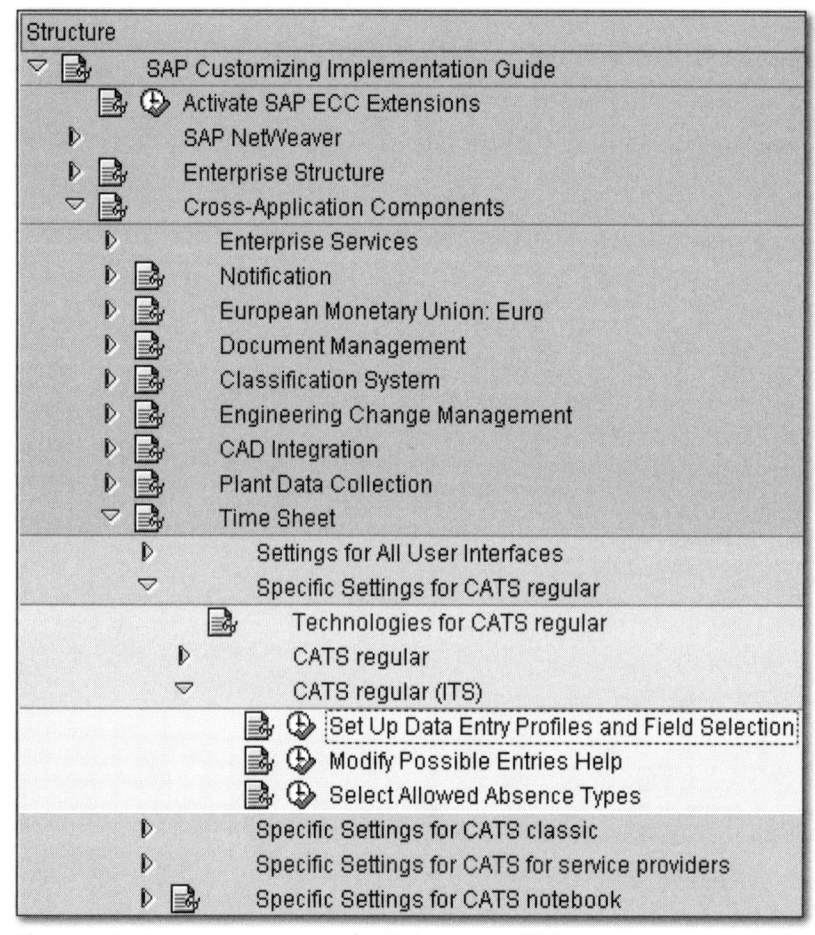

```
Structure
▽ 📄 SAP Customizing Implementation Guide
    📄 ⊕ Activate SAP ECC Extensions
    ▷    SAP NetWeaver
    ▷ 📄 Enterprise Structure
    ▽ 📄 Cross-Application Components
        ▷    Enterprise Services
        ▷ 📄 Notification
        ▷ 📄 European Monetary Union: Euro
        ▷ 📄 Document Management
        ▷ 📄 Classification System
        ▷ 📄 Engineering Change Management
        ▷ 📄 CAD Integration
        ▷ 📄 Plant Data Collection
        ▽ 📄 Time Sheet
            ▷    Settings for All User Interfaces
            ▽    Specific Settings for CATS regular
                📄    Technologies for CATS regular
                ▷    CATS regular
                ▽    CATS regular (ITS)
                    📄 ⊕ Set Up Data Entry Profiles and Field Selection
                    📄 ⊕ Modify Possible Entries Help
                    📄 ⊕ Select Allowed Absence Types
            ▷    Specific Settings for CATS classic
            ▷    Specific Settings for CATS for service providers
            ▷ 📄 Specific Settings for CATS notebook
```

Figure 2.28 Access to Customizing for Web-Enabled CATS

Figure 2.29 provides a detailed view of the popup customizing screen with the different customizing steps.

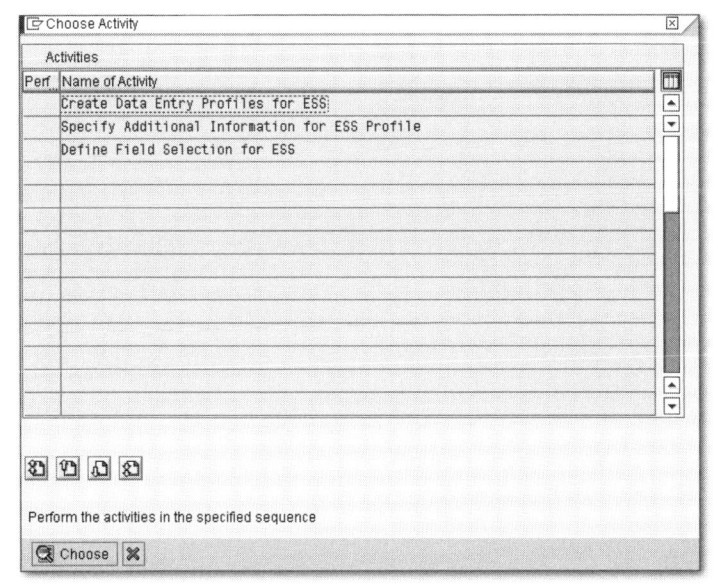

Figure 2.29 Popup Customizing Screen for ESS

2.3.4 Create Data-Entry Profile for ESS

Based on the assumption that the target users are likely to be different according to their modes of connection, we have to create additional data-entry profiles. In this case, they will only be relevant for ESS. Since the standard table contains data-entry profiles for the R/3 system and for the web enabled CATW service, we would advise the use of a clear naming convention. This will ensure that end users and administrators will be able to differentiate its use whether in the backend system or online.

> **Hint**
> Use ESS in the CATS abbreviation name.

2.3.5 Specify Additional Information for ESS Profile

While accessing this customizing screen, you must add the data-entry profile created earlier. Once it has been assigned to the table, the customizing process can proceed.

Since the integration with ESS allows additional flexibility, the following additional options are available.

Figure 2.30 provides the additional settings that can be enforced while working with the Web CATS version (service CATW), only when dealing with Internet Transaction Server. This screen has no impact on the new Web Dynpro screen. These settings are important as they provide a great flexibility throughout the screens provided by SAP.

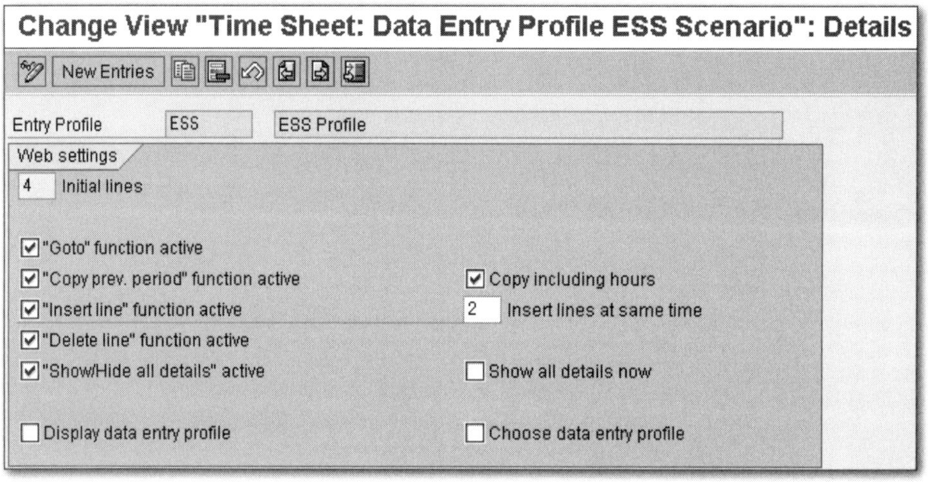

Figure 2.30 ESS Profile Web Settings

These settings are meant to tailor the user's screen to its best possibility, for instance with regard to its size. It is also a useful settings tool to hide functions to which the end-users are not entitled.

- **Initial lines**
  This option tells the system with how many lines the empty screen will initiate.

- **"Goto" function active**
  Should this option be selected, the icons go to will be enabled. This is a nice feature for allowing the end user to smoothly travel from one week to another.

- **"Copy prev. period" function active**
  Should this option be ticked, it will allow the end user to copy the past entries already done. It is a handy feature, especially with users working with the same activities every week; for instance, help desks, consultants, etc.

- **Copy including hours**
  Should the copy of the previous period be included? Theoretically, as the activities are likely to be the same, the time spent will differ. Therefore, most of the time this option is disabled.

- **"Insert line" function active**
  Can the end user add lines in his screen?

- **Insert lines at same time**
  If the end user can add lines, how many lines must be inserted? Please bear in mind that you are likely to be limited in screen space. Therefore, you should settle for five lines.

- **"Delete line" function active**
  Can the end user delete the lines?

- **"Show/Hide all details" active**
  In the standard screen, it is possible to go deeper in regards to the time entry details. Can the end user access it?

- **Show all details now**
  Show all details by default. Once again, as we are limited in screen space, this option is disabled all the time.

- **Display data entry profile**
  This option allows the end user to see which data-entry profile is used. Although it might be useful to know, for instance, for authorization purposes, this option is not enabled.

- **Choose data entry profile**
  This option allows the end users to choose their own data entry profile. Unless the end user is an administrator or a super-user, we would strongly advise not to enable this option.

By default, the CATS profile of the end user is defaulted by using the system parameter CVR in the SAP user's profile.

However, in most cases, we do need to enable this option as the end user is likely to select from the three basic data-entry profiles most companies use. These are:

- Daily profile
- Weekly profile
- Monthly profile

2.3.6 Define Field Selection for ESS

In order to enable the fields for the Web scenario CATW, the fields have to be re-enabled because the business requirements for the intranet/Internet solution can differ from those of the R/3 backend system.

Figure 2.31 provides the entry to the customizing screen, so managing the fields can be done through the Web-enabled Time Sheet. This customizing step is similar to the customizing steps for the regular backend screens. As with that, do not change the root of the customizing entry, switch to an influencing mode so that customizing effects will only apply for the selected data-entry profile.

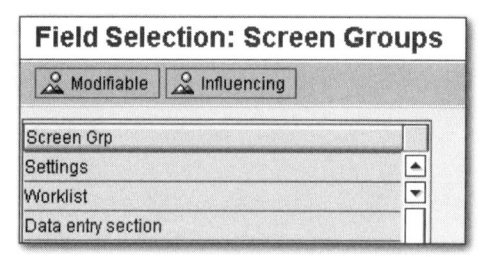

Figure 2.31 Entry to Customizing Screen

This is a useful feature, as it reduces the cost of development on the end user's interface. The main reason we are reducing the number of fields is because of the limited screen area. The options available are the same as those listed in the previous section, under the R/3 fields for the data-entry profile.

> **Hint**
> SAP HR users are aware of the table T588M, which is used to disable standard fields in the infotypes. A similar option is available for the Employee Self-Services (ESS) scenario using the table V_T588M_ESS (Control of Screen Fields for ESS Scenarios). You are advised to check these possibilities, rather than creating directly specific screens. This only applies for Internet Transaction Server based services. This table is obsolete when dealing with the new Web Dynpros.

2.3.7 Edit Possible Entries in the Search Help

We always aim to provide the best end user interface. Therefore, SAP also provides a way to assist the end user while searching for the information. Although the standard features provided are already adequate, this step could allow you to please the regular end user.

Figure 2.32 highlights the customizing entry where it is possible to define the help entries used in the Internet search engine. Figure 2.33 illustrates the detailed view of the possible help entries for the Internet search engine. This step could be very helpful if you enhance the CATS system by adding a specific field.

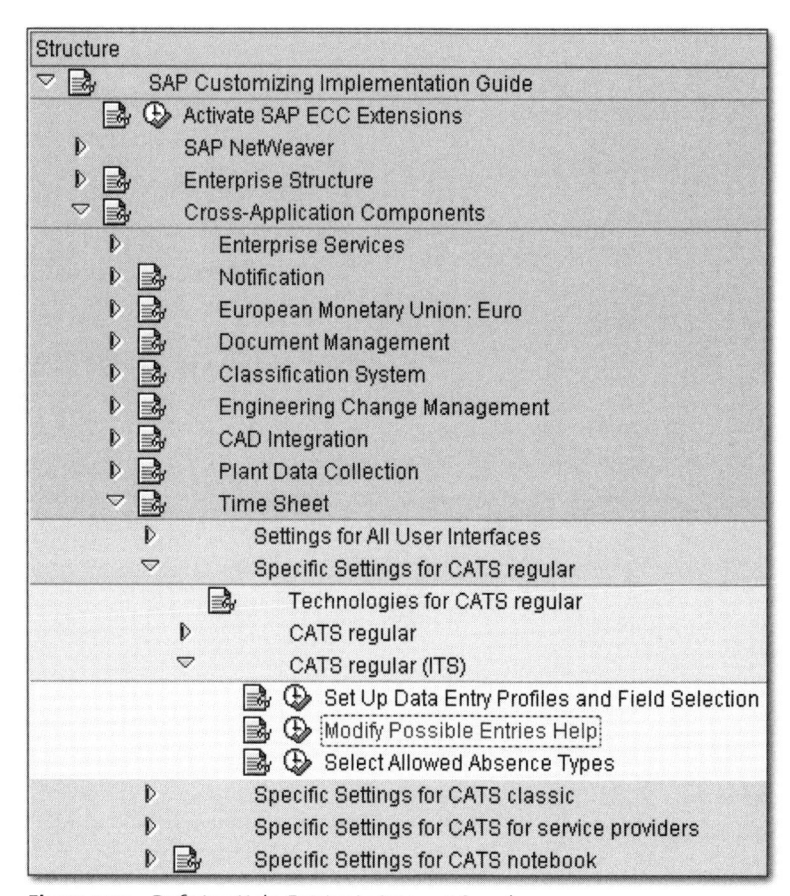

Figure 2.32 Defining Help Entries in Internet Search

2 | Customizing and Enhancing CATS

Field name	Srch help	Type
ARBPL	CRAMA	SH Search help
AUFKZ	AUFKN	FV Fixed values for domains
AUTYP	AUFTYP	FV Fixed values for domains
BEMOT	H_TBMOT	SH Search help
KAPAR	H_TC26	SH Search help
KOKRS	H_TKA01_CORE	SH Search help
LSTNR	ASMDH	SH Search help
OTYPE	H_T7780	SH Search help
PLANS	H_T528B	SH Search help
RAUFNR	ORDPA	SH Search help
RKDAUF	VMVAA	SH Search help
RKOSTL	KOSTN	SH Search help
RKSTR	KKPKA	SH Search help
RNPLNR	AUKOB	SH Search help
RPRZNR	COBPN	SH Search help
SEBELN	MEKKK	SH Search help
SKOSTL	KOSTN	SH Search help
SPRZNR	COBPN	SH Search help

Figure 2.33 Potential Help Entries for Internet Search

2.3.8 Select Allowed Absence Types

For Time Management, we are required to collect the relevant entries for the attendances and absences types. While we want to empower the end user, there are still certain attendances and absences types that can only be booked through a personnel administrator. These might include maternity leave, or a long-term illness.

Therefore, to restrict the view of the table and to secure the relevancy of the data, we can deactivate for CATS, all the irrelevant attendances and absences types.

Figure 2.34 illustrates the customizing step for selecting the allowed attendances and absences types to be used while working with the Web-enabled Time Sheet.

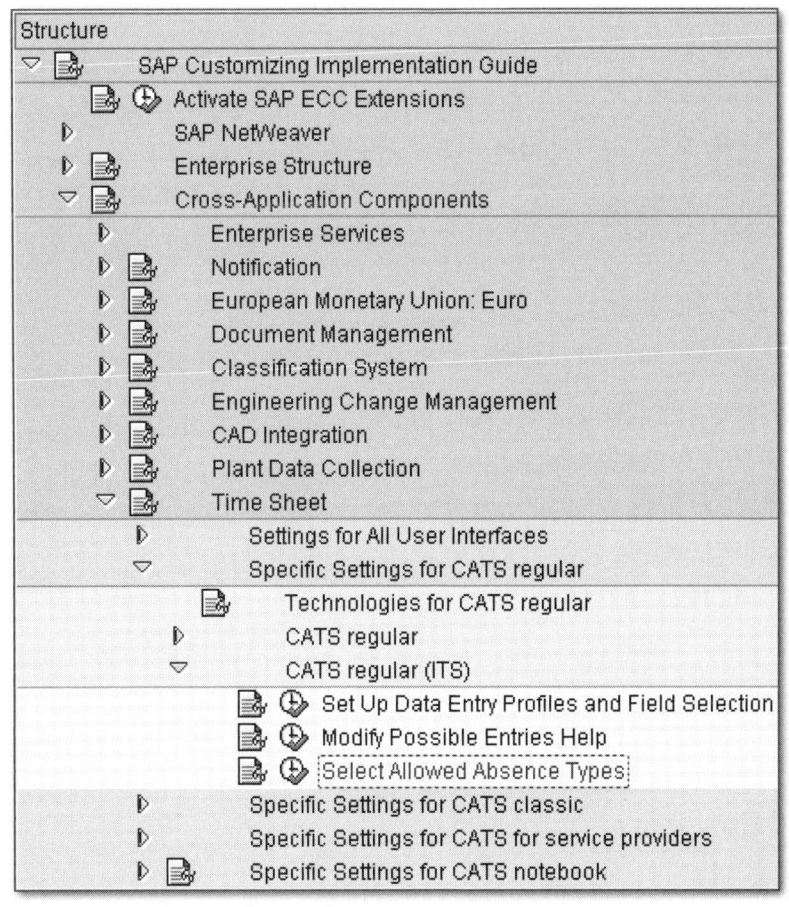

```
Structure
▽ 📄  SAP Customizing Implementation Guide
     📄 🕐  Activate SAP ECC Extensions
   ▷        SAP NetWeaver
   ▷ 📄    Enterprise Structure
   ▽ 📄    Cross-Application Components
       ▷           Enterprise Services
       ▷ 📄       Notification
       ▷ 📄       European Monetary Union: Euro
       ▷ 📄       Document Management
       ▷ 📄       Classification System
       ▷ 📄       Engineering Change Management
       ▷ 📄       CAD Integration
       ▷ 📄       Plant Data Collection
       ▽ 📄       Time Sheet
           ▷           Settings for All User Interfaces
           ▽           Specific Settings for CATS regular
                📄         Technologies for CATS regular
              ▷              CATS regular
              ▽              CATS regular (ITS)
                    📄 🕐 Set Up Data Entry Profiles and Field Selection
                    📄 🕐 Modify Possible Entries Help
                    📄 🕐 Select Allowed Absence Types
           ▷           Specific Settings for CATS classic
           ▷           Specific Settings for CATS for service providers
           ▷ 📄       Specific Settings for CATS notebook
```

Figure 2.34 Selecting Allowed Absence Types

After having carefully checked with the time administrators and the internal procedures, you can deactivate the attendances and absences types that you do not wish to be used through CATS.

Figure 2.35 illustrates the detailed view of the table V_T554S_ESSEX. This table allows a selection of the absence types that are allowed. It is easy as a mouse click: Simply flag the respective fields that have to be deactivated.

2 | Customizing and Enhancing CATS

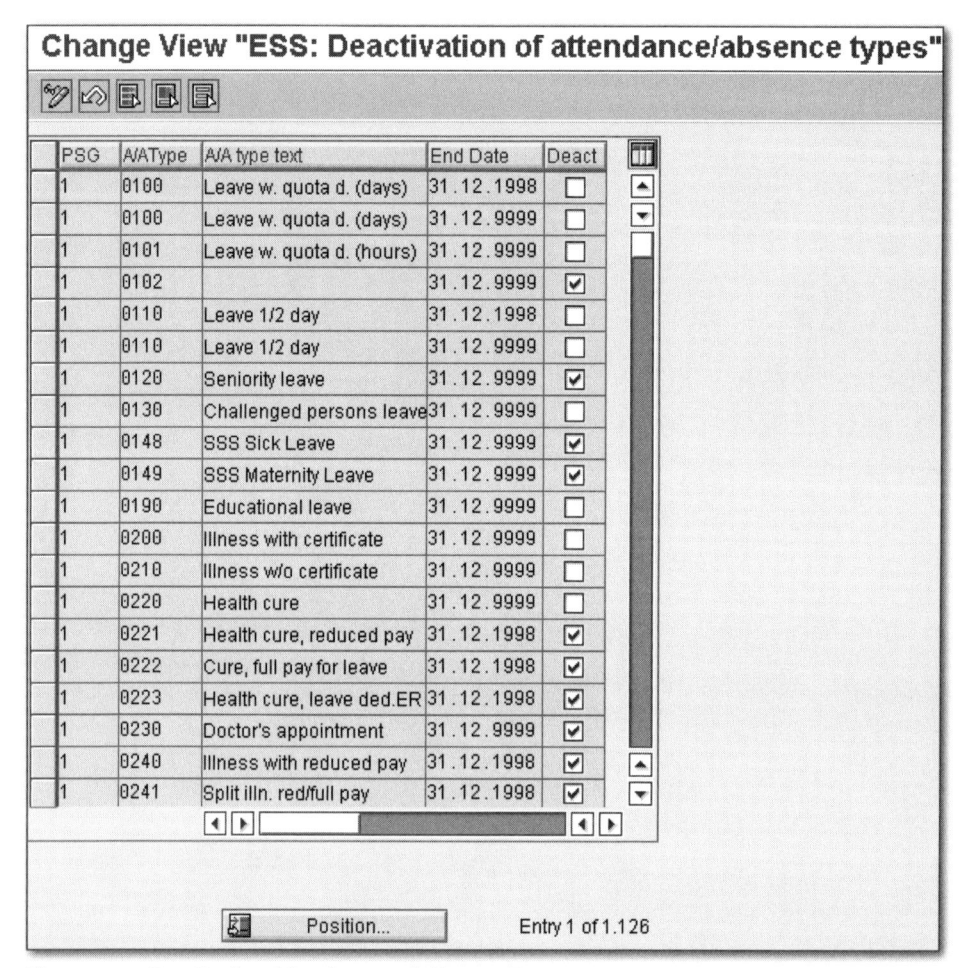

PSG	A/AType	A/A type text	End Date	Deact
1	0100	Leave w. quota d. (days)	31.12.1998	☐
1	0100	Leave w. quota d. (days)	31.12.9999	☐
1	0101	Leave w. quota d. (hours)	31.12.9999	☐
1	0102		31.12.9999	☑
1	0110	Leave 1/2 day	31.12.1998	☐
1	0110	Leave 1/2 day	31.12.9999	☐
1	0120	Seniority leave	31.12.9999	☑
1	0130	Challenged persons leave	31.12.9999	☐
1	0148	SSS Sick Leave	31.12.9999	☑
1	0149	SSS Maternity Leave	31.12.9999	☑
1	0190	Educational leave	31.12.9999	☐
1	0200	Illness with certificate	31.12.9999	☐
1	0210	Illness w/o certificate	31.12.9999	☐
1	0220	Health cure	31.12.9999	☐
1	0221	Health cure, reduced pay	31.12.1998	☑
1	0222	Cure, full pay for leave	31.12.1998	☑
1	0223	Health cure, leave ded.ER	31.12.1998	☑
1	0230	Doctor's appointment	31.12.9999	☑
1	0240	Illness with reduced pay	31.12.1998	☑
1	0241	Split illn. red/full pay	31.12.1998	☑

Figure 2.35 Deactivating Attendance and Absence Types

> **Hint**
>
> You might come across a similar table (V_T512Z_ESSEX - ESS: Deactivate Wage Types per Infotype) for the Wage Types. Unfortunately, this table is not meant for CATS. Rather, use the user exit CATS0003 – CATS: Validate recorded data.

2.4 Additional CATS Customizing

2.4.1 Define Print Report

The standard report (RCATSSP01) provided by SAP for printing CATS entries—whatever the target modules—can be overwritten by indicating its name here.

2.4.2 Define Authorization Groups

This table gathers the different authorization groups to be assigned to each data-entry profile. They will be used later on in the authorization setup, in order to restrict the access on a need to basis.

2.4.3 Specify Task Types, Components, and Levels

CATS is mostly used among the target modules already in place. However, it can also be used as a standalone system. Figure 2.36 illustrates the customizing access available to specify the tasks types, the components, and the different levels.

If this solution is selected, the following items must be defined in the customizing step:

- **Task type**
  The task type defines the activity that will be performed by an employee.
- **Component**
  The component will decline the different kind of activities within the task type (normal hours, overtime, on call, on duty, etc.)
- **Levels**
  This step will ensure that there is a different valuation, based on the component's information. An example would be overtime paid at 25% extra rate.

2 | Customizing and Enhancing CATS

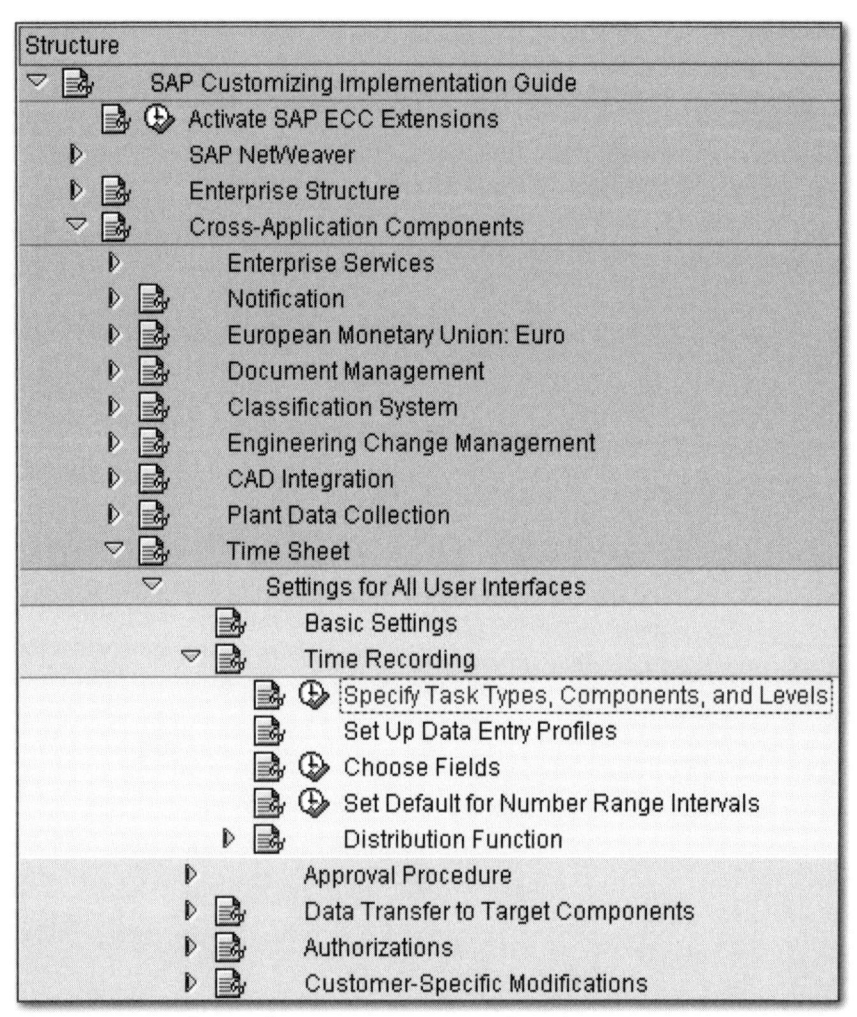

```
Structure
  ▽ 📄  SAP Customizing Implementation Guide
      📄 🕒  Activate SAP ECC Extensions
      ▷     SAP NetWeaver
      ▷ 📄  Enterprise Structure
      ▽ 📄  Cross-Application Components
          ▷     Enterprise Services
          ▷ 📄  Notification
          ▷ 📄  European Monetary Union: Euro
          ▷ 📄  Document Management
          ▷ 📄  Classification System
          ▷ 📄  Engineering Change Management
          ▷ 📄  CAD Integration
          ▷ 📄  Plant Data Collection
          ▽ 📄  Time Sheet
              ▽     Settings for All User Interfaces
                  📄  Basic Settings
                ▽ 📄  Time Recording
                    📄 🕒  Specify Task Types, Components, and Levels
                    📄     Set Up Data Entry Profiles
                    📄 🕒  Choose Fields
                    📄 🕒  Set Default for Number Range Intervals
                  ▷ 📄  Distribution Function
              ▷     Approval Procedure
              ▷ 📄  Data Transfer to Target Components
              ▷ 📄  Authorizations
              ▷ 📄  Customer-Specific Modifications
```

Figure 2.36 Specifying Task Types, Components, and Levels

Figure 2.37 provides a detailed view of the customizing table with the relevant entry for the tasks levels.

Additional CATS Customizing | 2.4

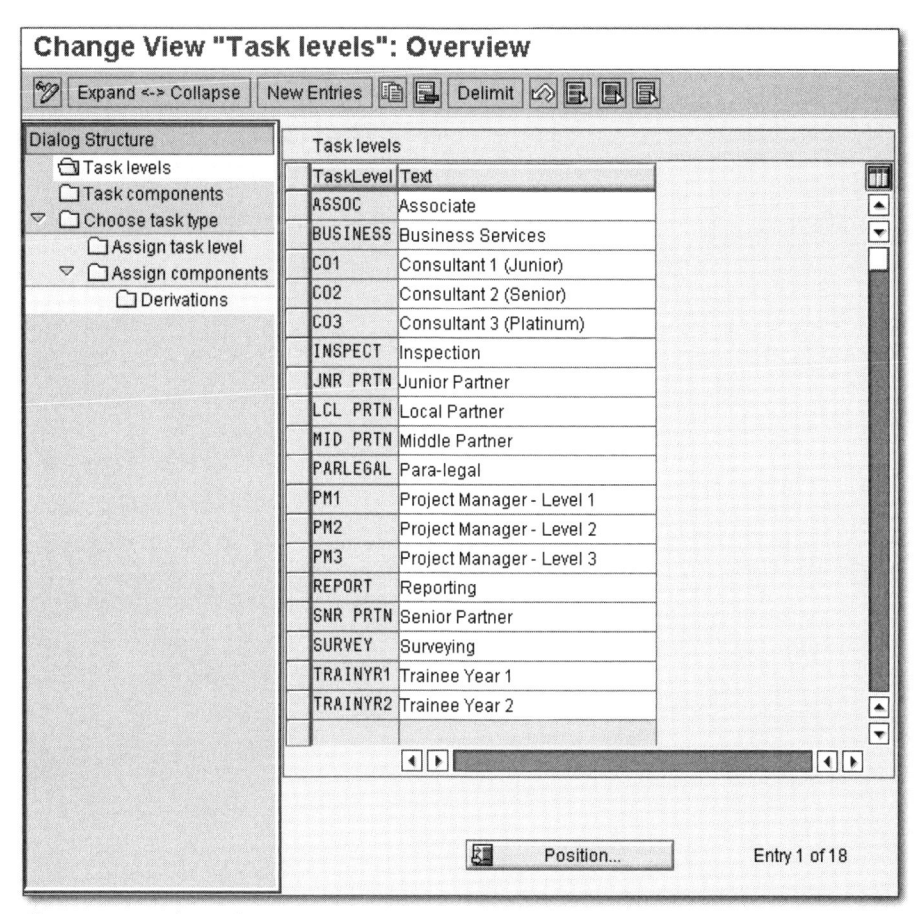

Figure 2.37 Task Level Overview Screen

2.4.4 Define Rejection Reasons for the Approval Process

The table depicted in Figures 2.38 and 2.39 shows the different rejection reasons likely to be used, if the approval phase is enabled in the CATS process. To set up the different rejection reasons that the approver will use, you have to customize the entry. Figure 2.38 illustrates the customizing access for defining the rejection reasons to be used in the approval process.

Figure 2.39 gives a detailed view of the customizing table, with the relevant rejection reasons created. If the company operates in an international environment, please remember to translate these rejection reasons. If the translation is missing, a blank line will be displayed in front of the rejection reason ID.

2 | Customizing and Enhancing CATS

```
Structure
  ▷    SAP NetWeaver
  ▷    Enterprise Structure
  ▽    Cross-Application Components
    ▷    Enterprise Services
    ▷    Notification
    ▷    European Monetary Union: Euro
    ▷    Document Management
    ▷    Classification System
    ▷    Engineering Change Management
    ▷    CAD Integration
    ▷    Plant Data Collection
    ▽    Time Sheet
      ▽    Settings for All User Interfaces
             Basic Settings
        ▷    Time Recording
        ▽    Approval Procedure
               Define Rejection Reasons
          ▷    Special Approval
          ▷    Approve Working Times
                 Determine Variant of Approval Report for Workflow
                 Workflow: Specify Method for Executing UWL Item
                 BAdI: CATS Approval
        ▷    Data Transfer to Target Components
        ▷    Authorizations
        ▷    Customer-Specific Modifications
      ▷    Specific Settings for CATS regular
      ▷    Specific Settings for CATS classic
```

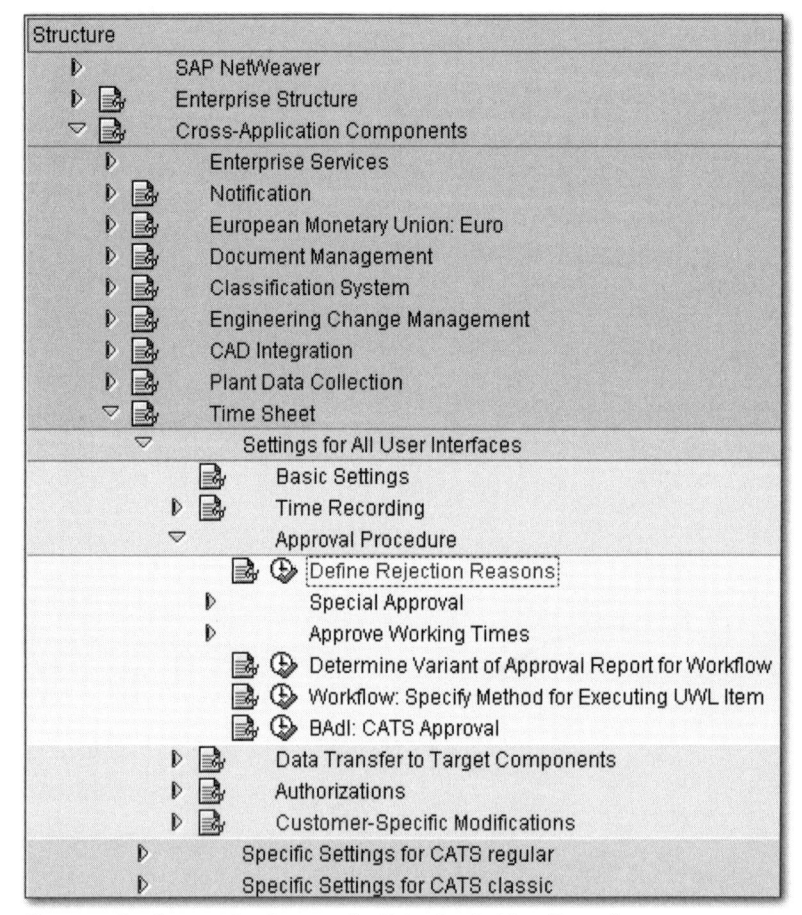

Figure 2.38 Customizing Reasons for Rejection in Time Recording

Please note, that for the R/3 Enterprise version, along with the rejection reason, you can add more detailed text if you want. Please select the box LT (Long Text) to enable this option.

Within the R/3 enterprise release, this option is only available with the following transactions:

▸ CATS_APPR: Approve Working Times (Power user)

▸ CATS_APPR_LITE: Approve Working Times

▸ ACTEXP_APPR: Approve Working Times and Trips

If you work on international projects, do not forget to translate these reasons.

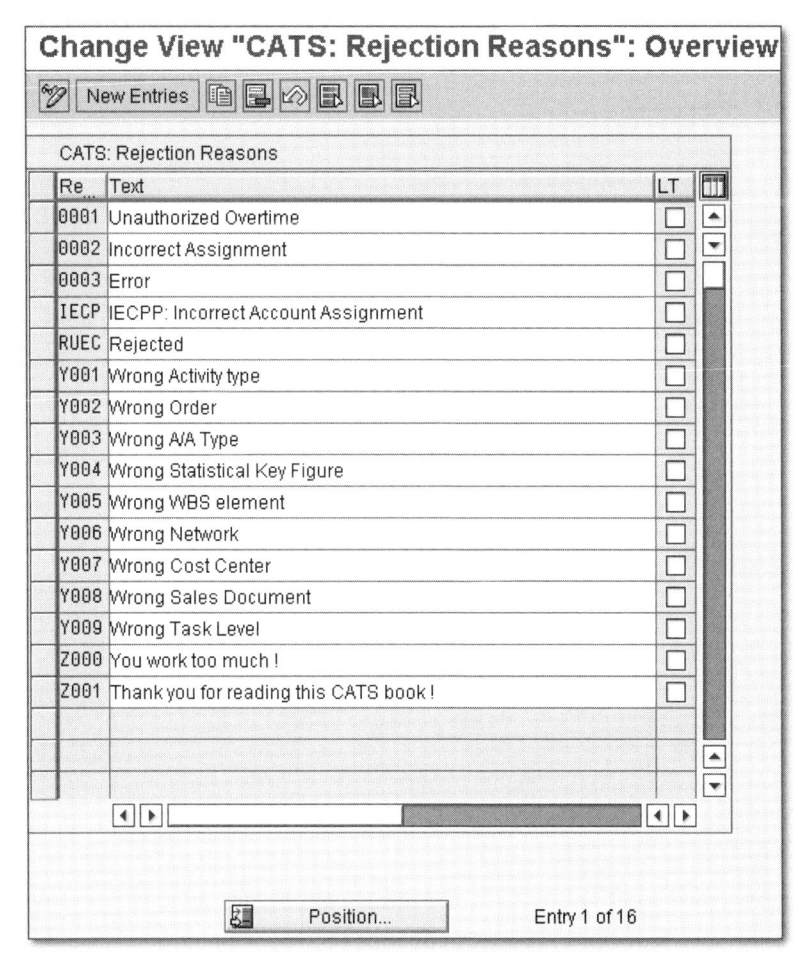

Re...	Text	LT
0001	Unauthorized Overtime	
0002	Incorrect Assignment	
0003	Error	
IECP	IECPP: Incorrect Account Assignment	
RUEC	Rejected	
Y001	Wrong Activity type	
Y002	Wrong Order	
Y003	Wrong A/A Type	
Y004	Wrong Statistical Key Figure	
Y005	Wrong WBS element	
Y006	Wrong Network	
Y007	Wrong Cost Center	
Y008	Wrong Sales Document	
Y009	Wrong Task Level	
Z000	You work too much !	
Z001	Thank you for reading this CATS book !	

Figure 2.39 List of CATS Rejection Reasons

2.4.5 Determine How to Fill CO Documents during Transfer to Controlling

Since CATS is receiving a lot of information, it is technically written in the tables relevant for each target module. This customizing step emphasizes the transfer to Controlling (CO). Indeed, we must verify with the controlling department what is best suited with regard to the activities collected through CATS. Figure 2.40 illustrates the customizing access for filling in the CO documents.

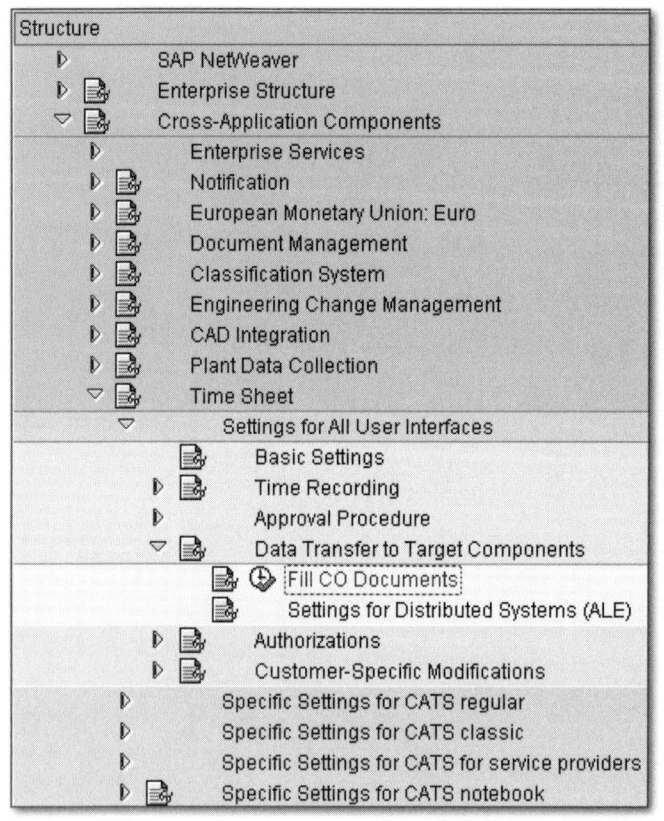

```
Structure
  ▷      SAP NetWeaver
  ▷ 📄   Enterprise Structure
  ▽ 📄   Cross-Application Components
      ▷      Enterprise Services
      ▷ 📄   Notification
      ▷ 📄   European Monetary Union: Euro
      ▷ 📄   Document Management
      ▷ 📄   Classification System
      ▷ 📄   Engineering Change Management
      ▷ 📄   CAD Integration
      ▷ 📄   Plant Data Collection
      ▽ 📄   Time Sheet
          ▽      Settings for All User Interfaces
              📄   Basic Settings
          ▷ 📄   Time Recording
          ▷      Approval Procedure
          ▽ 📄   Data Transfer to Target Components
              📄 ⊕ Fill CO Documents
              📄   Settings for Distributed Systems (ALE)
          ▷ 📄   Authorizations
          ▷ 📄   Customer-Specific Modifications
      ▷      Specific Settings for CATS regular
      ▷      Specific Settings for CATS classic
      ▷      Specific Settings for CATS for service providers
      ▷ 📄   Specific Settings for CATS notebook
```

Figure 2.40 Customizing Access for CO Documents

Figure 2.41 illustrates the different customizing options available for the filling up of the Controlling documents. Selecting the box in front of that option can easily enable the chosen option. The following options are possible:

- **One CO document per record**
  This option must be activated, if you need a detailed transcript of each time entry. Practically speaking, this is not what the controllers ask for.
- **All data records in one CO document**
  This option is the most common one used while setting up CATS, unless there needs to be a detailed subtotal by employee.
- **All data records of a personnel number in a CO document**
  This option is the most common one used while settings up CATS, if the HR module is in place.

- **All date records summarized into one CO document**
  This option will summarize all the entries into one CO document.

- **All data records of a personnel number summarized into one CO document**
  This option is a variant of the data recorded by personnel number into a CO document but it will be summarized. This will enhance the visibility of the data whilst the controllers will have access to it.

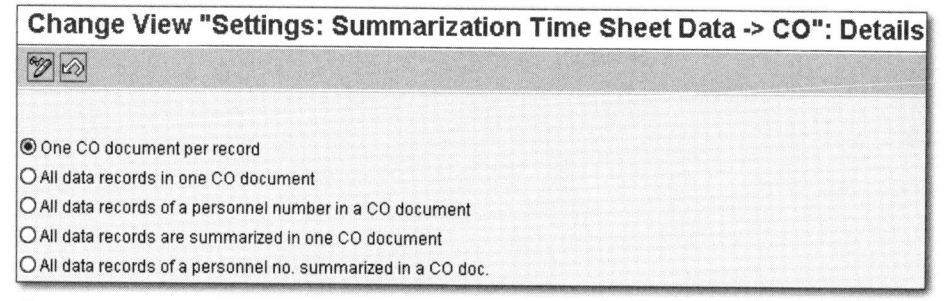

Figure 2.41 Summarizing Time-Sheet Data for Controlling

> **Note**
> This entry is critical as you are about to deal with a lot of CATS entries. Carefully check the requirement(s) from the controlling side.

2.5 Enhancing CATS

As we have seen in the previous sections, CATS provides many flexible settings for tailoring the user interface to the business requirements. Nevertheless, SAP provides a wide range of user-exits — shown in Figure 2.42 — that can extend CATS flexibility even further. The user-exits can be accessed via the transaction code SMOD. It is mandatory that user-exits be stored in a project, which must be activated prior to use.

The user-exits remain in effect when the SAP system is upgraded since the enhancements done in the system are not overwritten. They must, however, be revised and the source re-tested to guarantee consistency. As each requirement is different, you will find, whenever available, the sample source code provided by SAP.

Exit name	Short text
CATP0001	Determine target hours
CATS0001	CATS: Set up worklist
CATS0002	CATS: Supplement recorded data
CATS0003	CATS: Validate recorded data
CATS0004	CATS: Deactivate functions in the user interface
CATS0005	CATS: Customer field enhancements
CATS0006	CATS: Validate entire time sheet
CATS0007	CATS: Subscreen on initial screen
CATS0008	CATS: Determine workflow recipients for approval
CATS0009	CATS: Customer-Specific Text Fields in Data Entry Secti
CATS0010	CATS: Customer-Specific Text Fields in Worklist
CATS0011	CATS: Customer functions
CATS0012	CATS: Subscreen on data entry screen
CATSBW01	Customer Exit for Time Sheet Data Transfer -> BW

Figure 2.42 User-Exits Available for CATS

2.5.1 Determine the Target Hours

This user-exit CATP0001 can be used to enhance the determination of the target hours provided in CATS. The function module used is EXIT_SAPLCATP_001 and is shown here.

```
FUNCTION EXIT_SAPLCATP_001.
*"----------------------------------------------------------*"
*"Lokale Schnittstelle:
*"  IMPORTING
*"     VALUE(SAP_PERNR) LIKE P0001-PERNR
*"     VALUE(SAP_BEGDA) LIKE SY-DATUM
*"     VALUE(SAP_ENDDA) LIKE SY-DATUM
*"     VALUE(SAP_TIMETYPE) LIKE T555A-ZTART
*"     VALUE(SAP_SUBHRTIMES) LIKE RPTXXXXX-KR_FELD7
*"     VALUE(SAP_ADDOVERTIME) LIKE RPTXXXXX-KR_FELD7
*"  EXPORTING
*"     REFERENCE(SAP_TARGET_HOURS) TYPE
*"        CATS_HOURS_PER_DAY_TAB
*"  EXCEPTIONS
*"     NO_TARGETHOURS_DETERMINED
*"----------------------------------------------------------*"

INCLUDE ZXCATPU01 .
```

2.5.2 Compile the Worklist

This user-exit CATS0001 can be used to structure the contents of your worklist per your requirements. The worklist (based on the parameters of the data-entry profile) is copied to the table SAP_ICATSW. The table is defined in the function-module interface. It takes the format of the (DDIC) table CATSW and contains the contents of the worklist.

You can change or delete lines from the table, and this will be reflected in the setting up of the worklist. You can also insert new lines. You cannot, however, use this enhancement to insert new columns.

The table contents are displayed in the Time Sheet worklist. The data-entry profile (SAP_TCATS), the personnel number (SAP_PERNR), and the data-entry period (SAP_DATALEFT and SAP_DATERIGHT) are also copied into the table.

Understand that you must activate the customer-enhancement field in the worklist section when you maintain the settings for the data-entry profile you want to use.

The function module used is EXIT_SAPLCATS_001, detailed below.

```
FUNCTION EXIT_SAPLCATS_001.
*"----------------------------------------------------------
*"*"Lokale Schnittstelle:
*"  IMPORTING
*"     VALUE(SAP_TCATS) LIKE TCATS STRUCTURE TCATS
*"     VALUE(SAP_PERNR) LIKE CATSFIELDS-PERNR
*"     VALUE(SAP_DATELEFT) LIKE CATSFIELDS-DATELEFT
*"     VALUE(SAP_DATERIGHT) LIKE CATSFIELDS-DATERIGHT
*"     VALUE(SAP_DATEFROM) LIKE CATSFIELDS-DATEFROM OPTIONAL
*"     VALUE(SAP_DATETO) LIKE CATSFIELDS-DATETO OPTIONAL
*"  TABLES
*"     SAP_ICATSW STRUCTURE CATSW
*"     SAP_ICATSW_FIX STRUCTURE CATSW OPTIONAL
*"----------------------------------------------------------

INCLUDE ZXCATU01.
```

2.5.3 Supplement Recorded Data

This user-exit CATS0002 can be used to supplement the data entered using the Time Sheet. The internal table ENRICH_TABLE is used to communicate with the

SAP system. When the enhancement is called, the table contains one data record. You can then change the contents of the record and use the internal table ENRICH_TABLE to return it to the standard program.

Suppose you want to replace the receiver cost center 0000002200 Personnel, recorded on February 1st, 2005, with the cost center that is currently valid (cost center 0000002100 Logistics).

The sample code could be as follows:

```
LOOP AT ENRICH_TABLE.
IF ENRICH_TABLE_RKOSTL = ,0000002200'
AND ENRICH_TABLE-WORKDATE = ,20050201'.
ENRICH_TABLE-RKOSTL = ,0000002100'.
MODIFY ENRICH_TABLE.
ENDIF.
ENDLOOP.
```

The function module used is EXIT_SAPLCATS_002.

```
FUNCTION EXIT_SAPLCATS_002.
*"----------------------------------------------------------
*"*"Lokale Schnittstelle:
*"  IMPORTING
*"     VALUE(SAP_TCATS) LIKE TCATS STRUCTURE TCATS OPTIONAL
*"  TABLES
*"     ENRICH_TABLE STRUCTURE CATS_COMM
*"----------------------------------------------------------


INCLUDE ZXCATU02.
```

> **Hint**
> You can return more than one data record. The system then inserts another line for the additional record.

2.5.4 Validate Recorded Data

This user-exit CATS0003 can be used to validate any data already recorded. Validations are done at the cell level (an entry by one person on one day).

As an example let us suppose that you do not want SAP user MGILLET to record time data for the receiver cost center 0000002200 — Personnel.

The transfer structure is the structure FIELDS. This structure contains all the account- assignment fields relevant for you. If you wish to trigger and display a message to the standard program, you will also need to use the internal table I_MESSAGES.

Please refer to the table T100 where all SAP standard messages are stored. You will be required to add your own message class and messages. In this example, the error message 001 is triggered with message class ZZ, message type E (Error) and the parameter PLEASE DO NOT USE THIS COST CENTER.

Making entries in table I_MESSAGES is equivalent to using the command MESSAGE E001 (ZZ) with PLEASE DO NOT USE THIS COST CENTER. However, to ensure that all programs flows can run, fill the internal table I_MESSAGES instead of using this command.

The sample code for this example is as follows:

```
REFRESH I_MESSAGES.
IF FIELDS-RKOSTL = ‚0000002200' AND SY-UNAME = ‚MGILLET'.
I_MESSAGES-MSGTY = ‚E'.
I_MESSAGES-MSGID = ‚ZZ'.
I_MESSAGES-MSGNO = ‚001'.
I_MESSAGES_MSGV1 = ‚Please do not use this cost center'.
APPEND I_MESSAGES.
ENDIF.
```

The function module used is EXIT_SAPLCATS_003.

```
FUNCTION EXIT_SAPLCATS_003.
*"----------------------------------------------------------
*"*"Local interface:
*"  IMPORTING
*"     VALUE(FIELDS) LIKE CATS_COMM STRUCTURE CATS_COMM
*"     VALUE(SAP_TCATS) LIKE TCATS STRUCTURE TCATS OPTIONAL
*"     VALUE(OLD_DATA) TYPE BOOLEAN OPTIONAL
*"  TABLES
*"     I_MESSAGES STRUCTURE CATS_MESG
*"----------------------------------------------------------


INCLUDE ZXCATU03.
```

2.5.5 Deactivate Functions in the User Interface

This user-exit CATS0004 can be used to hide the function codes in the standard backend CATS transactions (i.e. CAT2). Along with the screen number and the processing mode, the data-entry profile with the current settings (TCATS) and the personnel number are transferred to the interface.

You can extend table T_CUAFC with function codes, using or not using the transferred information. The function codes are then deactivated in the graphical user interface (SAP GUI).

You can identify which screen is used in the transaction by using the menu path SYSTEM • STATUS. It provides the program name, the screen number, and the graphical user interface (GUI) status.

This information can be further used via the transaction code SE41 — Menu PAINTER.

The program name for CATS is SAPLCATS. Figure 2.43 provides an extensive list of the program statuses used in the CATS screens.

| Program Name | Report title |
Status	Description
SAPLCATS	Cross-Application Time Sheet
AGENTS	CATS: Agent
CELL	CATS: Information on an Input Cell
CUSTOM	CATS: Customer Fields
DETAIL	CATS: Detail Screen
DIST	CATS: Distribution
INIT	CATS: Initial Screen
LEGEND	CATS: Legend
PROFIL	CATS: Data Entry Profile
REASON	CATS: Rejection Reason (not currently used)
SEARCH	CATS: Find Entries
STATUS	CATS: Status Filter
TIMEAPPR	CATS: Approve Times (not currently used)
TIMED	CATS: Display Data Entry View
TIMEFRED	CATS: Release View in Display Mode
TIMEFREE	CATS: Release View
TIMEM	CATS: Data Entry View
TIMEOWN	CATS: Variable View
TIMEOWND	CATS: Variable View
WFAPPR	CATS: Workflow Approval

Figure 2.43 CATS Program Status Definitions

2.5 Enhancing CATS

The following GUI statuses are available: When selecting a status; such as TIMEM, you can find the internal names of the functions codes you might wish to hide. Figure 2.44 displays the GUI statuses used among the standard CATS screens.

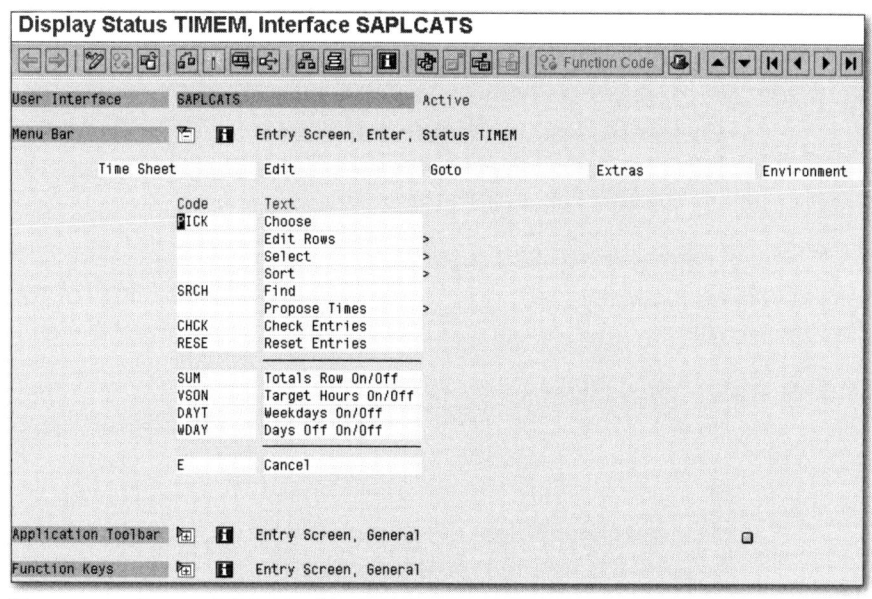

```
Display Status TIMEM, Interface SAPLCATS

User Interface    SAPLCATS                    Active
Menu Bar                          Entry Screen, Enter, Status TIMEM
         Time Sheet         Edit           Goto          Extras         Environment
                    Code   Text
                    PICK   Choose
                           Edit Rows        >
                           Select           >
                           Sort             >
                    SRCH   Find
                           Propose Times    >
                    CHCK   Check Entries
                    RESE   Reset Entries

                    SUM    Totals Row On/Off
                    VSON   Target Hours On/Off
                    DAYT   Weekdays On/Off
                    WDAY   Days Off On/Off

                    E      Cancel

Application Toolbar               Entry Screen, General
Function Keys                     Entry Screen, General
```

Figure 2.44 Status of GUIs Used in CATS Screens

We could, e.g., hide the function codes TRAV—Travel Expenses and WITH—Material withdrawal. The function module used is EXIT_SAPLCATS_004, detailed below.

```
FUNCTION EXIT_SAPLCATS_004.
*"----------------------------------------------------------
*"*"Lokale Schnittstelle:
*"  IMPORTING
*"     VALUE(DYNNR) LIKE SY-DYNNR
*"     VALUE(TCATS) LIKE TCATS STRUCTURE TCATS
*"     VALUE(MODE) LIKE TC10-TRTYP
*"     VALUE(PERNO) LIKE CATSDB-PERNR OPTIONAL
*"  TABLES
*"     T_CUAFC STRUCTURE CUAFCODE
*"----------------------------------------------------------


INCLUDE ZXCATU04.
```

2.5.6 Customer Fields Enhancements

This user-exit CATS0005 can be used to define specific customer fields and assign them to SAP predefined numbering. In the latest SAP release, ten extra fields are available for specific requirements.

There are two options available to set up these specific fields. The first option is to define the customer-specific fields in the customer include (CI_CATSDB) included in the ABAP/4 Dictionary for the CATS database (CATSDB). Only use fields type CHAR and/or NUMC. These fields must then be activated the transaction CAC5: Additional Customer Fields in CATS.

A second option is to trigger a dedicated popup screen for the specific fields. The advantage of this option is that you can output context-sensitive information. You have to define the customer include in the CI_CATSDB as seen in the first option.

Then you must define the subscreen SAPLXCAT 1000. This subscreen is then included in the dialog box that is then called. It will contain the specific screens defined.

You then must define a menu option to trigger the dialog box with your customer fields. You will also have to define a function module to receive data in the transfer structure FIELDS and then return the data to the calling program.

The function modules used are:

EXIT_SAPLCATS_005 (Export data to the customer dialog box) and

```
FUNCTION EXIT_SAPLCATS_005.
*"----------------------------------------------------------
*"*"Lokale Schnittstelle:
*"  IMPORTING
*"     VALUE(FIELDS) LIKE CATS_COMM STRUCTURE CATS_COMM
*"     VALUE(DISPLAY)
*"     VALUE(SAP_TCATS) LIKE TCATS STRUCTURE TCATS OPTIONAL
*"----------------------------------------------------------


INCLUDE ZXCATU06.
```

EXIT_SAPLCATS_008 (Import data to the customer dialog box).

```
FUNCTION EXIT_SAPLCATS_008.
*"----------------------------------------------------------
```

```
*"*"Lokale Schnittstelle:
*"  IMPORTING
*"     VALUE(SAP_TCATS) LIKE TCATS STRUCTURE TCATS OPTIONAL
*"  EXPORTING
*"     VALUE(FIELDS) LIKE CATS_COMM STRUCTURE CATS_COMM
*"----------------------------------------------------------
```

INCLUDE ZXCATU07.

2.5.7 Validate Entire Time Sheet

Business requirements often dictate the automatic validation of the entire Time Sheet, for specific entries (e. g., overtime hours).

To enable that, you can use the following user-exit.

```
FUNCTION EXIT_SAPLCATS_006.
*"----------------------------------------------------------
--
*"*"Lokale Schnittstelle:
*"  IMPORTING
*"     VALUE(DATEFROM) LIKE CATSFIELDS-DATEFROM
*"     VALUE(DATETO) LIKE CATSFIELDS-DATETO
*"     VALUE(SAP_TCATS) LIKE TCATS STRUCTURE TCATS OPTIONAL
*"  TABLES
*"     CHECK_TABLE STRUCTURE CATS_COMM
*"     I_MESSAGES STRUCTURE CATS_MESG
*"----------------------------------------------------------
```

INCLUDE ZXCATU05.

2.5.8 Subscreen on the Initial Screen

Sometimes, business requirements also require a reminder on the first CATS screen, to display all the times released, times pending approval, and times approved.

SAP provides the user-exit CATS0007 to adapt the program screen.

Figure 2.45 provides a detailed view of the user-exit CATS0007, which is designed for enhancing the initial screen, should this requirement arise on the CATS set-up list.

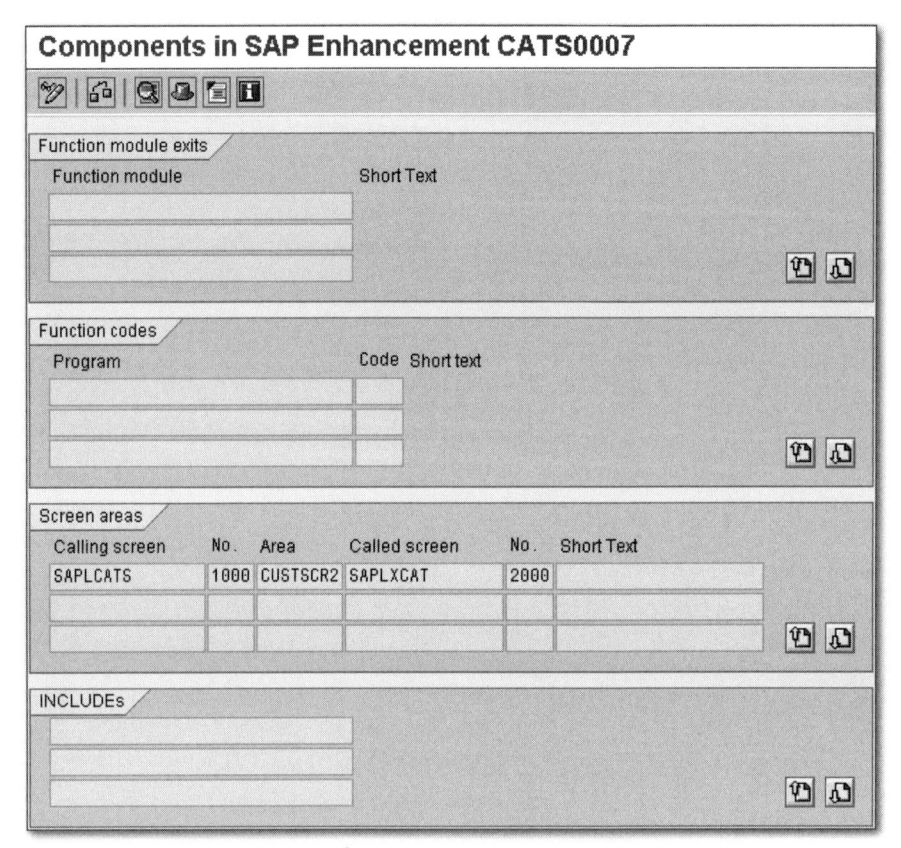

Figure 2.45 User-Exit CATS0007 for Screen Enhancement

2.5.9 Determine Workflow Recipient for Approval

As we have seen in the previous workflow section, SAP provides several possibilities to determine who is in charge for the approval process. Nevertheless, to secure its flexibility, SAP also provides a user-exit where you can set up the best option in the agent determination, to determine the person in charge.

```
FUNCTION EXIT_SAPLCATS_007.
*"----------------------------------------------------------------
*"*"Lokale Schnittstelle:
*"  IMPORTING
*"     VALUE(SAP_TCATS) LIKE TCATS STRUCTURE TCATS
*"     VALUE(SAP_PERNR) LIKE CATSFIELDS-PERNR
*"  EXPORTING
*"     VALUE(POSITION) LIKE AFRU_WF-AGNT_POSIT
```

```
*"  VALUE(USER) LIKE AFRU_WF-AGNT_USER
*"  VALUE(WORKCENTER) LIKE AFRU_WF-AGNT_PLACE
*"  VALUE(JOB) LIKE AFRU_WF-AGNT_JOB
*"  VALUE(UNIT) LIKE AFRU_WF-AGNT_ORGUN
*"  VALUE(AGENT) LIKE AFRU_WF-AGNT_OBJID
*"  VALUE(SCREEN_DARK) LIKE RC27X-FLG_SEL
*"  TABLES
*"  SAP_ICATSDB STRUCTURE CATSDBCOMM
*"  SAP_AGENTS STRUCTURE SWHACTOR
*"----------------------------------------------------------


INCLUDE ZXCATU08 .
```

2.5.10 Customer-Specific Text Fields in Data-Entry Profile

Since CATS is a standard delivery product, it knows which target module will be used. Therefore, you must manually match the receiver object's description with the two display fields provided by SAP. This option is available for the data-entry profile and for the worklist.

Description fields available in the customer-specific text fields for the data-entry profile and the worklist are:

- DISPTEXT1: Description text 1
- DISPTEXT2: Description text 2

```
FUNCTION EXIT_SAPLCATS_009.
*"----------------------------------------------------------
*"*"Lokale Schnittstelle:
*"  IMPORTING
*"  VALUE(TCATS_IMP) LIKE TCATS STRUCTURE TCATS
*"  VALUE(CATSD_IMP) LIKE CATSD_EXT STRUCTURE CATSD_EXT
*"  VALUE(DISPTEXT1_IMP) LIKE CATSFIELDS-DISPTEXT1
*"  VALUE(DISPTEXT2_IMP) LIKE CATSFIELDS-DISPTEXT2
*"  EXPORTING
*"  VALUE(DISPTEXT1_EXP) LIKE CATSFIELDS-DISPTEXT1
*"  VALUE(DISPTEXT2_EXP) LIKE CATSFIELDS-DISPTEXT2
*"----------------------------------------------------------


INCLUDE ZXCATU09 .
```

2.5.11 Customer-Specific Text Fields in Worklist

Use the same procedure here as for the data-entry profile. The main difference is that it is only relevant for the worklist.

```
FUNCTION EXIT_SAPLCATS_010.
*"----------------------------------------------------------
*"*"Lokale Schnittstelle:
*"  IMPORTING
*"     VALUE(TCATS_IMP) LIKE TCATS STRUCTURE TCATS
*"     VALUE(CATSW_IMP) LIKE CATSW STRUCTURE CATSW
*"     VALUE(DISPTEXTW1_IMP) LIKE CATSFIELDS-DISPTEXTW1
*"     VALUE(DISPTEXTW2_IMP) LIKE CATSFIELDS-DISPTEXTW2
*"  EXPORTING
*"     VALUE(DISPTEXTW1_EXP) LIKE CATSFIELDS-DISPTEXTW1
*"     VALUE(DISPTEXTW2_EXP) LIKE CATSFIELDS-DISPTEXTW2
*"----------------------------------------------------------


INCLUDE ZXCATU10 .
```

2.5.12 Customer Functions

In the standard R/3 screen, you can add additional icons. This will enable, e. g., the creation of a link to the remaining Leave Entitlements for the users. This user-exit enables the activation of such an additional icon. Naturally, the content of the link must be coded, if this is not a standard program or feature.

```
FUNCTION EXIT_SAPLCATS_011 .
*"----------------------------------------------------------
*"*"Lokale Schnittstelle:
*"  IMPORTING
*"     VALUE(SAP_FCODE) LIKE SY-UCOMM
*"     VALUE(SAP_TCATS) LIKE TCATS STRUCTURE TCATS OPTIONAL
*"     VALUE(SAP_CATSFIELDS) LIKE CATSFIELDS_COMM
*"      STRUCTURE CATSFIELDS_COMM OPTIONAL
*"     VALUE(SAP_CATSD) TYPE CATSD_EXT_TAB OPTIONAL
*"     VALUE(SAP_CATSW) TYPE CATSW_TAB OPTIONAL
*"     VALUE(SAP_PERNRLIST) TYPE PERNR_LIST_TAB OPTIONAL
*"     VALUE(SAP_CURSOR_FIELD) TYPE TEXT70 OPTIONAL
*"     VALUE(SAP_CURSOR_CATSDLINE) LIKE SY-STEPL OPTIONAL
*"----------------------------------------------------------


INCLUDE ZXCATU12 .
```

2.5.13 Subscreen on Data-Entry Screen

This user-exit enables the organization of the data-entry screen. We could, for instance, take the transaction PA61 — Maintain Time Data — for the Time Administrator as a root.

```
FUNCTION EXIT_SAPLCATS_012 .
*"----------------------------------------------------------
*"*"Lokale Schnittstelle:
*"  IMPORTING
*"     VALUE(SAP_TCATS) LIKE TCATS STRUCTURE TCATS OPTIONAL
*"     VALUE(SAP_CATSFIELDS) LIKE CATSFIELDS_COMM
*"      STRUCTURE CATSFIELDS_COMM OPTIONAL
*"     VALUE(SAP_PERNRLIST) TYPE PERNR_LIST_TAB OPTIONAL
*"  EXPORTING
*"     VALUE(NO_OTHER_HEADER_INFO) TYPE XFELD
*"----------------------------------------------------------


INCLUDE ZXCATU13 .
```

2.5.14 Exit for Time Sheet Transfer to BW

If you have in place a business intelligence tool such as SAP BW, you can enhance the data transfer by using this user-exit.

```
FUNCTION EXIT_SAPLTSBW_001.
*"----------------------------------------------------------
*"*"Lokale Schnittstelle:
*"  IMPORTING
*"     VALUE(XCATSDB) LIKE CATSDB STRUCTURE CATSDB
*"  CHANGING
*"     VALUE(ISOURCE) LIKE CATS_IS_1 STRUCTURE CATS_IS_1
*"----------------------------------------------------------


INCLUDE ZXTSBWU02
```

The user-exits are likely to be the most used features while setting CATS. However, more flexibility is available thanks to the Business Application Program Interface (BAPI): transaction BAPI.

2 | Customizing and Enhancing CATS

For information purposes Figure 2.46 provides an extensive view of the available BAPIs for CATS. A BAPI is a standard piece of code provided by SAP. It can be widely used by programmers in specific programs. Since it is already provided by SAP, its main assets are: faster implementation since already provided, data integrity is secured, in case of issues; it is supported by SAP. The Business Add-In (BAdI): transaction is SE18.

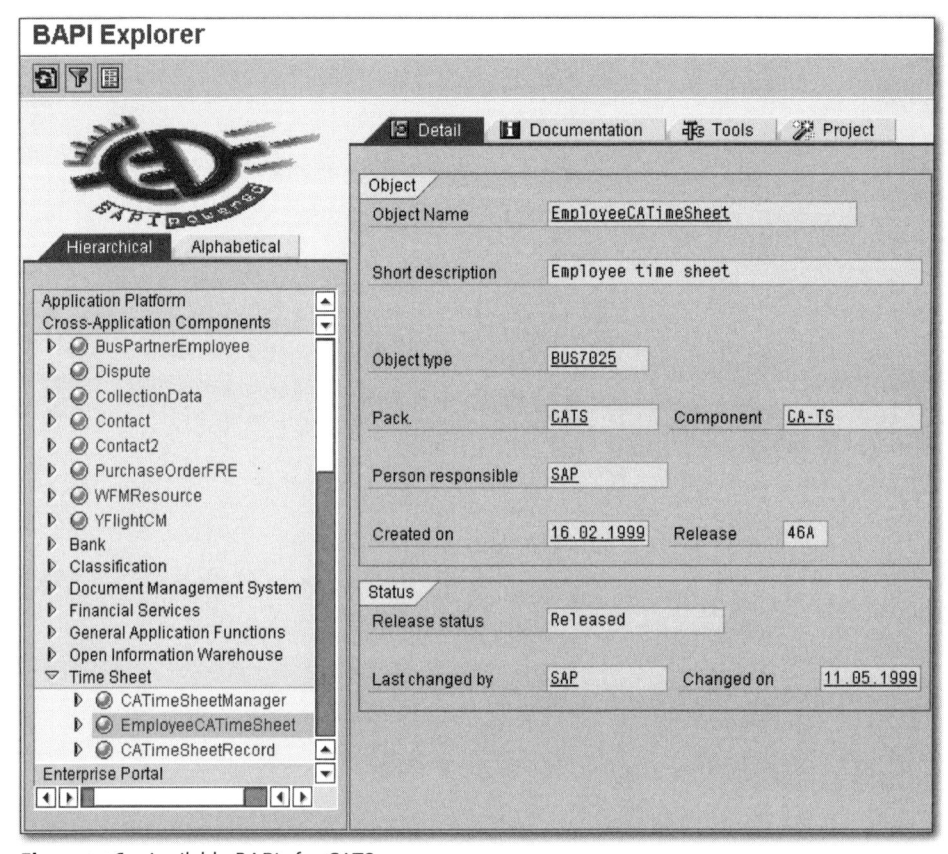

Figure 2.46 Available BAPIs for CATS

Figure 2.47 shows details of the available BAdIs for CATS. A BAdI provides another way to open a back door in SAP. These can also be accessed through customizing.

Name of a BAdI Definition	Enhancement Spot	Description
BADI_CATS_APPROVAL	CATS_APPROVAL	CATS Approval
BADI_CATS_ESA_PICKLS	PAOC_CATS_SERVICES	
BADI_CATSTCO_ADD_DATA	ES_CATSTCO_BADI	Additional data for CATS transfer to CO
CATS_DERIVATIVES	CATS_DERIVATIVES	
CATS_REPORTING		CATS Reporting and Approval
CATS_WORKLIST_ADDIN	CATS_WORKLIST_ADDIN	
CATSBW_CUST_ISOURCE		Transfer Control of Time Sheet Data into BW
CATSXT_EVENT		CATSXT: Customer Fields and Data Checks
ET_QUERY_TS_CONV	PAOC_CATS_XI_PROXY	
HRCATS_APPR_CUST	APPR_CUST	
OFFLINE_APPL		Customer Exit for Offline Application with WAF
TS_CHANGE_CHECK_CONV	PAOC_CATS_XI_PROXY	
TS_CHANGE_CONV	PAOC_CATS_XI_PROXY	
TS_COMPLETE_CONV	PAOC_CATS_XI_PROXY	
TS_CONFIG_CONV	PAOC_CATS_XI_PROXY	
TS_QUERY_CONV	PAOC_CATS_XI_PROXY	

Figure 2.47 BAdI Definitions

Figure 2.48 highlights the customizing access path for managing the setting up of the relevant BAdIs for CATS.

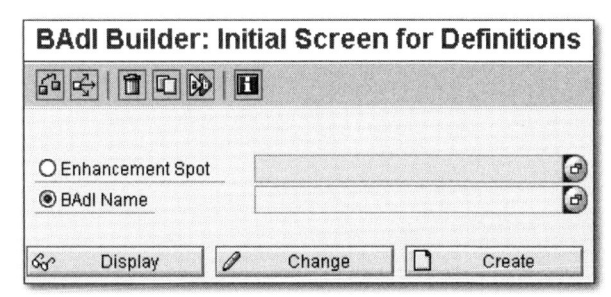

Figure 2.48 BAdI Setup

Figure 2.46 illustrates any BAPI choices within CATS while Figure 2.47 gives BAdI definitions and descriptions. Look at Figure 2.49 for the access to the customizing of CATS dedicated enhancements.

2 | Customizing and Enhancing CATS

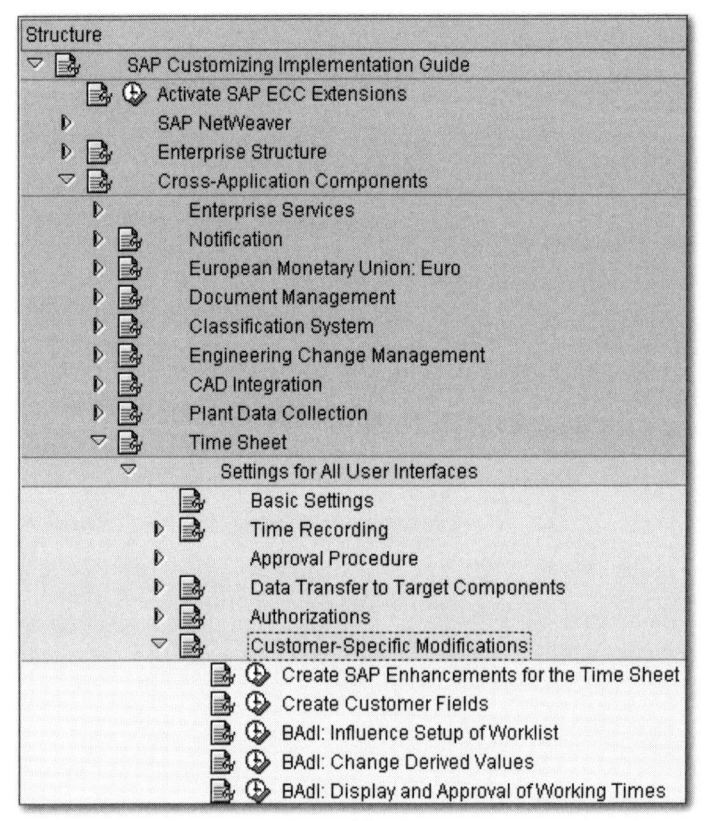

Figure 2.49 Customer Specific modifications

2.6 Lessons Learned

The purpose of this chapter was to run through the customizing options to take the lead in setting up CATS or to be able to read the customizing already implemented. The chapter also provided you with a checklist of the common customizing steps to undertake.

We have added the latest functionalities provided by SAP in release ERP 6.0 so that you can take full advantage of the standard product.

We trust it helped you to fully understand the CATS customizing concept and to know what lies behind the functional screens.

In addition to the standard customizing available, we also informed you of the different user-exits. Prior to investigating any application development, you should check carefully the flexible solutions provided by SAP, thanks to the user-exits.

For background information, we introduced the concepts of a BAPI and a BAdI. This introduction will help emphasize the standard tools already available within SAP before you consider full specific development.

Now that we are all on the same page about the foundations of the CATS setup, let's examine the functional modules. Let's see what is required to run each module and understand the impact of such use.

> **Hint**
> Due to its flexibility and its many options, we recommend the documentation of every step undertaken, including the customizing and the user-exits, the BAPIs and the BAdIs. This will save valuable time when upgrading your system and testing the adjustments made to CATS.

3 Integration with Human Resources

Although the Cross Application Time Sheet is widely used throughout SAP, the Human Resources (HR) module is a crucial partner for enabling CATS. Even if SAP HR is not currently implemented in your organization, it must contain the mini-master data required to run CATS, such as the Organizational Assignment, the identity, and the CATS default values.

If SAP HR is already in place, it will require a close partnership with Time Management and Payroll in order to guarantee data accuracy. Doing several checks along the CATS process will enforce this. HR is also a preferred partner since it might provide an organizational structure to set up the Workflow.

This chapter will provide the basic information needed to set up HR. HR users can review this checklist of its integration points.

3.1 Background Information for the Human Resources Module

SAP HR is divided into two major sections:

- Personnel Administration (PA) which gathers all the administrative information for the employees (administrative information, time management, etc.)
- Personnel Development (PD), which gathers all the relevant information for the employee's development (qualification, organizational management, etc.)

All the information in SAP HR is stored in screens, which are called infotypes (information types). Each infotype consists of a four-digit sequence.

Each HR sub-module owns its range:

- 0000–0999 = Personnel Administration (PA)
- 1000–1999 = Personnel Development (PD)
- 2000–2999 = Personnel Time Management (PT)

- 4000–4999 = Personnel Recruitment (RC)
- 9000–9999 = Customer Include (CI)

Keep in mind that time settings are very important in SAP HR. Each infotype is set to a time constraint allowing different records, gaps, overlapping, and other attributes.

With CATS, the time constraint is set to 2, which means that the record may include gaps but should have no overlapping.

Each record stored in the infotypes has a start date and an end date. This is essential for maintaining data integrity. All the personnel administration infotypes can easily be accessed through the maintenance and display screens available under PA. Alternatively, you can use transaction code PA30 to call the maintenance mode.

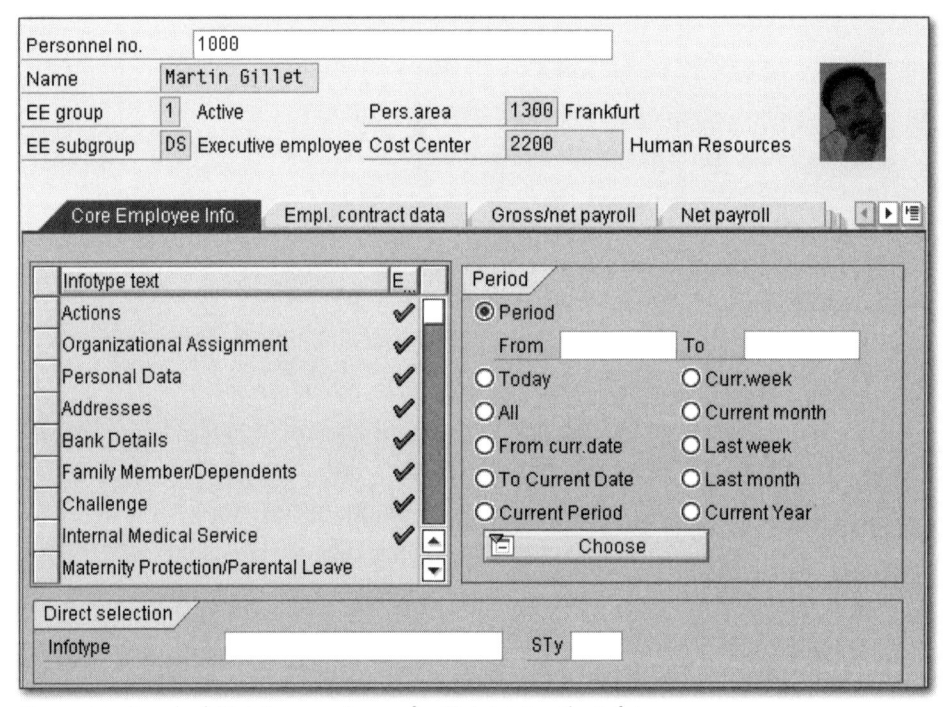

Figure 3.1 Standard Maintenance Access for Maintaining the Infotypes

For users who have never used the HR module, Figure 3.1 introduces the main maintenance screen for personal information, through the functional transaction PA30.

Figure 3.2 illustrates the concept of an enterprise structure, used in SAP to identify the main foundations of the SAP HR module. This Figure also gives an overview of the system's setup and shows how all the relevant information is tightly linked.

To ensure that we are all on the same page about terminology, here are the standard definitions:

- **Client**
  The client is defined at the system level. It contains its own data and customizing. It represents a unique key within SAP.

- **Company Code**
  The company code is provided by the finance and controlling departments. It depicts how they are structured.

Furthermore, the five foundations of the SAP HR module are divided into two main areas, the enterprise structure and the personnel structure.

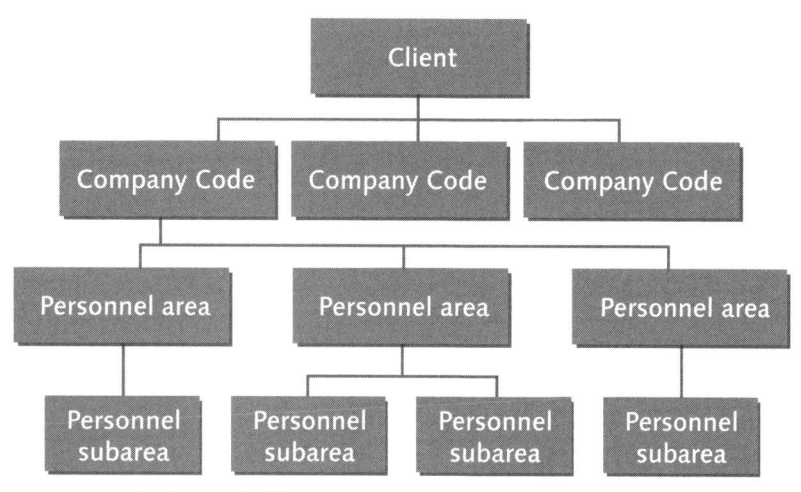

Figure 3.2 The Enterprise Structure

3.1.1 Enterprise Structure

- The personnel area, only used in Personnel Administration, is unique in each client. It consists of a four-character alphanumeric combination. It must be linked to Finance (FI) and Controlling (CO) through the company code. (This is where the integration is done between HR and FI-CO).

▸ Personnel Subarea only used in Personnel Administration, is unique in each client. It consists of a four-character alphanumeric combination. It must be linked to a personnel area. It is the smallest element of the enterprise structure.

3.1.2 Personnel Structure

▸ **Employee Group**
The employee group is used to classify employees in general terms. It defines the position of the employee within the company's workforce. Example: Active employee

▸ **Employee Subgroup**
Employee groups are divided into employees' subgroups. Active employee can be split up into different categories according to their status. Please note that all control features for the personnel structure are defined at the employee subgroup level. Example: Salaried employee

The Personnel Structure concept in SAP HR, as illustrated in Figure 3.3, allows a more accurate description of the personnel.

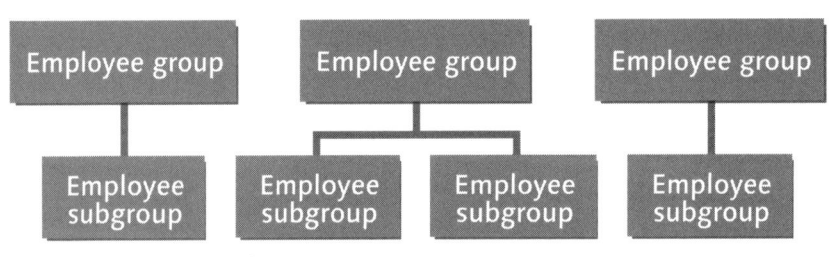

Figure 3.3 The Personnel Structure in SAP HR

The personnel number (with no more than eight digits) that identifies each associate in the company is the key information for all related HR master data.

> **Caution**
> Please pay extra attention when defining the enterprise or personnel structure, as it could play a major role in the system as regards master data groupings, authorizations, default values, and reporting.

3.2 Human Resources Mini-Master Data

The SAP HR module doesn't have to be implemented in order to run CATS. However, certain infotypes are recommended in order to set up a SAP HR Mini Master Data.

The infotypes for the personnel administration are as follows:

3.2.1 0000—Actions (Must Have)

This stores the employee's entry into the company, the reason for the hiring and its personnel group and subgroup. Figure 3.4 illustrates the initial Infotype 0000—Personnel Actions, with the standard information header of the employee. It provides the reason for the action triggered for each employee.

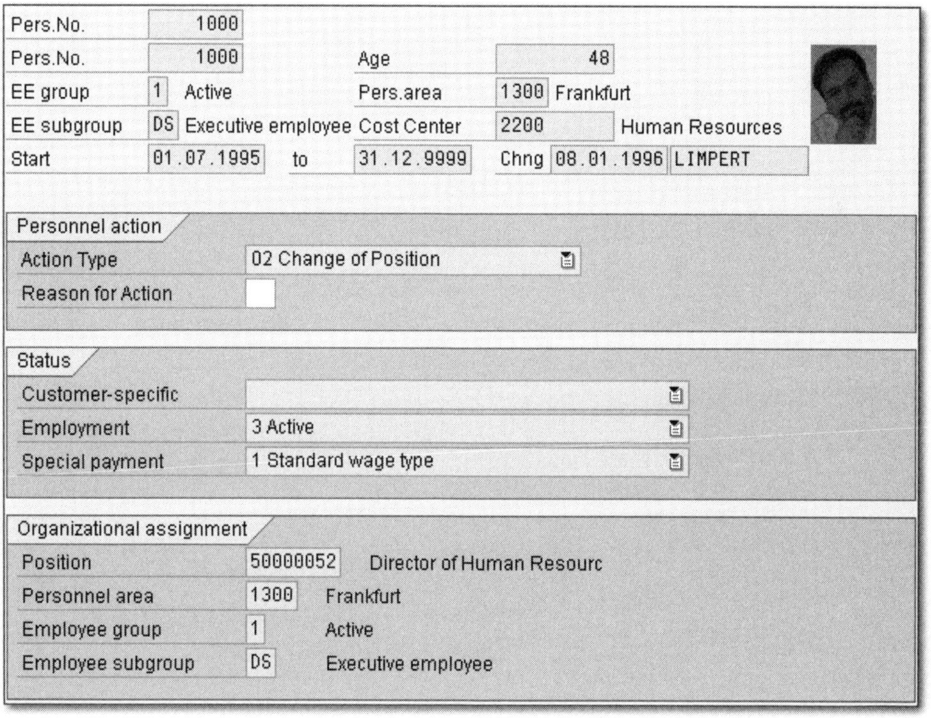

Figure 3.4 Initial Infotype 0000—Personnel Actions

3.2.2 0302—Additional Actions in Infotype 0000—Actions (Nice to Have)

Please note that an additional screen might be added at the bottom of the screen. It is known as the Infotype 0302—Additional actions. Its aim is to sort out all actions if they occur on the same day. This additional infotype is a virtual infotype and cannot, therefore, be maintained directly. Figure 3.5 illustrates the optional additional actions that can be enabled, if needed, in the Infotype 0000—Personnel Actions.

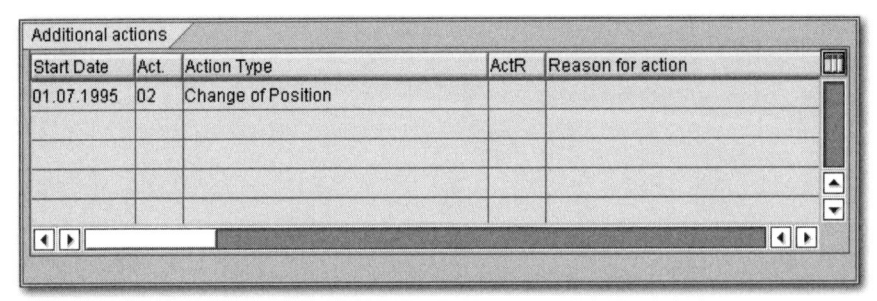

Figure 3.5 Additional Actions in Infotype 0000

3.2.3 0001—Organizational Assignment (Must Have)

It stores, above all, the employee Organizational Assignment, as well as its personnel administrators, its payroll area, its place in the personnel area and subarea, the personnel grouping, and subgrouping, etc. Please bear in mind that the link with the Organizational Structure is nice to have but is not mandatory.

Figure 3.6 illustrates the Infotype 0001—*Organizational Assignment* with its subsections:

- Enterprise structure
- Personnel structure
- Organizational Plan (Shall the integration with the organizational structure in Personnel Development be enabled)
- Administrator

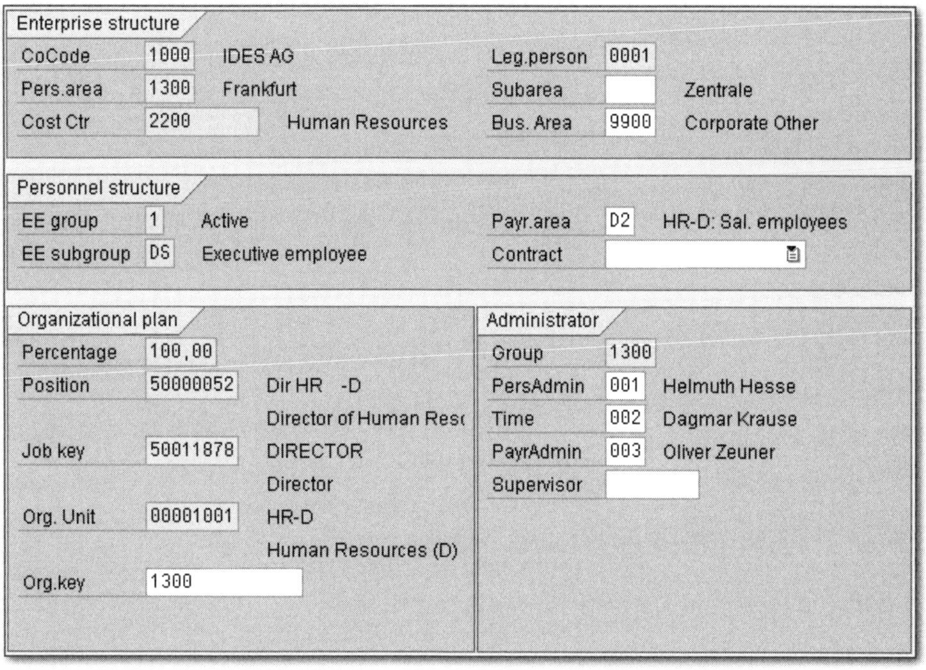

Enterprise structure						
CoCode	1000	IDES AG		Leg.person	0001	
Pers.area	1300	Frankfurt		Subarea		Zentrale
Cost Ctr	2200		Human Resources	Bus. Area	9900	Corporate Other

Personnel structure						
EE group	1	Active		Payr.area	D2	HR-D: Sal. employees
EE subgroup	DS	Executive employee		Contract		

Organizational plan				Administrator		
Percentage	100,00			Group	1300	
Position	50000052	Dir HR -D		PersAdmin	001	Helmuth Hesse
		Director of Human Resc		Time	002	Dagmar Krause
Job key	50011878	DIRECTOR		PayrAdmin	003	Oliver Zeuner
		Director		Supervisor		
Org. Unit	00001001	HR-D				
		Human Resources (D)				
Org.key	1300					

Figure 3.6 Structure of Infotype 0001—Organizational Assignment

3.2.4 0002—Personal Data (Must Have)

This infotype stores personnel information such as last name, first name, and date of birth. CATS requires the last name and the first name to use them in standard screen headers.

Figure 3.7 illustrates the standard Infotype 0002 which contains the personal data of the employee. Please note that according to the country settings, screens may differ slightly. The screen is taken from the country grouping 01 which stands for Germany.

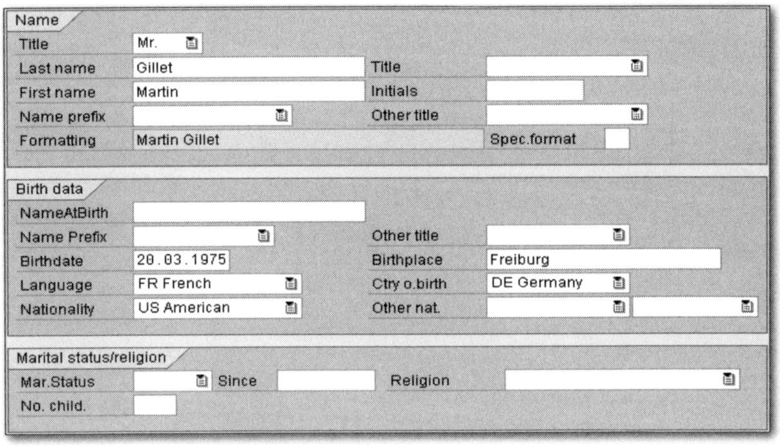

Figure 3.7 Standard Infotype 0002—Personnel Data

3.2.5 0315—CATS Time Sheet Defaults (Nice to Have)

Although this infotype is not mandatory, setting it up will greatly enhance the user's work. Indeed, this infotype stores default values in order to reduce the employee labor while collecting time entries. Please pay attention to the cost center number, as it should match the cost center already set up in the Infotype 0001—*Organizational Assignment*.

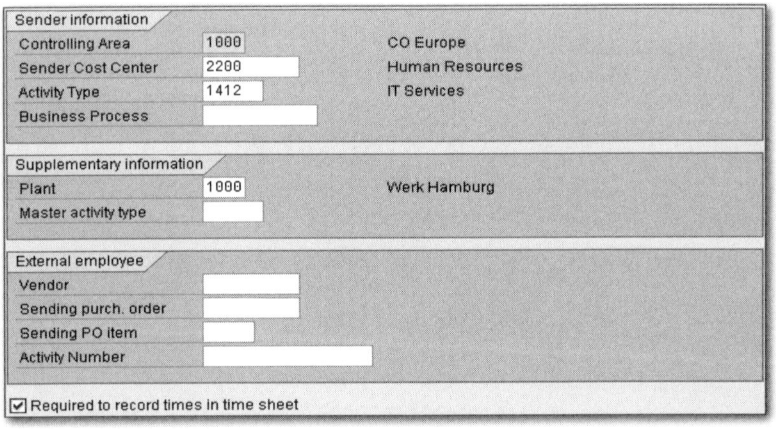

Figure 3.8 Infotype 0315—Time Sheet Defaults

Figure 3.8 illustrates the most relevant infotype for CATS: the Infotype 0315, which contains the CATS defaults. The infotype is divided into three main sections:

- Sender Information
- Supplementary information
- External Employee

Each section is described below.

Sender Information (Integration to Controlling)

- **Controlling Area**
  Identifies the highest organizational unit in Controlling
- **Sender Cost Center**
  Identifies the cost center selected as the sender cost center
- **Activity Type**
  Identifies the activity produced by a cost center and is measured in units of time and quantity
- **Business Process**
  Identifies the business process.

Supplementary Information (Integration to Plant Maintenance)

- **Plant**
  Identifies the plant to be used
- **Master activity type**
  Identifies the master activity type with which the employee activities can be further allocated internally

External Employee (Integration to Materials Management)

- **Vendor**
  Alphanumeric key identifying the vendor
- **Sending purch. order (Purchase Order, PO)**
  Identifies the sender purchase order
- **Sending PO item**
  Identifies the Purchase Order item within the purchase document
- **Activity number**
  Identifies the number of the service master record

If the option REQUIRED TO RECORD TIMES IN TIME SHEET is flagged, it means that the employee has to collect all his or her time entries through CATS.

> **Hint**
> According to the customizing setup, these default values prompted in the time sheet screens can be hidden, in display mode only, or changeable.

3.3 Time Management Infotypes

Personnel time management will add value to your CATS installation. In deciding how the system will be used, consider whether you will record the standard hours as is and book only the exceptions, or if you will book every type of attendance and absence.

The infotypes for personnel time management are as described below.

3.3.1 0007 — Personal Work Schedule (Nice to Have Even Without Time Management)

Even if Time Management is not implemented, this infotype will greatly enhance CATS configuration, as it gathers the default work schedule, workdays, and breaks for the employee. It will be used in the user's Time Sheet to default a schedule in his or her time-entry screen. It will also be useful for managers when they are running reports concerning hours collected versus the planned working time.

Figure 3.9 illustrates Infotype 0007, which contains, according to SAP, the *Planned Working Time*. Most regular users refer to this infotype as the default schedule, which makes more sense to them.

Time Management Infotypes | 3.3

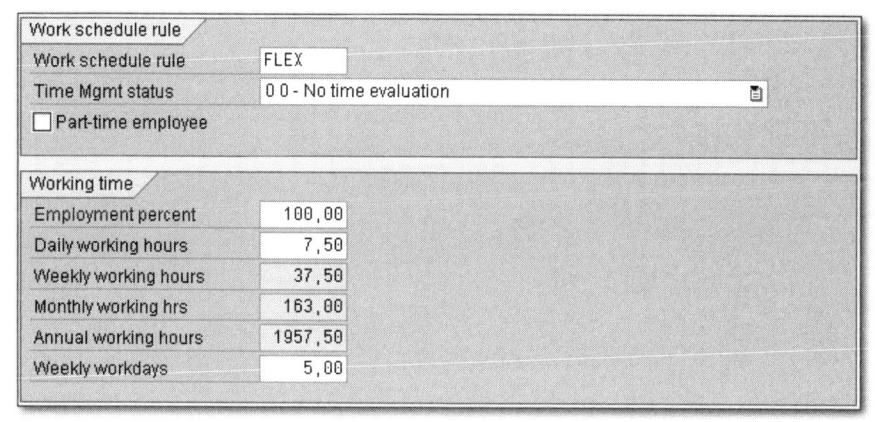

Figure 3.9 Infotype 0007—Planned Working Time

A sample view of a weekly planned working time can be found under the transaction PA61, in time management. Figure 3.10 provides a detailed view.

Figure 3.10 Weekly Schedule Assigned to Employee

3.3.2 2006—Absence Quotas (to be Set Up with Time Management)

This infotype holds the employee's leave entitlement. It is greatly appreciated by the time administrators since the employees, depending on the settings, cannot book their own holidays if no entitlement exists. This information is also used in the leave-request process.

Figure 3.11 illustrates the standard Infotype 2006 which contains the *Absence Quotas*. In fact, most end users refer to this infotype as the leave entitlement for each employee.

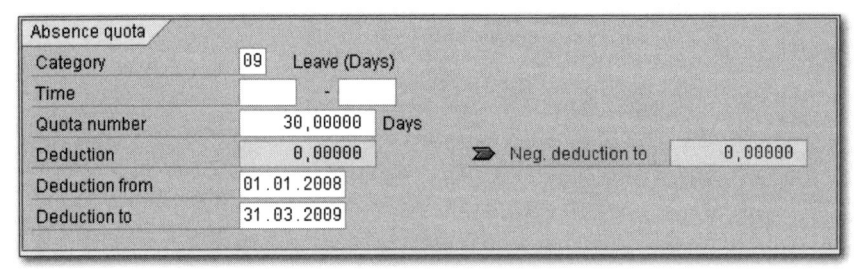

Figure 3.11 Infotype 2006—Absence Quotas

There are three ways to populate this infotype:

- Manually feed into the infotype (single and/or mass entry through transaction code PA61)
- Generation via the program RPTQTA00 (no time evaluation in use)
- Automatic generation and update via the program RPTIME00 (time evaluation in use)

Figure 3.12 illustrates the common access to the absence quotas screen. This screen can be easily reached by calling the standard Transaction code PA61.

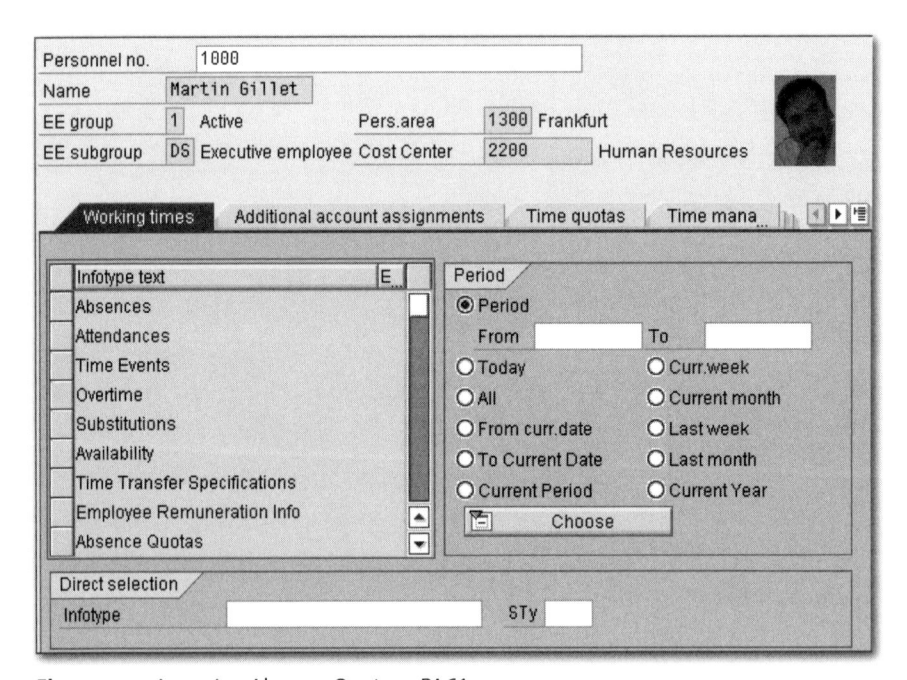

Figure 3.12 Accessing Absence Quotas—PA61

Time Management Infotypes | 3.3

Automatic generation through the program "Generate absence quotas"

Figure 3.13 shows the initial selection screen for the quota generation. The name of this program is RPTQTA00. This program can also be easily called by the standard transaction code PT_QTA00.

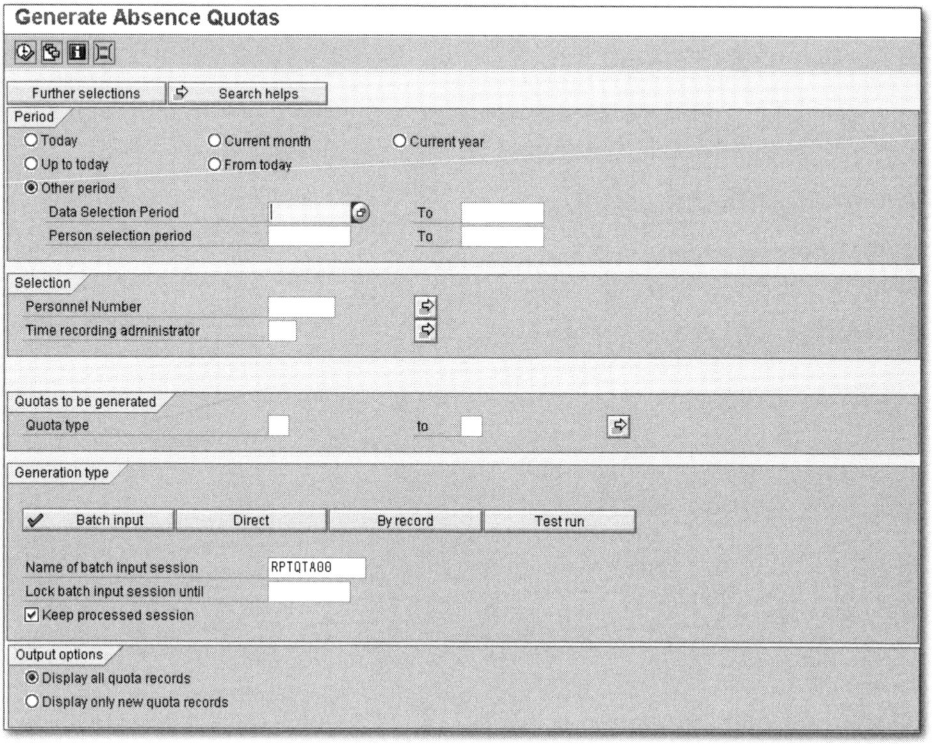

Figure 3.13 Initial Selection Screen for Quota Generation

Full program documentation is available, if you have further questions about the absence-quota generation. Please refer to the online documentation available in the selection screen under the appropriate icon. Figure 3.14 shows you the icon on which to click to access the full program documentation.

3 | Integration with Human Resources

Figure 3.14 Icon to Click to Access Full Program Documentation

Automatic generation through the program Time Evaluation

Figure 3.15 displays the initial selection screen for the program Time Evaluation. The program's technical name is RPTIME00. Full program documentation is available, should you have further questions regarding the Time Evaluation.

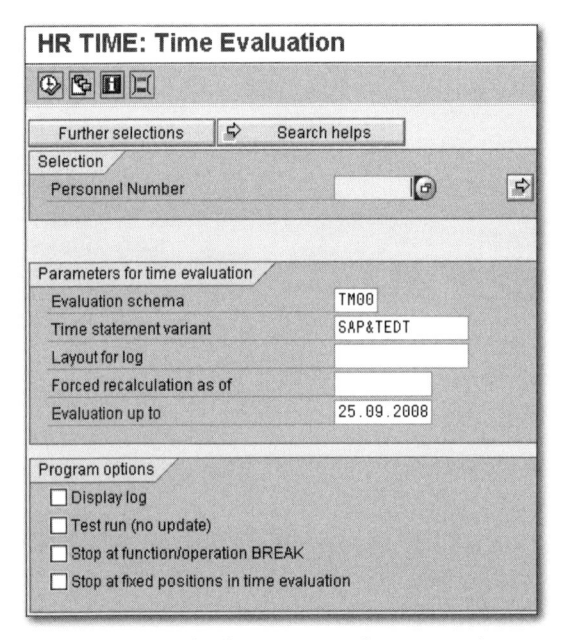

Figure 3.15 Initial Selection Screen for Time Evaluation

3.3.3 2001—Absences (to be Set Up with Time Management)

This infotype stores the different absence types collected for the associate throughout his professional time. It holds all kind of absences, from sickness to training, and from short term to long term. Figure 3.16 illustrates the Infotype 2001 which contains *Employee Absence*. It provides a sample of an authorized leave.

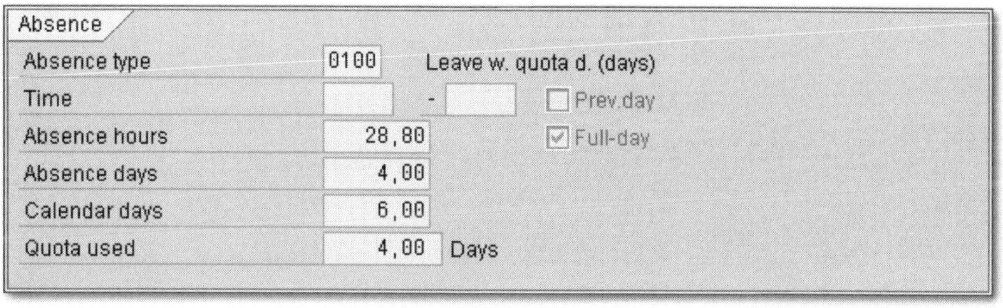

Figure 3.16 Infotype 2001—Employee Absence

3.3.4 2002—Attendances (to be Set Up with Time Management)

This infotype stores the different attendance types collected for the employee throughout his professional time. It holds all kind of attendances, from standard attendance to union meetings, from short term to long term. Figure 3.17 illustrates the Infotype 2002 which contains *Employee Attendance*. It also provides an example of regular attendance hours, with its impact on payroll.

> **Caution**
> Both Infotypes, 2001 and 2002, require the setup of absence and attendance types.

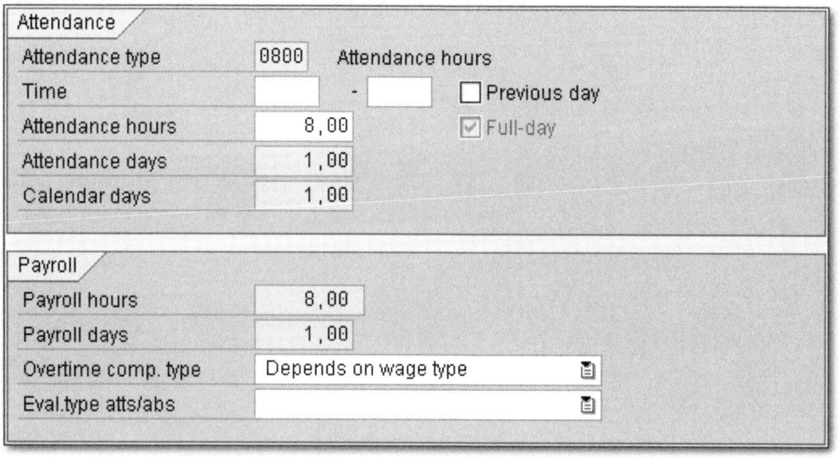

Figure 3.17 Infotype 2002—Employee Attendance

3.3.5 2010—Employee's Remuneration Statement (to be Set Up with Time Management)

This infotype gathers the manually calculated wage-type amount, bonus, or any other wage type that cannot be planned. This infotype is to be used in connection with the Payroll module.

Figure 3.18 illustrates the Infotype 2010, which contains the *Employee's Remuneration Statement*. This Figure provides an example of a bonus relating to time allocated to a work council. This remuneration statement can be easily used through the Time Sheet in order to collect unusual activities that are likely to impact the Payroll process.

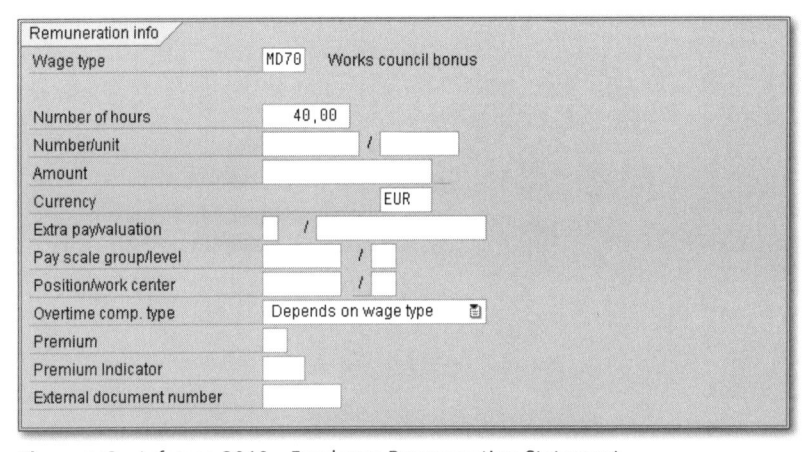

Remuneration info		
Wage type	MD70	Works council bonus
Number of hours	40,00	
Number/unit	/	
Amount		
Currency	EUR	
Extra pay/valuation	/	
Pay scale group/level	/	
Position/work center	/	
Overtime comp. type	Depends on wage type	
Premium		
Premium Indicator		
External document number		

Figure 3.18 Infotype 2010—Employee Remuneration Statement

> **Hint**
> All fields are not mandatory in all infotypes. You can easily tune up the fields' attributes (mandatory, hidden, etc.) through the standard table T588M.

> **Hint**
> To populate this master data, we suggest using the administrative action CATS mini master already provided by SAP in transaction code PA40.

Figure 3.19 illustrates the personnel action flow used to populate master data. This flow is also meant to centralize the information recording into one streamline so that we can avoid data inconsistency. This is the best-case scenario, as opposed to individual data recording one infotype at a time.

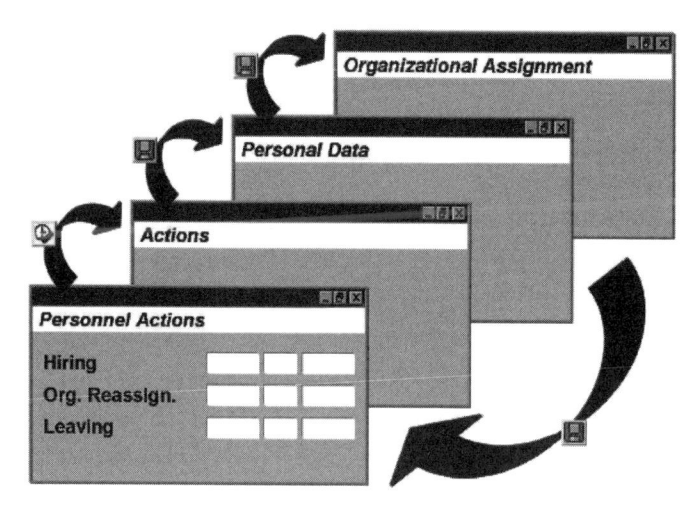

Figure 3.19 Populating Master Data

3.4 Human Resources Personnel Development

Although the use of Personnel Development is not mandatory, the CATS processes could be greatly enhanced by setting up the organizational structure. Like the other sub-modules belonging to Personnel Development, it is of object-oriented design. Each item of relevant information is stored in infotypes but is also identified by a letter or a two-letter code (e.g., Person = object P).

The Personnel Development sub-module is focused on Infotypes 1000 through 1999.

The most important Infotypes are:

- 1000 — *Object*
- 1001 — *Relationships*

Figure 3.20 illustrates the Organizational Management concept and its integration with Personnel Administration. Additional information (such as cost distribution, or description) can also be stored in other infotypes.

Prior to installation, the integration flag must be switched on in the central SAP HR table, known as T77SO. The flag is named under PLOGI — ORGA. Once the switch is activated, the organizational information provided in the Infotype 0001 — *Organizational Assignment* can be changed only through the Organizational Structure.

3 | Integration with Human Resources

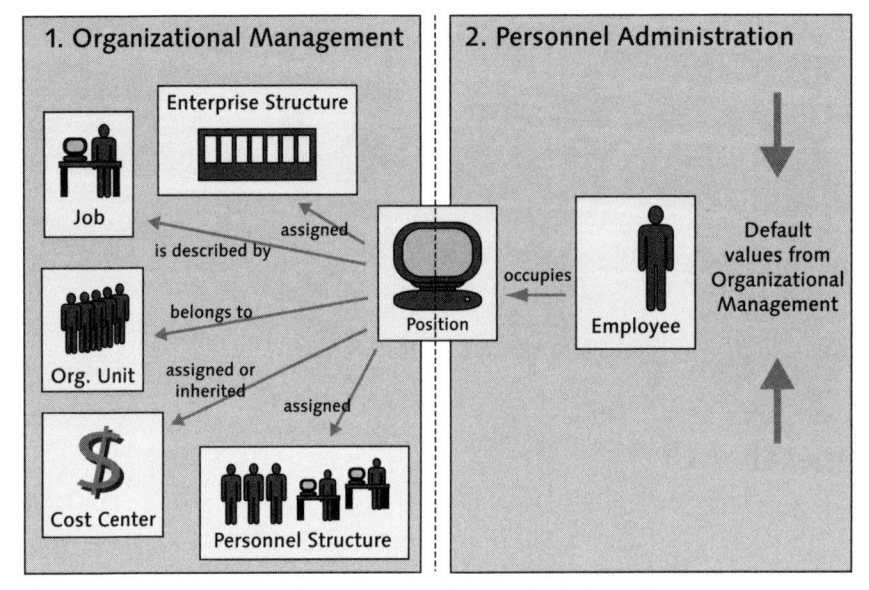

Figure 3.20 Organizational Management in Personnel Administration

In order to build a basic Organizational Structure, you must use the following objects.

- Object O: Organizational Structure
- Object S: Position
- Object P: Person
- Object K: Cost Center

Figure 3.21 illustrates how the objects can be linked one to another.

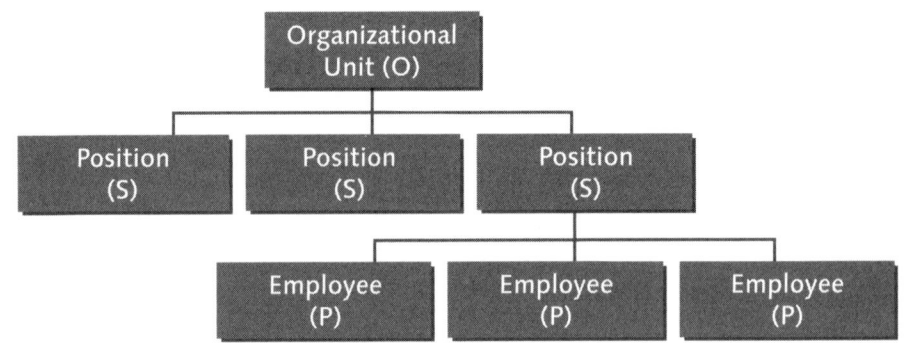

Figure 3.21 Object Links Within Organizational Structure

Figure 3.22 provides a sample of an Organizational Structure, displaying Objects O-S-P. It provides a clearer picture of what regular users would expect from an Organizational Structure.

You can set up the Organizational Structure for the following reasons:

- For search and selection in standard programs
- For structural authorizations
- For further additional features such as workflow

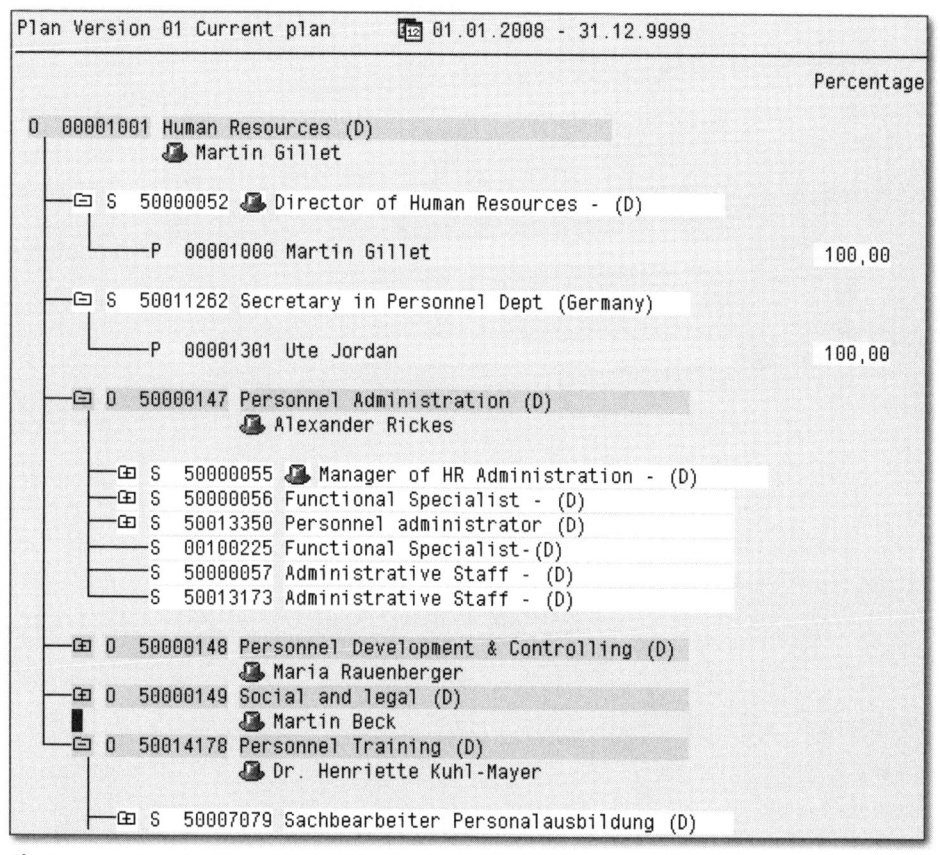

```
Plan Version 01 Current plan        01.01.2008 - 31.12.9999
                                                                    Percentage
O   00001001 Human Resources (D)
             Martin Gillet
      S   50000052  Director of Human Resources - (D)
          P   00001000 Martin Gillet                                   100,00
      S   50011262 Secretary in Personnel Dept (Germany)
          P   00001301 Ute Jordan                                      100,00
      O   50000147 Personnel Administration (D)
             Alexander Rickes
          S   50000055  Manager of HR Administration - (D)
          S   50000056 Functional Specialist - (D)
          S   50013350 Personnel administrator (D)
          S   00100225 Functional Specialist-(D)
          S   50000057 Administrative Staff - (D)
          S   50013173 Administrative Staff - (D)
      O   50000148 Personnel Development & Controlling (D)
             Maria Rauenberger
      O   50000149 Social and legal (D)
             Martin Beck
      O   50014178 Personnel Training (D)
             Dr. Henriette Kuhl-Mayer
          S   50007079 Sachbearbeiter Personalausbildung (D)
```

Figure 3.22 Sample Organizational Structure

3.5 Practical Applications

Let us look at the setup of the Infotype 0007—Planned Working Time—and its impact.

Even without Time Management, if you have work-schedule rules assigned to specific employees through their Infotypes 0007—*Planned Working Time* the employees will be able to display their schedules in their Time Sheets under the data-entry view, as shown in Figure 3.23.

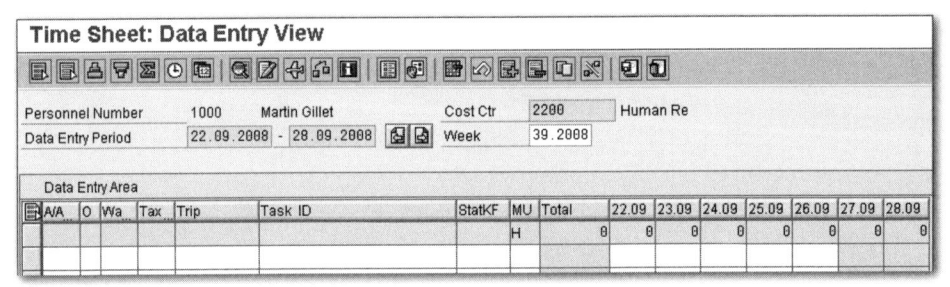

Figure 3.23 CATS Data-Entry View with the Target Hours Switched Off, Through the Standard R/3 Back-End Screen.

To enable (switch on) the option target hours, to display the planned working time, either click on the icon, press F7 on your keyboard, or go to the menu, under EDIT • TARGET HOURS ON/OFF. Now the standard work schedule assigned to the employee will be displayed. Figure 3.24 shows the common icon, a clock that is used to switch on/off the target hours as they are provided from the Infotype 0007 that contains the employee's schedule. Figure 3.25 illustrates the outcome, with CATS data-entry view with the target hours switched on.

Figure 3.24 Clock Icon

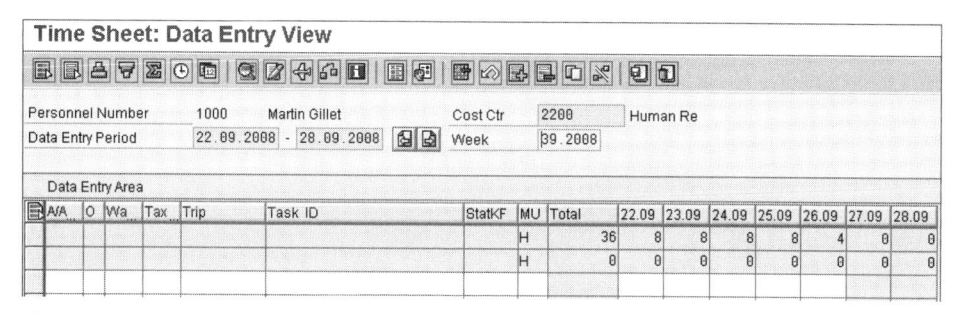

Figure 3.25 Time Sheet Data-Entry View

3.5.1 Option Required to Record Times in Time Sheet Enabled

If the option REQUIRED TO RECORD TIMES IN TIME SHEET is switched on, it means that all time entries from now on will be done through CATS. Using this option generates an important piece of information that could be used in the CATS Time-Leveling report (program RCATSCMP—transaction code CATC), to compare the time entries collected against the following options.

- Time sheet for employees required to enter their time through CATS (flag in Infotype 0315—Field "Required to record times in Time Sheet").
- Time sheet for which no times or quantities have been recorded
- Time sheet with no times recorded
- Against a specified number of hours
- Against the target hours stored under *Planned Working Time* (Infotype 0007)

Figure 3.26 provides the initial selection entry screen for the CATS Time-Leveling report. Special attention should be paid to the subsection REPORT SPECIFIC SELECTION OF EMPLOYEES, which contains the option EMPLOYEE REQUIRED TO RECORD TIMES IN TIME SHEET.

The transfer to HR can also be done by using the transaction code CAT6. Often, standalone transfer is not permitted since additional information may be in use from another target component. In this case, use the transaction code CATA.

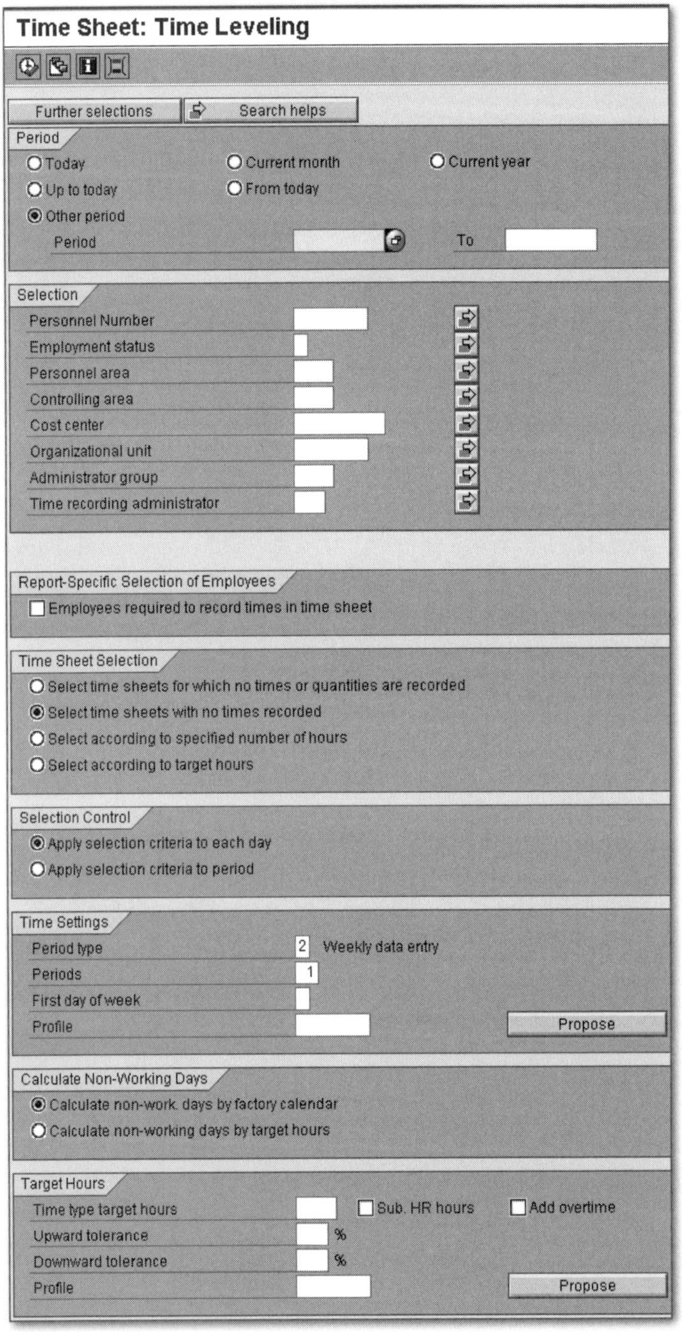

3 | Integration with Human Resources

Figure 3.26 CATS Time-Leveling

Figure 3.27 focuses on the subsection from the CATS Time-Leveling Report and contains the output settings.

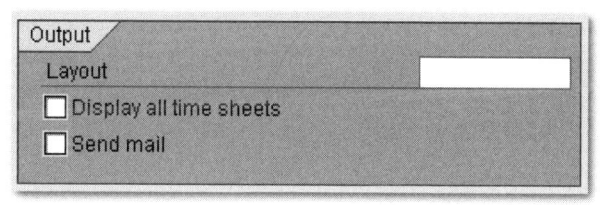

Figure 3.27 Output Settings for CATS Time-Leveling

3.6 Lessons Learned

CATS is integrated with the HR module with respect to the Time Management submodule. It centralizes the absence and attendance time entries through a single point of entry, with or without a release-and-approval process.

The data is then transferred to HR for updating the relevant master data and — if applicable — for further processing into the Time Evaluation and Payroll processes. Figure 3.28 illustrates an executive summary of the CATS integration with HR.

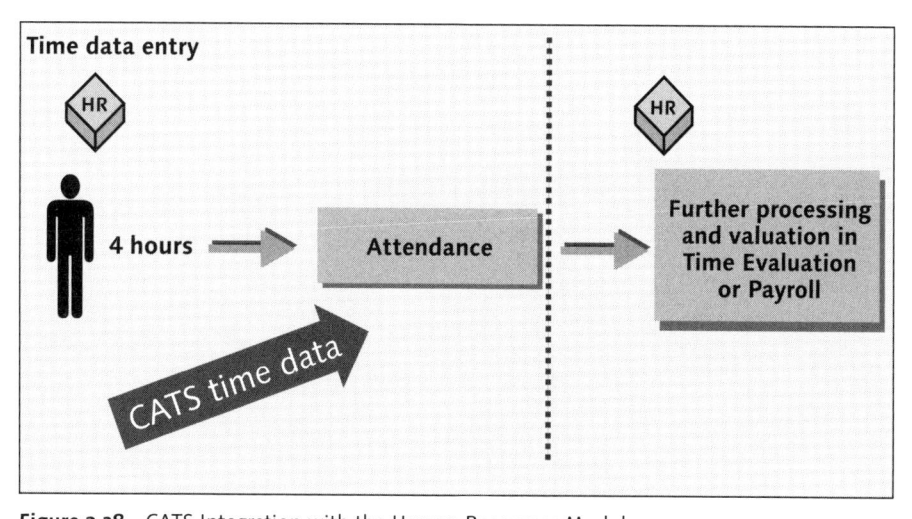

Figure 3.28 CATS Integration with the Human Resources Module

Now that we have looked at HR, let's turn to the other important modules: Finance and Controlling. Let's find out what is required for them and, most importantly, let's look at financial consequences and how we can proceed with the cost allocation.

4 Integration with Finance and Controlling

4.1 Background Information for Financial Accounting

Financial information is crucial to today's business processes, which involve state-of-the art budgeting, invoicing, cost posting, and other related work.

Financial Accounting — through the SAP modules Financials (FI) and Controlling (CO) — creates in most cases the biggest demand for CATS installation. The simplicity of CATS enables the smooth booking of financial-accounting information.

Although we are dealing with Controlling, we also refer to it as the Financial-Accounting (Controlling) module, also known as FI-CO. It is truly the backbone of the SAP system, as it collects the figures and the relevant information for the financial and non-financial managers.

4.1.1 Key Elements for Integrating CATS with Financial Accounting

This section will highlight the integration points with CO, providing a checklist and pointing out the key transaction codes required to handle the basic processes within the CO and FI modules.

The integration of CATS among these two modules is needed to trigger the cost allocation. It is also useful information that will be provided to the managers and team leaders, as they will be able to manage their cost centers and the internal rate they will be charged for an activity.

Figure 4.1 illustrates the place of CATS among the integration with the target component — Controlling.

4 | Integration with Finance and Controlling

Internal activity allocations

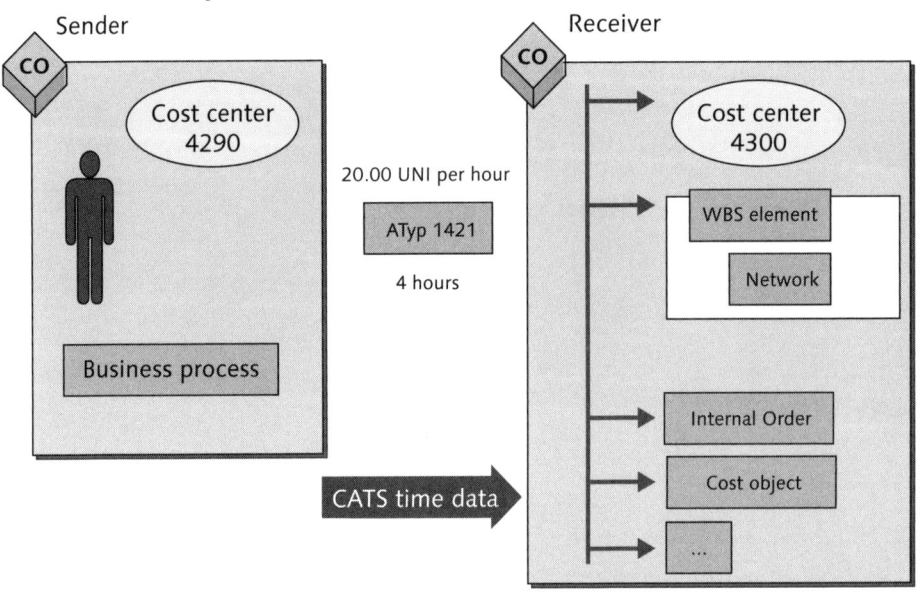

Figure 4.1 CATS Time Data and Controlling

For common background knowledge, the following information will be reviewed:

- The importance of the cost center
- The impact of the activity type
- The liaison between the price planning cost center and the activity type
- The optional object receiver that could be used: the internal order

All the information provided, even if not immediately relevant can be used as a checklist for documentation and test purposes.

> **Caution**
>
> It is likely that the use of these transactions and these business processes require an SAP authorization clearance. Talk to your authorization system administrators. If your request is declined, you can always request a standard display mode, in order to view the different pieces of information.

4.1.2 CATS Integration in Financial Accounting

This section will focus on CATS integration, including the relevant fields to be used, the specific default information available through the Infotype 0315, and the options available through CATS customizing.

We will pay special attention to the integration of FI-CO and—if they are enabled in your company—Payroll and time management. These options will be introduced under the cost-accounting variant feature.

In order to comply with the controlling department, we will review the different available options for the document generation in the system.

> **Hint**
> To ensure a smooth CATS setup, make sure you involve your controlling department to receive the relevant information. Most common controlling issues arise due to incorrect information being collected in the system and, most of all, due to a lack of communication between teams.

4.1.3 Integration between Human Resources and Financial Accounting

Prior to any installation, it is wise to check the integration between the Human Resources (HR), FI and CO modules.

Although this integration is quite basic, it will secure data integrity and enable data posting after data has been collected.

To access this customizing step, simply execute the node under the path shown in Figure 4.2.

The table V_T500P contains the linking between the personnel area (an organizational unit within HR) and the company code (an organizational unit within Financial Accounting.

This company-code assignment is crucial because it will drive all financial accounting related information, such as the cost centers and activity types.

4 | Integration with Finance and Controlling

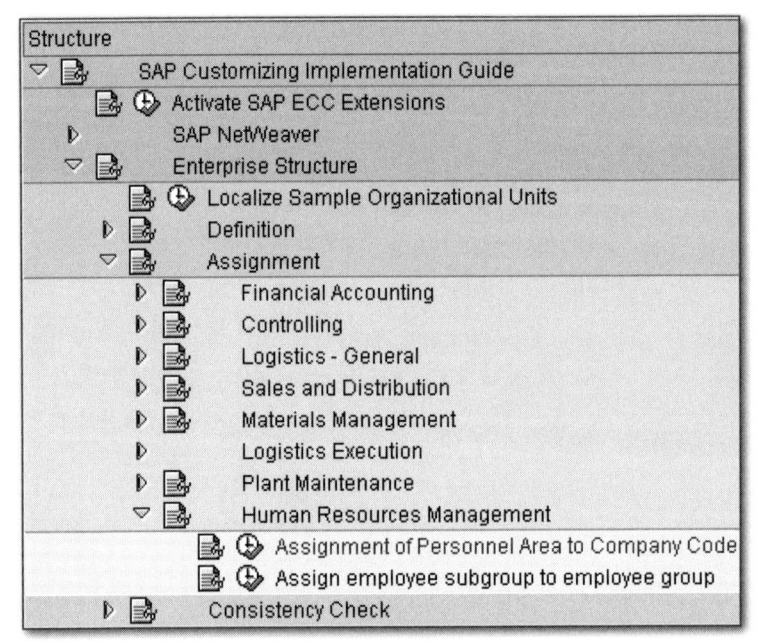

```
Structure
  ▽ 📄    SAP Customizing Implementation Guide
       📄 ⊕  Activate SAP ECC Extensions
       ▷         SAP NetWeaver
       ▽ 📄    Enterprise Structure
              📄 ⊕  Localize Sample Organizational Units
              ▷ 📄   Definition
              ▽ 📄   Assignment
                     ▷ 📄   Financial Accounting
                     ▷ 📄   Controlling
                     ▷ 📄   Logistics - General
                     ▷ 📄   Sales and Distribution
                     ▷ 📄   Materials Management
                     ▷      Logistics Execution
                     ▷ 📄   Plant Maintenance
                     ▽ 📄   Human Resources Management
                           📄 ⊕  Assignment of Personnel Area to Company Code
                           📄 ⊕  Assign employee subgroup to employee group
              ▷ 📄   Consistency Check
```

Figure 4.2 Customizing Access Path for Integration Between HR and FI/CO

Figure 4.3 illustrates the content of the table used to maintain the assignment of the company code and the country grouping to the personnel area.

Change View "Assignment of Personnel Area to Company Code": Overview

Pers.area	Personnel Area Text	Company Code	Company Name	Ctry Grpg
1000	Hamburg	1000	IDES AG	01
1100	Berlin	1000	IDES AG	01
1200	Dresden	1000	IDES AG	01
1300	Frankfurt	1000	IDES AG	01
1400	Stuttgart	1000	IDES AG	01

Figure 4.3 Assigning Company Codes

Like the Personnel Area definition available in the HR module, the company code is defined and maintained by the financial accounting department.

Once your system is in production, SAP recommends that you not change the company-code assignment to protect the master data and to avoid major inconsistencies. Should a change be necessary, SAP provides the report RPUP0001.

Background Information for Financial Accounting | **4.1**

The working assumption made in this Essentials guide is that we have integrated Personnel Administration and Personnel Development (Checkbox PLOGI ORGA activated—X in the main HR table T77S0). This means that the cost center cannot be directly assigned in the Infotype 0001—*Organizational Assignment*; it comes from the Organizational Structure.

Figure 4.4 illustrates the main table T77S0 used for the HR switches. This Figure focuses on the maintenance for the group PLOGI.

Change View "System Table": Overview

Group	Sem.abbr.	Value abbr	Description
PLOGI	ADAYS		Waiting Period Personnel Planning
PLOGI	APPNT	1	Appointment calendar integration switch
PLOGI	APPRA	1	Integration switch for appraisal
PLOGI	BSPAY	X	Integration IT1005 - IT0008
PLOGI	COSTD		Integration of Cost Distribution PersAdm/OrgManag
PLOGI	COSTI		Integration switch for cost center accounting
PLOGI	DIFMA		Company codes from different FM areas
PLOGI	EVCCC	02	Master data action: company code change
PLOGI	EVCRE	X	Generate event with entry T77INT (action designat.
PLOGI	EVEGC	02	Master data action: employee subgroup change
PLOGI	EVENB		Enhanced integration (X= on, Space= off)
PLOGI	EVPAC	02	Master data action for country reassignment
PLOGI	ORGA	X	Integration Switch: Organizational Assignment
PLOGI	PDCON		HR: Context Authorization Check in PD
PLOGI	PLOGI	01	Integration Plan Version / Active Plan Version
PLOGI	PRELI	99999999	Integration: default position
PLOGI	PRELU	0	Integration: PA update online or batch
PLOGI	QUALI	1 A032 Q	Integration switch for qualifications
PLOGI	SPLIT		Integration: New IT 0001 record at name change
PLOGI	TEXTC		Integration: transfer short text of job

Figure 4.4 Switching Within the Organizational Structure

Should the checkbox PLOGI ORGA be disabled, the cost center can be directly managed in the Infotype 0001—*Organizational Assignment*.

111

4.1.4 Basic Information about Financial Accounting

In order to help you integrate CATS with FI-CO, this chapter will highlight basic transactions. Although this information is usually handled by financial consultants, a basic knowledge will ease the implementation or testing process of testing CATS and will also help solve financial issues should they arise while booking time entries.

Create, maintain, or display a cost center

The cost center is widely used within HR, in the Infotype 0001 — *Organizational Assignment*, the Infotype 0315 — *CATS Default values* and the Organizational Structure.

Figure 4.5 provides a quick reference list for creating, maintaining and displaying a cost center. This transaction codes could be added in the SAP user's favorites, for quicker access.

KS01	Create cost center
KS02	Change cost center
KS03	Display Cost Center

Figure 4.5 Cost Center Basic Screen

This transaction will enable you to either create the new cost center required for the setting up of CATS or just to check the current available entries in the system.

The transaction display cost center (transaction code KS03) is useful for displaying the business card of the cost center, as shown in Figure 4.6.

Create, maintain or display an activity type

Although the cost center compiles the cost inherent to an activity and is likely to be provided by the financial department, the activity type is key information for project and line managers, as it will reflect the financial charge due for an activity performed by an individual.

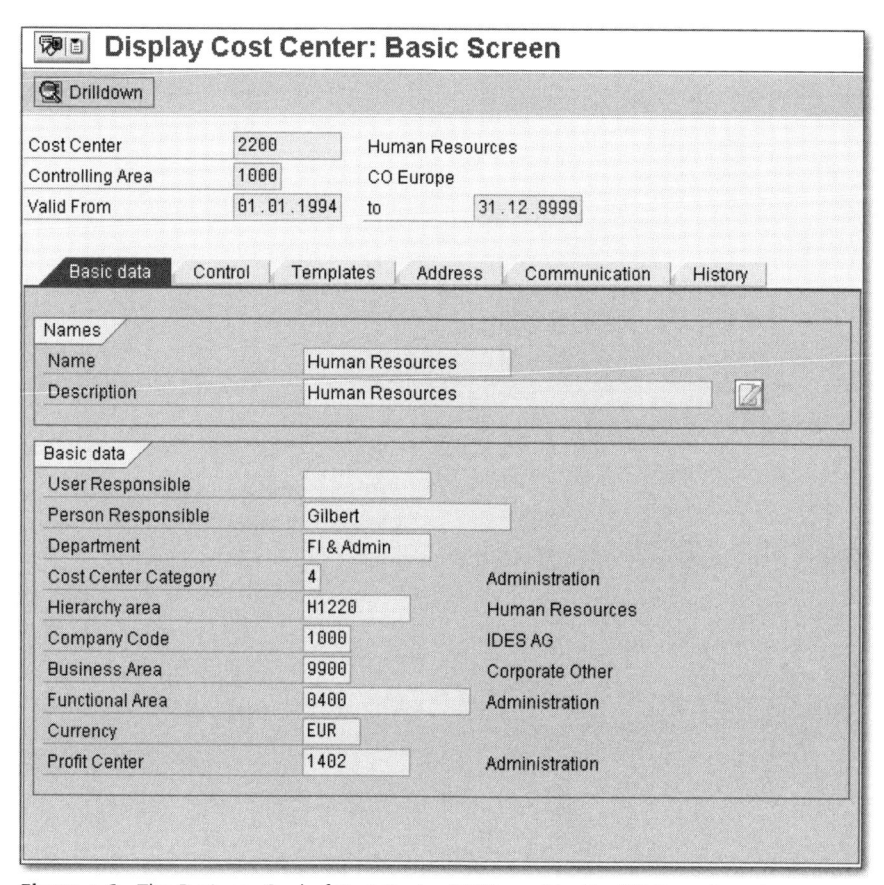

Background Information for Financial Accounting | 4.1

```
Display Cost Center: Basic Screen
  Drilldown

Cost Center        2200        Human Resources
Controlling Area   1000        CO Europe
Valid From         01.01.1994  to    31.12.9999

 Basic data | Control | Templates | Address | Communication | History

 Names
   Name               Human Resources
   Description        Human Resources

 Basic data
   User Responsible
   Person Responsible    Gilbert
   Department            FI & Admin
   Cost Center Category  4              Administration
   Hierarchy area        H1220          Human Resources
   Company Code          1000           IDES AG
   Business Area         9900           Corporate Other
   Functional Area       0400           Administration
   Currency              EUR
   Profit Center         1402           Administration
```

Figure 4.6 The Business Card of Cost Center 2200 used by the HR Department

For instance, we can identify several activity types with regard to the different consulting levels: junior, confirmed, and senior consultant. Each activity type will apply a different rate, according to the respective level of expertise. Figure 4.7 provides a short list of the activity types' transactions codes, while Figure 4.8 shows access to a sample activity-type business card.

```
KL01    Create Activity Type
KL02    Change Activity Type
KL03    Display Activity Type
```

Figure 4.7 Activity Type Transactions Codes

4 | Integration with Finance and Controlling

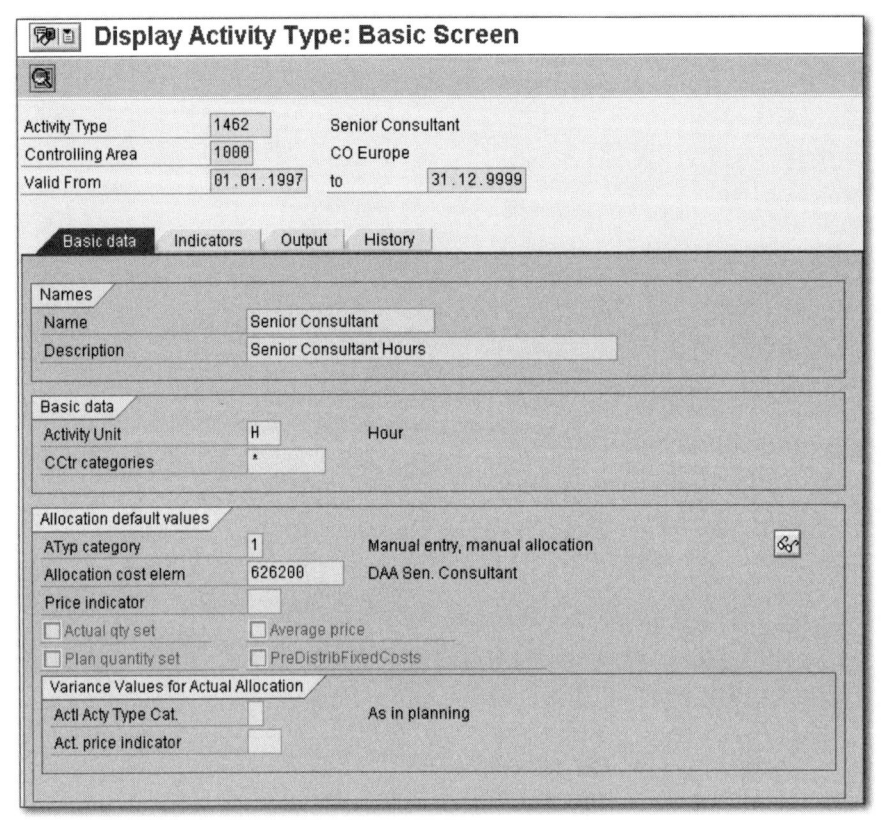

Figure 4.8 Activity Type 1462, Meant for a Senior Consultant

These transactions are useful for creating the new required activity types for CATS, or to just simply check the current activity types already available.

The sender cost center, the business process, and the activity type can be defaulted for each individual, thanks to the Infotype 0315—*Time Sheet Default*, shown in Figure 4.9.

Figure 4.9 Close-Up of the Sender Information in the Infotype 0315—Time Sheet Defaults

Background Information for Financial Accounting | 4.1

Maintain the price planning for the activity type

Although the cost center and the activity type are set up, an important step remains. The cost center and the activity type must be assigned a price for a selected period.

The transaction code KP26 is used to achieve that major step. Alternatively, the transaction code KP27 can be used for display purposes only. Both are shown in Figure 4.10.

| KP26 | Change Plan Data for Activity Types |
| KP27 | Display Plan Data for Activity Types |

Figure 4.10 Plan Data for Activity Types Transactions

This step is crucial and has a deep financial impact. We would recommend letting the Controlling department handle it.

In order to set up the plan data for activity types, the following information is required (entry mode OVERVIEW SCREEN).

Figure 4.11 displays the initial screen for choosing the cost center and the activity type to be linked. This Figure provides a sample example for the cost center 2200 (Human Resources) and the activity type 1462 (Senior Consultant hours). This screen can easily be accessed through the transaction code KP26.

Change Activity Type/Price Planning: Initial Screen

Layout	1-201	Activity types with prices: standard
Variables		
Version	0	Plan/actual version
From period	1	January
To period	12	December
Fiscal year	2008	
Cost Center	2200	Human Resources
to		
or group		
Activity Type	1462	Senior Consultant Hours
to		
or group		

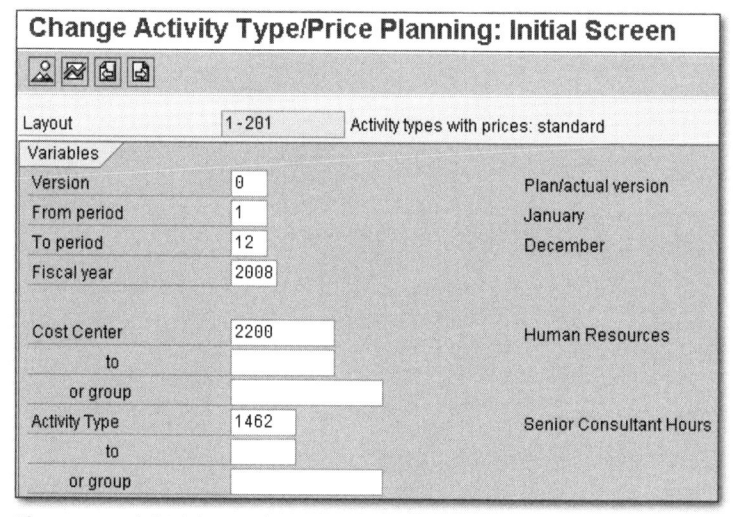

Figure 4.11 Initial Screen for Cost Center and Activity Type

4 | Integration with Finance and Controlling

> **Caution**
>
> Since all these steps are likely to impact the financial accounting department, check with your controlling department if you are entitled to achieve these steps. This will help to avoid unpleasant surprises when posting the financial data from CATS to Controlling.

This step will ensure that the most common error — indicated by the message KL001 – CREATE A MASTER RECORD — will not occur or will at least be minimized while employees book their times.

To resolve this problem, maintain the price planning for the cost center and the activity type.

Figure 4.12 provides the detailed log error for the error message requiring the creation of a master record for the cost center and the activity type. Figure 4.13 shows the error message CREATE A MASTER RECORD FOR XXXX (COST CENTER) / YYYY (ACTIVITY TYPE), as it appears at the bottom of the end user's screen.

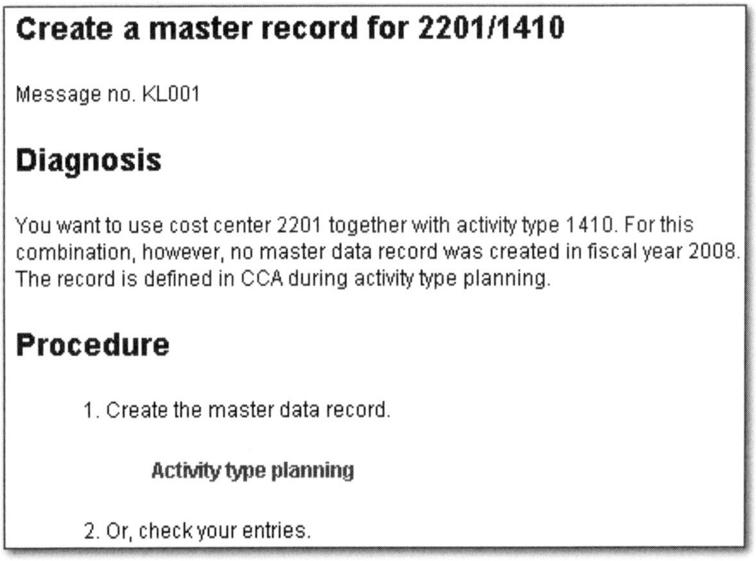

Create a master record for 2201/1410

Message no. KL001

Diagnosis

You want to use cost center 2201 together with activity type 1410. For this combination, however, no master data record was created in fiscal year 2008. The record is defined in CCA during activity type planning.

Procedure

1. Create the master data record.

    Activity type planning

2. Or, check your entries.

Figure 4.12 Detailed Log Error for the Error Message

The error message in Figure 4.13 will appear at the bottom of the user's screen if the master record is missing. It will highlight the basic information: cost center/ activity type.

116

> ⊗ Create a master record for 2201/1410

Figure 4.13 Copy of the Error Message

Create, Maintain, or Display an Internal Order

As we noted in Chapter 1, there are several ways to collect and charge hours and activities within SAP.

Although this information is normally not provided to end users, it is useful to highlight the common transactions for creating, maintaining, or by merely displaying the relevant information at hand for the internal cost center. Figure 4.14 provides a short list of the useful transaction codes used for an internal order.

> **Caution**
> Internal ordering will only be used internally and will not allow post-processing.

Alternatively, you could use service order, maintenance order, purchase order, or a Work Breakdown Structure (WBS) element.

KO01	Create Internal Order
KO02	Change Order
KO03	Display Internal Order

Figure 4.14 Internal-Order Transaction Codes

Figure 4.15 displays the business card from an internal order. This Figure provides a sample example of the internal order number 400078, which is used in the system for the Cebit convention in Hannover, Germany.

If these transactions are not included in your user profile, ask your authorization system administrator to assign the display transactions codes to your profile. They could be added in a CATS basic display authorization profile.

4 | Integration with Finance and Controlling

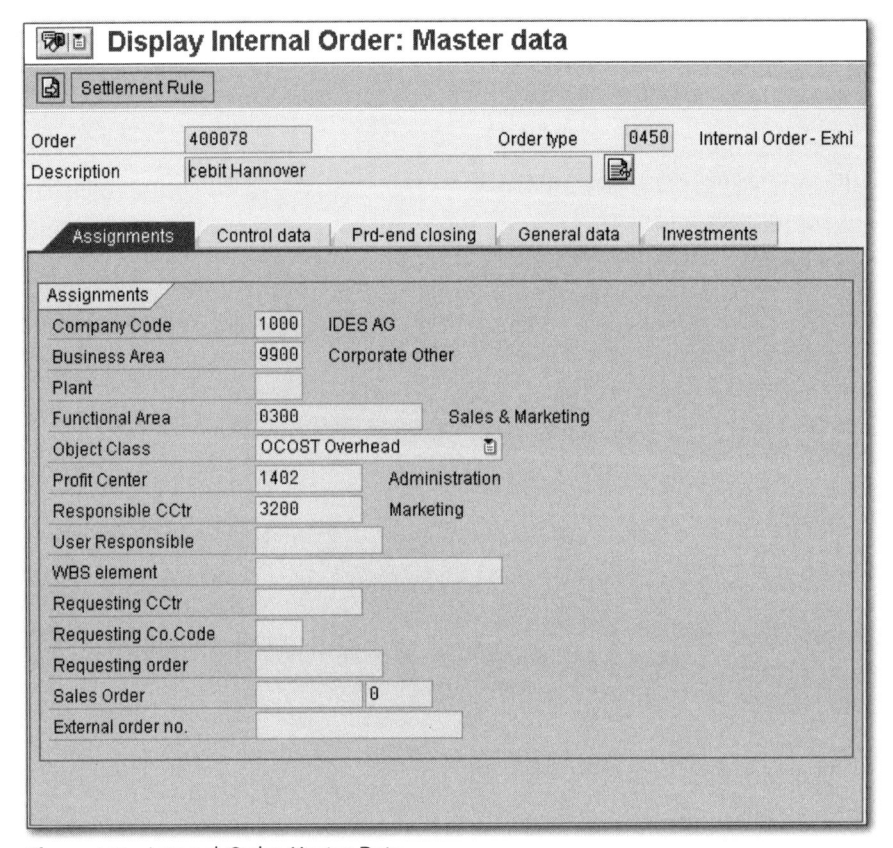

Figure 4.15 Internal-Order Master Data

4.2 CATS Customizing Integration with Financial Accounting

Now that we have revised the basic Financial Accounting elements, let's focus on the customizing possibilities for integrating CATS with Financial Accounting.

Determining the Actual Costs

Because CATS does not evaluate working times, it is unable to determine if the time entries booked are regular hours, overtime, worked with a specific code (i.e. on call, or on duty), or worked on a public holiday. Therefore, we have three ways to determine the costs:

- **Determining the cost using the plan activity type**
  This is the most common option setup. Refer to the transaction KP26.
- **Assigning the activity price directly while booking the time entries**
  This will mean that the user will have to set the value while booking his or her time entries. Do not forget to enable the field in the customizing options (transaction code CAC2).

Determining the activity type, using the user-exit—CATS0002—CATS: Supplement recorded data (function module EXIT_SAPLCATS_002)

This will mean that the user will see the value populated, thanks to a user-exit.

Do not forget to enable the field in the customizing options (transaction code CAC2).

Managing the Cost-Accounting Variant

If you have set up the payroll process in your system, several cost-accounting variants are available, depending on your payroll scenario(s).

In the customizing setup, under the transaction code CAC1, and after having chosen a CATS profile, the section cost-accounting variant allows a number of switches that we will describe

The customizing screen in Figure 4.16 lists the options available for CATS.

- **Assignment of personnel costs to master cost center**
  In the Infotype 0001—*Organizational Assignment*, each employee has been assigned a cost center. The personnel costs are normally considered as primary costs and are charged to this cost center. However, in certain cases, the employee is likely to spend time on other cost centers or on other receiving objects.

In order to open the system to these possibilities, these additional options have been offered:

- **Assignment of personnel costs to receiver object**
- **Assignment of personnel costs to sender**
- **Activity allocation master/sender**
- **Account assignment to activity type**

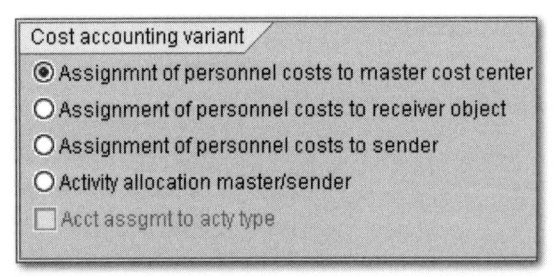

Figure 4.16 Cost Accounting Variants

Enabling Default Values

With regard to the CO module, the following fields can be switched on.

- **Controlling area**
  Should this field be enabled, the system will propose the controlling area, based on the employee's Infotype 0001—Organizational Assignment master data.

- **Master cost center**
  If this field is enabled, the system will propose the master cost center as it has been collected through the Infotype 0000—*Personnel Actions*, while setting the employee's position.

- **Cost center**
  Should this field be enabled, the system will propose the sender cost center, based on the information stored in the employee's Infotype 0315—*Time Sheet Default*.

- **Activity type**
  If this field is enabled, the system will propose the activity type, based on the information stored in the employee's Infotype 0315—*Time Sheet Default*.

- **Sender Business process**
  With this field enabled, the system will propose the sender business process, based on the information stored in the employee's Infotype 0315—*Time Sheet Default*.

> **Hint**
> Depending on the customizing settings for each field, the value generated can be overwritten by the user.

CATS Customizing Integration with Financial Accounting | 4.2

Figure 4.17 provides a reminder of the default values that are likely to be set up. This Figure displays a sample customizing action, where the default values controlling area, master cost center, cost center, and activity type have been enabled.

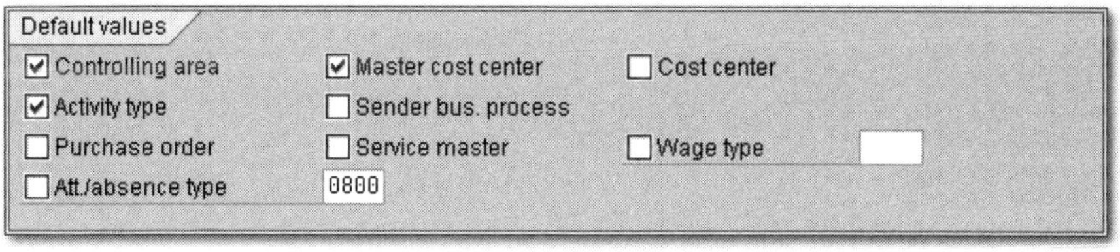

Figure 4.17 Default Values Enabled in Customizing

4.2.1 Focusing on the Available Fields for Controlling

As we have seen in the customizing of the CATS interface, a wide range of fields are available. These fields can be set up under the CATS customizing or simply by calling the transaction code CAC2.

With regard to Controlling (CO), several fields are available for customizing the user interface through the screens, as shown in table 4.1.

Technical Field	Field Description
CATSFIELDS-KOSTLLTXT	Description
CATSD-RAUFNR	Receiver Order
CATSD-RPRZNR	Receiver Business Process
CATSD-RKOSTL	Receiver Cost Center
CATSD-RKSTR	Receiver Cost Object
CATSD-RKDPOS	Receiver Sales Item Object
CATSD-RKDAUF	Receiver Sales Order
CATSD-RPROJ	Receiver WBS Element
CATSD-UNIT	Internal Unit of Measure
CATSD-KOKRS	Controlling Area
CATSFIELDS-SKOSTL	Cost Center
CATSD-LSTAR	Activity Type
CATSD-SKOSTL	Sender Cost Center

Table 4.1 Fields Available for the CO Module

Technical Field	Field Description
CATSD-SPRZNR	Sender Business Process
CATSD-STATKEYFIG	Statistical Key Figure
CATSD-PRICE	Price
CATSD-TCURR	Transaction Currency

Table 4.1 Fields Available for the CO Module (Cont.)

4.2.2 Focusing on Document Generation

While working with CATS, every time entry will populate lines at different levels in the R/3 system. Figure 4.18 depicts the document reduction possible in CATS while working in CO.

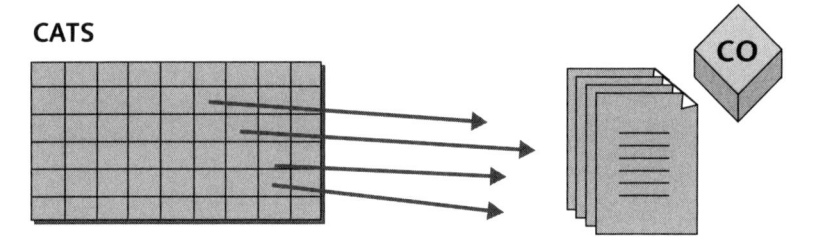

Options for organizing your data
- All documents
- All documents for one personnel number
- All documents with the same sender and receiver account assignments
- All documents for one personnel number with the same sender and receiver account assignments

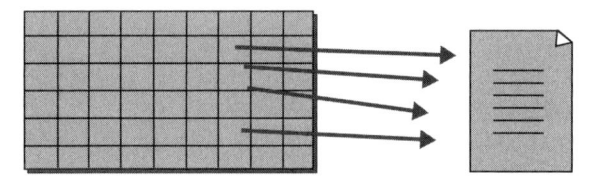

Figure 4.18 How CATS Can Reduce the Number of Documents

In order to optimize the CATS processes and to reduce the number of lines, the system could be adapted simply by adjusting the customizing flag as seen in Chapter 2. The following options are available:

CATS Customizing Integration with Financial Accounting | 4.2

- One CO document is filled for each data record (= no grouping)
- All data records in one CO document (= grouping)
- All data records of a personnel number in a CO document (= grouping)
- All data records are summarized in one CO document; the time entries from all records with the same combination of sender and receiver objects are combined (smart grouping)
- All data records of a personnel number are summarized in a CO document; all the time entries from all records for one personnel number, with the same combination of sender and receiver object, are combined (= smart grouping)

Figure 4.19 provides the customizing access path for maintaining the CATS document reduction while using the CO module. This is very useful for the controlling department, as it deals with a large number of entries all year long. Setting up the option suitable according to their requirement will secure the right number of documents.

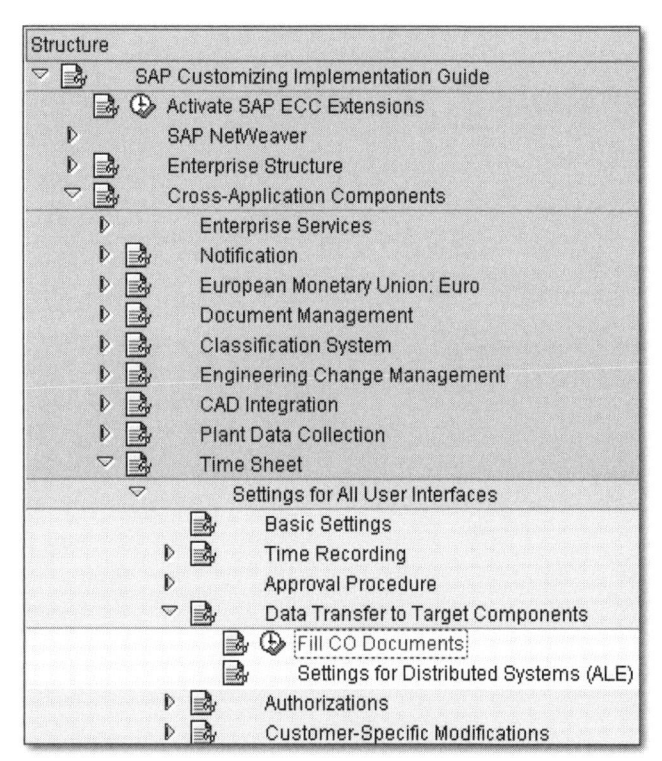

Figure 4.19 Customizing Access While Using CO

Figure 4.20 provides a detailed look at the customizing options. This Figure provides an example where the option ONE CO DOCUMENT PER RECORD has been enabled.

Change View "Settings: Summarization Time Sheet Data -> CO": Details

◉ One CO document per record
○ All data records in one CO document
○ All data records of a personnel number in a CO document
○ All data records are summarized in one CO document
○ All data records of a personnel no. summarized in a CO doc.

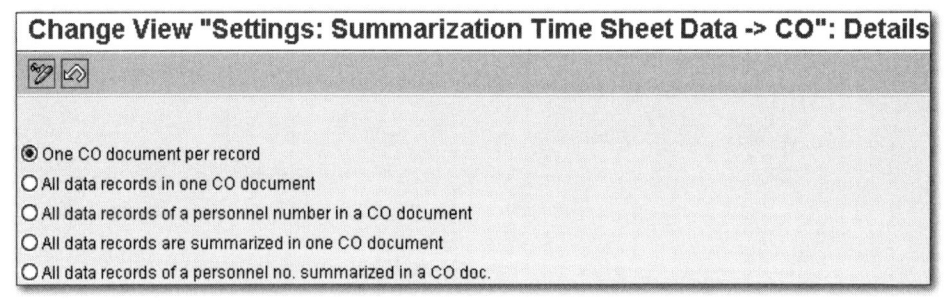

Figure 4.20 Time-Sheet Customization Details

4.2.3 Available User-Exit to Enhance CATS Flexibility in Controlling

Although CATS is flexible, there is still an open door available in R/3 under the common name user-exit. Since each user-exit is used differently according to each business requirement, we will simply point out the names of these extensions.

- The user-exit CATS0002, as introduced earlier
- The user-exit CATS0003–Validate Recorded Data (function module EXIT_SAPLCATS_003), accessible through the transaction code SMOD, can be used to personalize further the CATS process

4.2.4 CATS and Controlling Transfer

Once we have complied with the business processes in CATS, (book, release, and approve time entries), we can run the transfer for CO. Figure 4.21 illustrates the transfer from the data collected through the Time Sheet (CATS) to Controlling. The report used to run the transfer is called RCATSTCO (transaction code CAT7).

To run a mass transfer, you can also use the report RCATSAL (transaction code CATA). SAP recommends setting this program in the background job chain so that it runs every night.

Since CO is usually fed directly by the SAP surrounding modules, and we want to avoid double cost posting. Therefore, time entries collected in CATS can only be transferred directly to CO if you are working only with HR and CO.

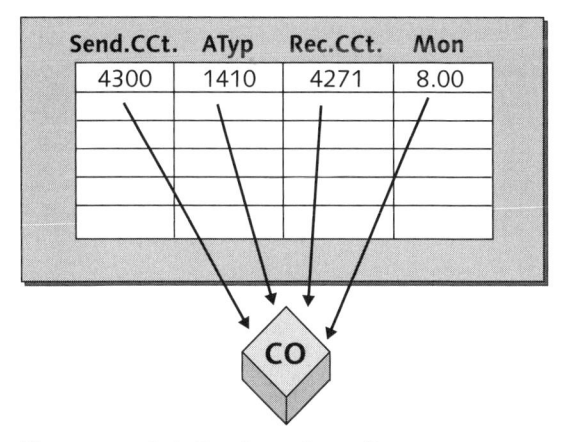

Figure 4.21 Data Transfer to Controlling

Other combinations will feed CO indirectly through their respective target modules.

Table 4.2 depicts the allowed transfer combinations between Controlling and the other modules. Once again, please notice that Controlling is always indirectly fed unless there is a transfer to HR, which can be combined with the Controlling module.

CO	HR	MM-SRV	PM/CS	PS
X	X			
	X	X		
	X		X	
	X			X
	X	X	X	
	X	X		X
		X	X	
		X		X

Table 4.2 Transfer Between CO and Other SAP Modules

4.3 Lessons Learned

This chapter introduced the basis of the Controlling integration by describing the main key features: the cost center, the activity type, and the plan data for the activity type. We have explained the importance of making sure that the integration between Human Resources and Financial Accounting was done correctly.

We also introduced the Controlling receiver object, the internal order that can be used to collect time activities. More closely related to CATS, we have reviewed the relevant fields to be enabled in the data-entry profile as well as the basic options for the document transfer to Controlling. Last but not least, we highlighted the transfer program used to run the transfer from CATS to Controlling.

Now that we have secured the two most important forms of mini-master data from HR and CO, let's investigate the alternative receiver objects that the system provides. Let's have a closer look at the Plant Maintenance and the Customer Service modules.

5 Integration with Plant Maintenance and Customer Service

Important Notice: Since the Plant Maintenance (PM) and the Customer Service (CS) modules are based on a common receiving order, the integration with CATS will be illustrated through the PM module. This should not present a problem, as both modules are based on the same transaction code with regard to the orders.

5.1 Background Information for Plant Maintenance

5.1.1 Key Elements for Integrating CATS with PM and CS

This first section will highlight the integration points with PM, providing a checklist and pointing out the key transaction codes required to handle the basic processes within PM. Figure 5.1 depicts PM and its integration with CATS.

The following information will be reviewed:

- Work Center
- Maintenance order and its operations
- Confirmation of a maintenance order

All the information provided, even if not immediately relevant, can be used as a checklist for documentation and testing.

Using these transactions and business processes might require an SAP authorization clearance. Refer to your authorization-system administrators. If your request is declined, you can always request a standard display mode, in order to view the different pieces of information.

Section 5.2 will focus on CATS integration, including the relevant fields to be used, the specific default information available through Infotype 0315, and the options available through CATS customizing.

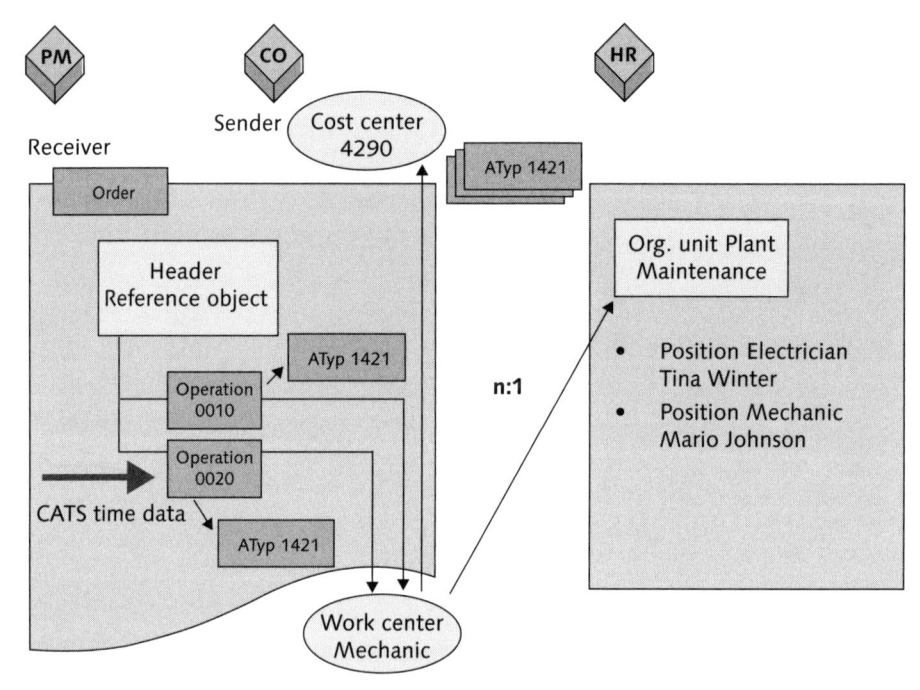

Figure 5.1 How CATS Time Data Interacts with PM

5.1.2 Basic Information about PM

To help you integrate CATS with PM, this chapter will highlight basic transactions. Although this information is normally handled by logistics consultants, understanding it yourself will help to smoothly implement or test CATS, and may enable you to solve other issues while booking time entries.

Create, Maintain or Display a Work Center

The work center is widely used within the Logistics module, including PM and CS. Its aim is to structure Logistics into organizational units. It can identify different types of:

- Machines
- People
- Production Lines
- Groups of craftsmen

With respect to its integration with Personnel Time Management, the work center represents suitably equipped physical locations where work can be performed.

Figure 5.2 lists the transaction codes used to create, maintain, and display a maintenance work center.

IR01	Create Work Center
IR02	Change Work Center
IR03	Display Work Center

Figure 5.2 Work-Center Transaction Codes

The transaction display work center (transaction code IR03) is useful for displaying the business card of the work center, with work center category PM. Figure 5.3 provides the business card of the work center. This Figure provides a sample example of the work center 2200, used in the system for mechanical maintenance.

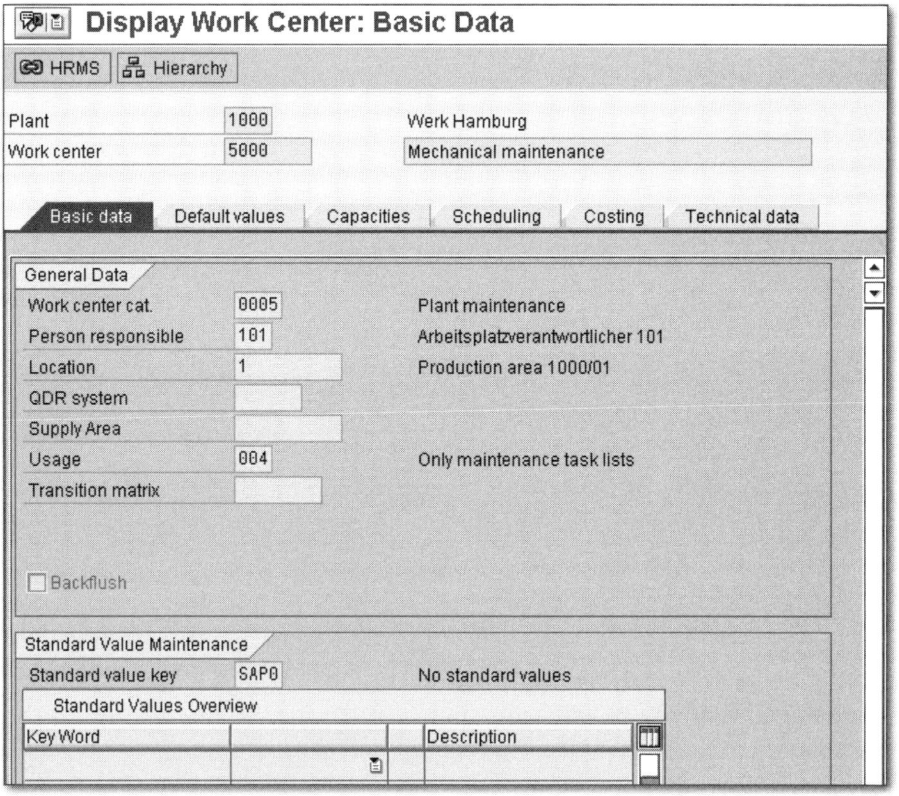

Figure 5.3 Basic Data for Work Center 2200

Create, Maintain, or Display a Maintenance Order

In a standard process, we can identify different events in the PM process. We could start with the assumption that we use mainly preventive maintenance (in other words, a production-line mechanical maintenance), and that for the maintenance requested beyond that a notification has been issued.

The Maintenance Order will be the main receiver object for collecting time spent on scheduled operations. Figure 5.4 provides an example of a maintenance order. The example provided displays the standard fields available in the system. For CATS, pay close attention to the start date, which is a crucial element, along with the status RELEASED for allocating time entries. The bottom of the screen shows the first operation named SAMPLE ORDER FOR COLLECTING CATS.

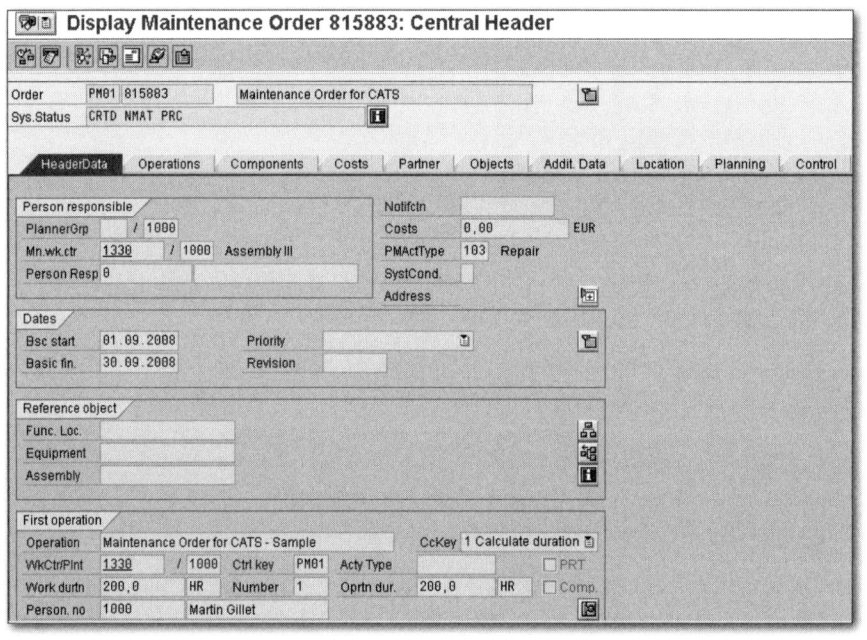

Figure 5.4 Central Header Data for Maintenance Order

Each maintenance order can be organized in several steps known as operations. Although it is likely that most of the maintenance order will be built with a single operation, this functionality will be useful in distributing the different operations to carry on the requested activity.

Background Information for Plant Maintenance | **5.1**

An operation is an activity within the order itself. It can be organized in a sequence so that the process can be divided into different steps, as shown in Figure 5.5.

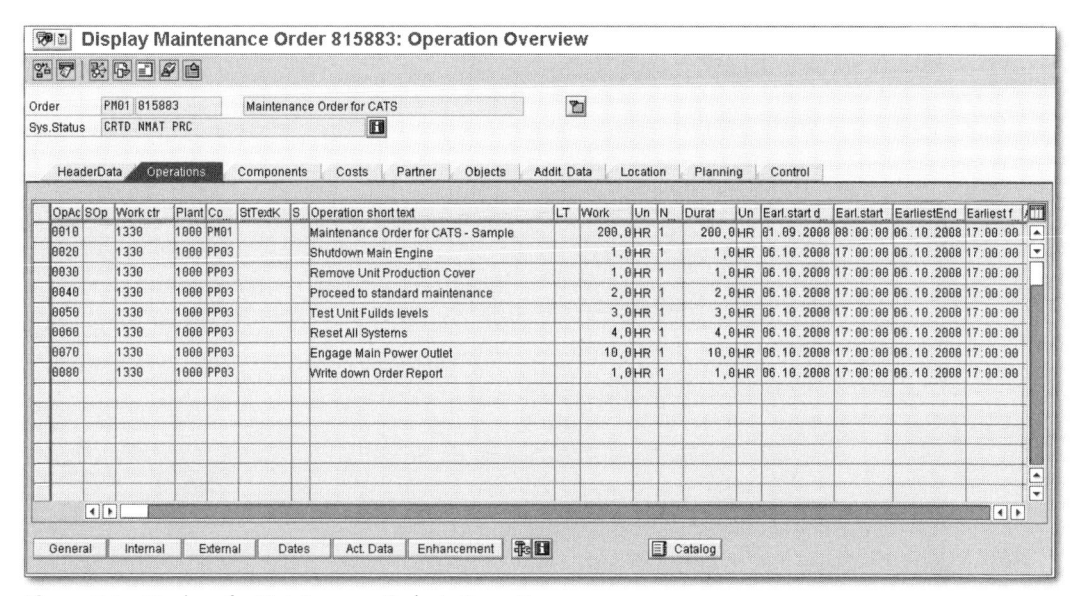

Figure 5.5 Display of a Maintenance Order's Operation

Figure 5.5 illustrates a maintenance order with nine operations, all sequenced in a unique order. Each operation has its own attributes with regard to the time, the duration, the cost allocation and the number of workers assigned to it. Please note the activity-type information, located on the far right column. For information about integrating CATS with FI-CO, refer to Chapter 4.

> **Hint**
>
> Carefully check the maintenance order's system status.

Look at Figure 5.6 for a closer look into the system status, showing the status created (CRTD) once the order has been created and saved. Figure 5.7 provides the description of each system status.

Figure 5.6 Created System Status

131

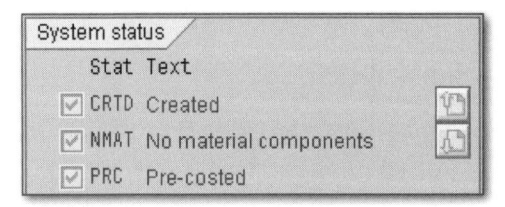

5 | Integration with Plant Maintenance and Customer Service

Figure 5.7 System Status Descriptions

Having the order in CREATED status will not enable time bookings through CATS. In order to achieve that, the order must have been released and bear the status REL. This step will ensure that the order is open for time collection.

Figure 5.8 provides a closer look at the system status once the order has been released (REL). Releasing the order enables time-collection. Figure 5.9 displays a more detailed description of the system status.

Figure 5.8 System Status with Maintenance Order Released

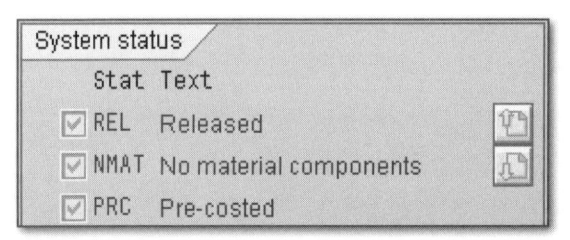

Figure 5.9 Maintenance Order Status Details

> **Caution**
>
> All these steps are likely to affect the plant-maintenance department's planning, so check with your maintenance department whether you are authorized to perform these steps. This will help prevent unpleasant surprises when releasing the maintenance order.

The transactions shown in Figure 5.10 are likely to be useful while setting up CATS. These transactions will be useful for reviewing the open maintenance order in the system. They also could provide the information needed to start investigating the integration of the PM module and CATS.

IW31	Create Order
IW32	Change Order
IW33	Display PM Order

Figure 5.10 Transactions for Creating, Editing, and Displaying a Maintenance Order

This step will ensure that the most common error, indicated by the message BS013—SYSTEM STATUS CRTD IS ACTIVE. To resolve this error, maintain the system status of the maintenance order by releasing it. Please notice that the technical name of the message is BS013.

System status CRTD is active (ORD 815884)

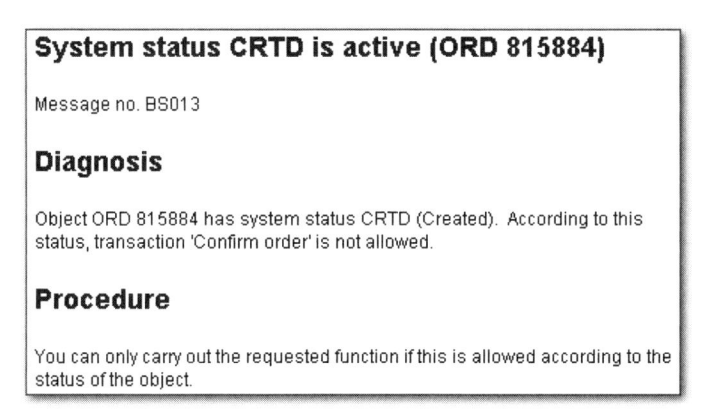

Message no. BS013

Diagnosis

Object ORD 815884 has system status CRTD (Created). According to this status, transaction 'Confirm order' is not allowed.

Procedure

You can only carry out the requested function if this is allowed according to the status of the object.

Figure 5.11 Detailed Log of Error Message "System status CRTD is active"

⊗ System status CRTD is active (ORD 815884)

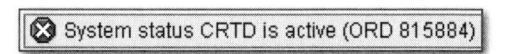

Figure 5.12 CRTD Error Message Log

This message will appear at the bottom on the user's screen, as shown in Figure 5.12, if the system status CRTD is active. It will highlight the basic information the order number.

IW41	Enter PM Order Confirmation
IW42	Overall Completion Confirmation
IW43	Display PM Order Confirmation

Figure 5.13 Error message on End User's Screen

Create, maintain, or display an order confirmation

After creation of the maintenance order, let's assume that time entries have been collected through CATS. For clear integration reasons, once the process for collecting time entries through CATS has been determined, direct stand-alone confirmations must be avoided.

This section will provide the stand-alone confirmation transactions. This information is provided to check that the time entries collected through CATS have been transferred to the target module.

Figure 5.14 lists transaction codes used for the order confirmation. Because the time collection will be done through the Time Sheet, the transaction IW43 is likely the one to remember, as it provides only a display.

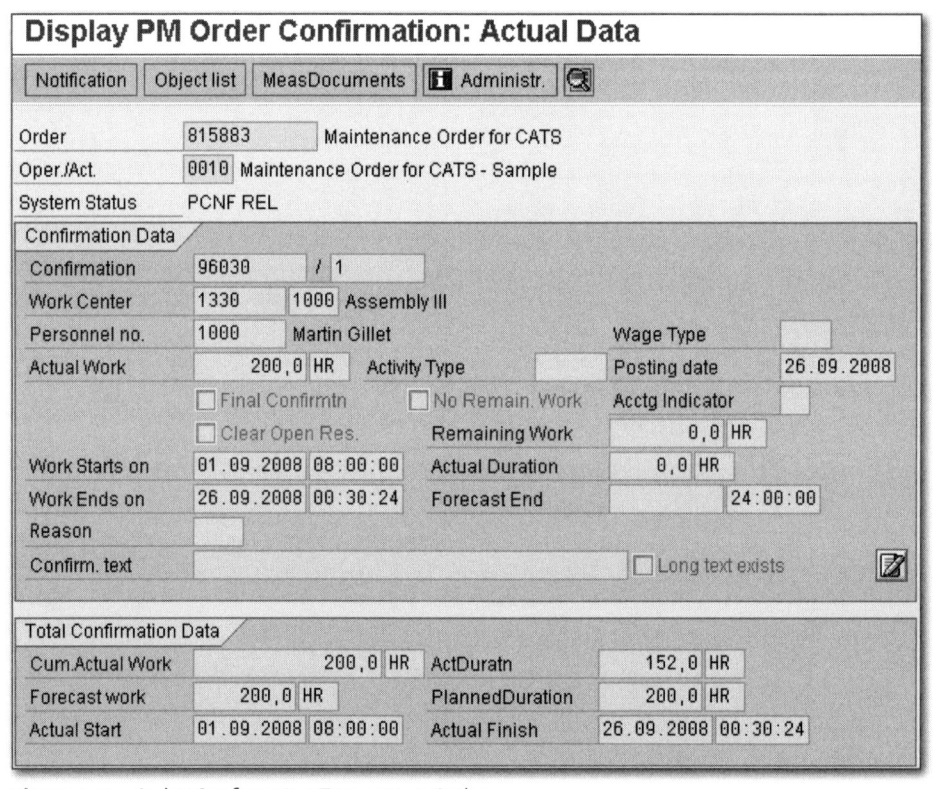

Figure 5.14 Order-Confirmation Transaction Codes

These transactions are useful because they will allow the display of the confirmation details allocated to the maintenance order, once the transfer has run from CATS to the PM module.

Table 5.1 displays the information gathered from CATS and sent out onto the maintenance order. It shows the details of the confirmation allocated to the maintenance order.

> **Hint**
>
> If these transactions are not included in your user profile, ask your authorization- system administrator to assign the display transactions codes to your profile. They can be added in a CATS basic display authorization profile.

Technical Field	Field Description
CATSD-ARBPL	Work Center
CATSD-BEMOT	Accounting Indicator
CATSD-RAUFNR	Receiver Order
CATSFIELDS-DISPTEXT1	(Order) Description
CATSFIELDS-DISPTEXT2	(Order) Description
CATSD-RAUFNR	Receiver Order
CATSDB-AUERU	Final Confirmation
CATSD-KAPAR	Capacity Category
CATSD-KOKRS	Controlling Area
CATSDB-LTXA1	Short Text
CATSFIELDS-PERNR	Personnel Number
CATSDB-PEDD	Forecast Finish Date
CATSDB-OFMNW	Remaining Work
CATS-SPLIT	Split Number
CATSFIELDS-AUSTAT	Det. Status Auto.
CATSDB-ERUZU	Partial Confirmation
CATSDB-UVORN	Suboperation
CATSD-VORNR	Operation
CATSD-WERKS	Plant

Table 5.1 Order Confirmation Details for Plant Maintenance

5.2 CATS Integration for PM

5.2.1 Focusing on Available Fields for PM

As we have seen in the customizing of the CATS interface, a wide range of fields are available. These fields can be set up under CATS customizing or simply by calling the Transaction code CAC2. Several fields are available for the PM and the CS module, as shown in Figure 5.15

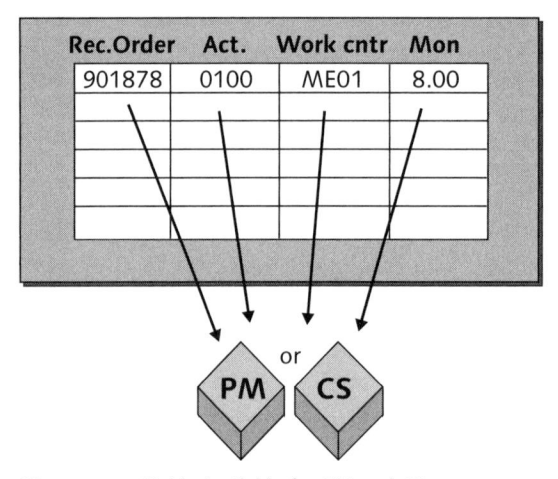

Figure 5.15 Fields Available for PM and CS

5.2.2 Available User-Exit to Enhance CATS Flexibility

Even though CATS is extremely flexible, there is still an open door available in R/3 under the common name user-exit. Since each user-exit is used differently according to the specific business requirement, we will just point out the name of these extensions.

- The user-exit CATS0002, as already introduced
- The user-exit CATS0003, as already introduced

Furthermore, SAP also provides two user-exits for displaying the order description in the collection section or in the worklist section.

- The user-exit CATS0009, Customer-Specific Text Fields in DATA-ENTRY Section, based on the function module EXIT_SAPLCATS_009

- The user-exit CATS0010, Customer-Specific Text Fields in WORKLIST, based on the function module EXIT_SAPLCATS_010

Both these user-exits require mapping of the display field to the PM description field.

5.2.3 CATS and Plant Maintenance Transfer

Once you have complied with the business processes in CATS, (book, release, and approve time entries), you can run the transfer for PM.

Table 5.2 depicts the transfer of the data collected through CATS to the PM and the CS modules.

CO	HR	MM-SRV	PM/CS	PS
X	X			
	X	X		
	X		X	
	X			X
	X	X	X	
	X		X	X
		X	X	
		X		X

Table 5.2 Data Transfer to Plant Maintenance and Customer Service Modules

The report used to run the transfer is called RCATSTPM (transaction code CAT9).

To run mass transfers, you can also use the report RCATSAL (transaction code CATA). SAP recommends setting this program in the background job chain so that it runs every night.

Since CO is usually fed indirectly by the surrounding SAP modules, and because we want to avoid double cost-posting, time entries collected in CATS can only be directly transferred to CO, and only if you are only working with the HR and CO modules. Other combinations will feed PM and other target modules.

Table 5.2 gives a graphic view of the allowed transfer combinations for PM and CS.

5.3 Lessons Learned

This chapter reviewed the key elements for integrating PM or CS to CATS. It has provided the basic useful transactions codes and the user-exits for optimizing the use of CATS. This chapter also illustrated the transfer program to the target component.

Let's now move on to the next chapter, where we will investigate the integration with the Project System and its object receiver, the Work Breakdown Structure (WBS) element.

6 Integration with Project System

6.1 Background Information for Project System

Like similar software handling tasks and activities, SAP contains a module called Project System (PS). The main purpose of this module is it to describe project activities through receiver objects such as networks and work breakdown structure (WBS) elements. As this is one of the potential receiver objects, it is important to understand how to integrate it with the CATS.

This section will highlight the key integration points with the Project System (PS) module, providing a checklist and identifying the key transaction codes required to handle the basic processes within PS.

Figure 6.1 provides an overview of PS and its main elements:

- Work center
- Work Breakdown Structure (WBS) element and its operations
- Confirmation of a WBS element

These elements will be reviewed as background information. They all play roles in CATS integration. If the information provided here is not immediately relevant, it may be used as a checklist for documentation and test purposes.

Using these transactions and business processes will require an SAP authorization clearance. Refer to your authorization system administrators. Should your request be declined, you can always request a standard display mode, in order to view the different pieces of information.

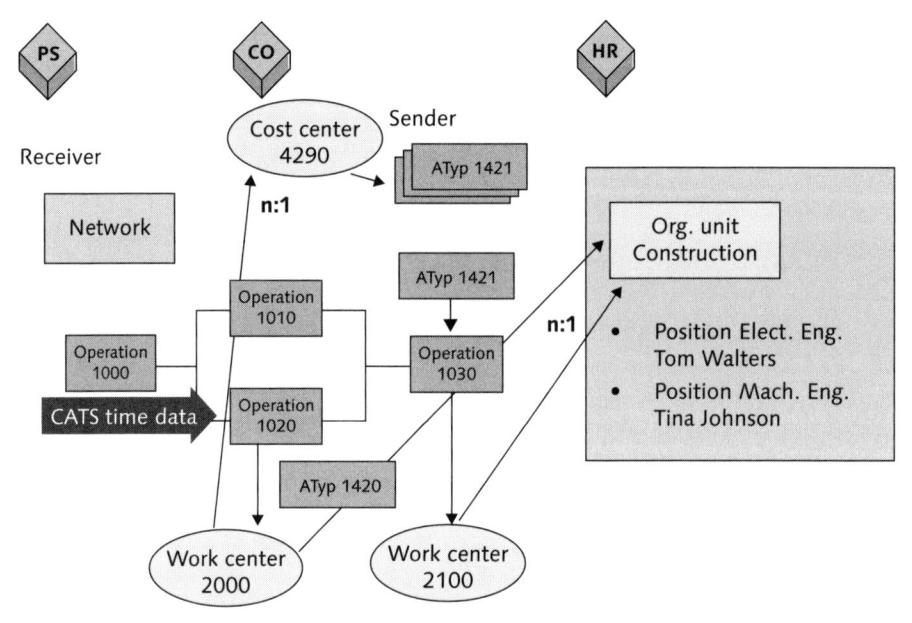

Figure 6.1 Project System (PS) and Its Integration Within CATS

6.2 Setting Up CATS Integration with the Project System Module

Section 6.2 will focus on CATS integration aspects, including the relevant fields to be used and the options available through the CATS customizing.

6.2.1 Basic Information About PS Transactions to Be Integrated

To help you integrate CATS with PS, this chapter will highlight the basic transactions to be integrated. Although logistics consultants normally handle this information, this knowledge will enable you to implement or test CATS smoothly and also to solve basic problems that arise while booking time entries.

These transactions will be handy, as they will be used to review the current settings.

Create, Maintain, or Display a Work Center

The work center is widely used within Logistics. Its aim is to structure the Logistics into organizational units.

6.2 Setting Up CATS Integration with the Project System Module

With regard to its integration with Personnel Time Management, it represents a suitably equipped physical location where work can be performed.

Figure 6.2 shows the transactions that are likely to be useful while setting up the integration between CATS and the PS core module. The transactions shown are the transactions used to maintain the work center.

CNR1	Create Work Center
CNR2	Change Work Center
CNR3	Display Work Center

Figure 6.2 Different Access Modes for the Project System Work Center

The transaction display work center (transaction code CNR3) is useful in displaying the business card of the work center, with work-center category Project Management. Figure 6.3 provides a reference snapshot of a work center belonging to the Project System.

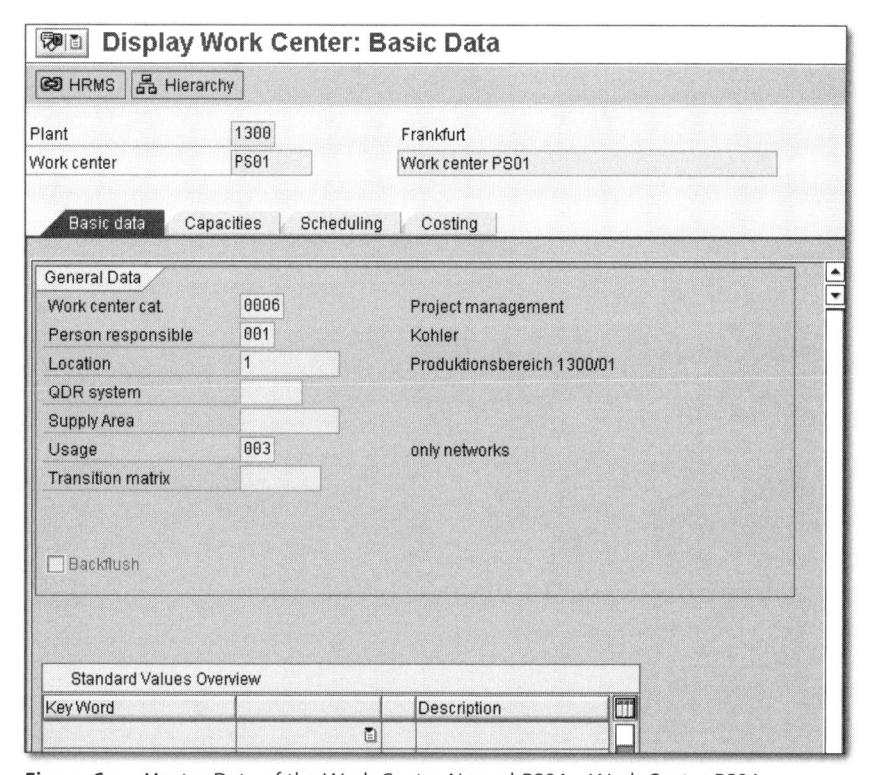

Figure 6.3 Master Data of the Work Center Named PS01 — Work Center PS01

141

6 | Integration with Project System

We assume that all the required data has been created by the logistics team. However, the basic transactions will help you to monitor the PS module. Within PS, we could use several receiver objects such as the WBS, a statistical figure, or a network activity.

In order to illustrate the integration with CATS, we will focus on the Project Builder, the most common receiver element used in the modules. The construction of the WBS elements can be achieved through the Project Builder.

The Project Builder

The Project Builder, transaction code CJ20N, can be used to centralize the different elements belonging to the PS component. Its major asset is to gather all the relevant information into one screen, as shown in Figure 6.4.

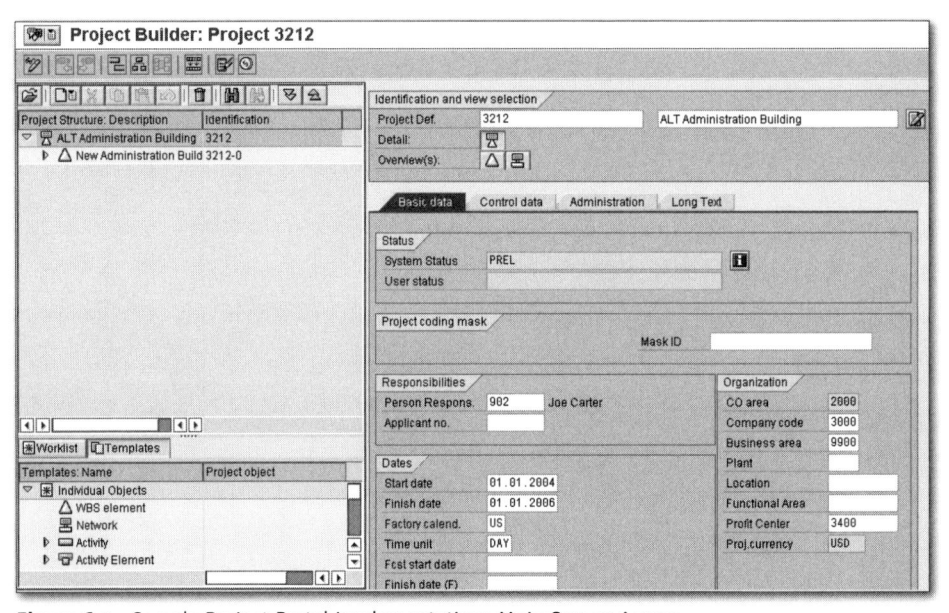

Figure 6.4 Sample Project Portal Implementation: Main Screen Access

Create, Maintain, or Display a WBS

As usual in SAP, there are several transaction codes used to maintain, change, and display a Work Breakdown Structure. Figure 6.5 shows the different transaction codes used to handle the different steps for a Work Breakdown Structure.

Please carefully note that the acronym WBS, which stands for Work Breakdown Structure, is widely used in the system instead of its full name.

CJ01	Create Work Breakdown Structure
CJ02	Change Work Breakdown Structure
CJ03	Display Work Breakdown Structure

Figure 6.5 Reference Transactions to Create, Change, and Display the WBS Element

We assume that the main data has been created prior to the installation of CATS. However, since CATS is integrated with the target modules which are theoretically already in place, it might be useful to check and identify the WBS elements required for the time bookings.

In order to display the WBS master data, the transaction CJ03 can be used.

In the example illustrated next in Figure 6.6, one WBS element is displayed. However, it is likely that the project will contain more than one WBS. Figure 6.6 provides a snapshot of a WBS element within a project.

During CATS project implementation, you might be asked to assign the relevant WBS elements to the employees working on this element. This is not possible through the Infotype 0315 — *CATS Default*. The best solution would be to create a dedicated infotype to gather all the relevant WBS assigned to the employees. This will ensure that:

- Time bookings are done on the correct receiver object
- The selection process will be easier (no scrolling down a search list)
- The WBS elements can also be included in the worklist, in order to find them easily should they occur frequently

The basic transaction to create an infotype is the transaction PM01.

6 | Integration with Project System

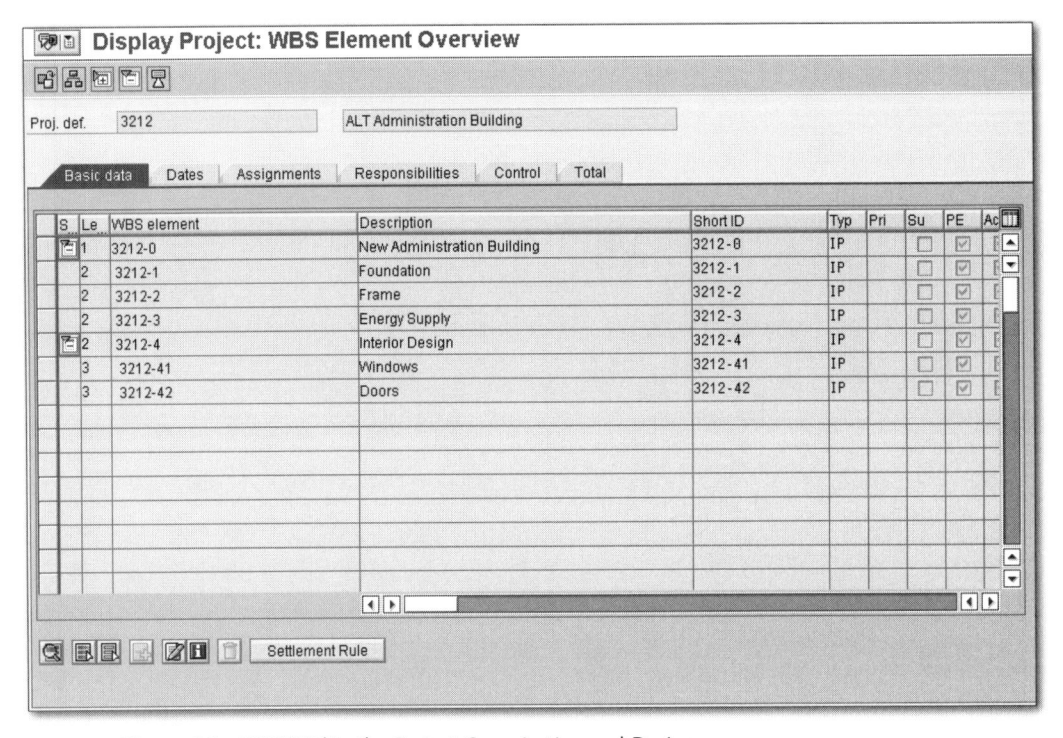

Figure 6.6 WBS Within the Project Organization and Design

Create, Maintain, or Display a WBS Confirmation on a Network

To further explore the creation of the WBS element, let's assume that time entries have been collected through CATS.

For integration reasons, direct stand-alone confirmations must be avoided once the process has been determined for collecting time entries through CATS.

For information purposes, this section will provide the stand-alone confirmation transactions. This information is provided so you can check that the time entries collected through CATS have been transferred to the target module. Figure 6.7 displays the confirmation transactions for the network activities.

CN25	Confirm Completions in Network
CN27	Collective confirm.
CN28	Display Network Confirmations
CN29	Cancel Network Confirmation

Figure 6.7 Transaction Codes Used to Allocate Time Activities on a WBS

If these transactions are not included in your user profile, ask your authorization system administrator to assign the display transactions codes to your profile. They could be added in a CATS basic display authorization profile.

6.3 CATS Integration for Project System

6.3.1 Focusing on the Available Fields for PS

As we have seen in the customizing of the CATS interface, a wide range of fields is available. These fields can be set up under the CATS customizing or simply by calling the transaction code CAC2.

Table 6.1 illustrates the different fields available for PS within CATS. It provides a quick reference snapshot of the technical field name and its description.

Technical Field	Field Description
CATSD-ARBPL	Work Center
CATSD-BEMOT	Accounting Indicator
CATSD-RAUFNR	Receiver Order
CATSFIELDS-DISPTEXT1	(Order) Description
CATSFIELDS-DISPTEXT2	(Order) Description
CATSD-RAUFNR	Receiver Order
CATSD-AUERU	Final Confirmation
CATSD-KAPAR	Capacity Category
CATSD-KOKRS	Controlling Area
CATSDB-LTXA1	Short Text

Table 6.1 PS Fields and Their Descriptions

CATSFIELDS-PERNR	Personnel Number
CATSDB-PEDD	Forecast Finish Date
CATSDB-OFMNW	Remaining Work
CATSD-SPLIT	Split Number
CATSFIELDS-AUSTAT	Det. Status Auto.
CATSDB-ERUZU	Partial Confirmation
CATSD-UVORN	Suboperation
CATSD-VORNR	Operation
CATSD-WERKS	Plant

Table 6.1 PS Fields and Their Descriptions (Cont.)

6.3.2 Available User-Exit to Enhance CATS Flexibility

Although CATS is quite flexible, there is still an open door available in R/3 under the common name USER-EXIT. Since each user-exit is used differently according to each business requirement, we will simply point out the name of these extensions:

- The user-exit CATS0002, as already introduced earlier
- The user-exit CATS0003, as already introduced earlier

Furthermore, SAP also provides two user-exits for displaying the order description in the collection section and/or in the worklist section.

- The user-exit CATS0009, Customer-Specific Text Fields in Data Entry Section, based on the function module EXIT_SAPLCATS_009
- The user-exit CATS0010, Customer-Specific Text Fields in Worklist, based on the function module EXIT_SAPLCATS_010

Both of these user-exits require the mapping of the display field to the plant-maintenance description field.

6.3.3 CATS and PS Transfer

Once we have complied with the business processes in CATS, (book, release, and approve time entries), we can run the transfer for PS. Figure 6.8 provides the key elements for transferring the data to the Project System.

CATS Integration for Project System | **6.3**

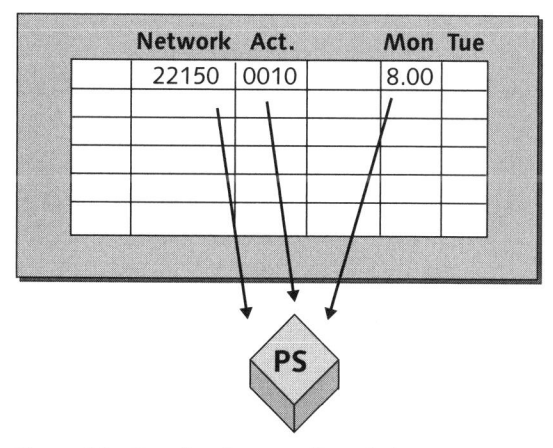

Figure 6.8 Transfer of Data Collected Through CATS to Target Component PS

The report used to run the transfer is called RCATSTPS (transaction code CAT5).

To run mass transfer, you could also use the report RCATSAL (transaction code CATA). SAP recommends setting this program in the background job chain so that it runs every night.

Since Controlling (CO) is usually fed indirectly by the surrounding SAP modules, and because we want to avoid double cost-posting, time entries collected in CATS can only be directly transferred to CO, and only if you are working with the Human Resources (HR) and CO.

Other combinations will feed PS and other target modules. Table 6.2 shows the authorized combinations for PS.

CO	HR	MM-SRV	PM/CS	PS
X	X			
	X	X		
	X		X	
	X			X
	X	X	X	
	X	X		X
		X	X	
		X		X

Table 6.2 Transfer Types Allowed for PS

6.4 Lessons Learned

This chapter examined the key elements in the structure of the Project System module. We covered the integration aspects, including the available fields for customizing the user interface. It also described the transfer feature for Project System.

We also looked at most of the target modules. Now only Materials Management (MM) remains. It will be introduced in the next chapter.

7 Integration with External Services Management

7.1 Background Information for External Services Management

In this chapter you will learn about the key elements for integrating CATS with External Services Management, through Materials Management (MM). We will highlight the integration points CATS has with MM, providing a checklist and highlighting the information required for assigning the purchase order into the provider's default values.

Figure 7.1 illustrates the flow, from the creation of the purchase order in MM, to the time sheet activities collection. The MM module is tricky in the sense that once the CATS time entries have been approved and transferred to it, these time entries must be submitted to a reception process.

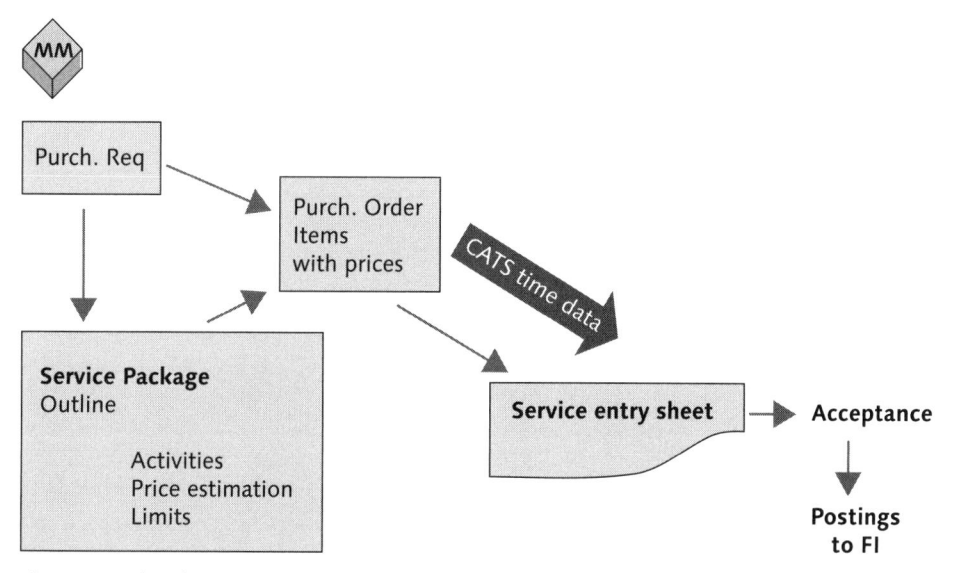

Figure 7.1 Flow from Creation of Purchase Order in MM

We assume that you know the reception process for your core environment. SAP assumes that the CATS approval process (if enabled) and the reception process in MM are performed by two different persons. Therefore, this is a standard process.

All the information provided in this section, even if it does not seem immediately relevant, can be used as a checklist for documentation and test purposes.

These transactions and business processes might require an SAP authorization clearance. Please communicate with your authorization system administrators. If your request is declined, you can request a **standard display mode** so you can view the different pieces of information.

7.1.1 Basic Information for MM

To integrate CATS with External Services Management, which is part of the MM module, this chapter will highlight the basic transactions you need to know. Although this information is normally handled by logistics consultants, knowledge of these facts will ensure a smooth process while implementing or testing CATS while also making it possible to solve basic issues that arise when booking time entries.

Create a Purchase Order

A purchase order is the receiver object for collecting time activities from external providers. The following transactions are useful while setting up CATS, if they provide the direct transaction access code. Figure 7.2 illustrates the basic ways to create a purchase order for external providers. Let's look at four possibilities:

- The vendor is known
- The vendor is unknown
- The purchase order is created via the requisition assignment list
- The purchase order is created automatically via the Purchase Requisitions

Let's assume that the vendor is known, and we can, therefore, use the transaction code ME21N.

ME21N	Create Purchase Order
ME25	Create PO with Source Determination
ME58	Ordering: Assigned Requisitions
ME59N	Automatic generation of POs

Figure 7.2 Basic Ways to Create Purchase Order for External Providers

Background Information for External Services Management | 7.1

Maintain and display a purchase order

It might be useful to know the transaction to maintain and mass-process the purchase order. Figure 7.3 shows the transaction codes for maintaining individually and mass- processing these purchase orders.

ME22N	Change Purchase Order
ME23N	Display Purchase Order
MEMASSPO	Mass Change of Purchase Orders

Figure 7.3 Transaction Codes for Individual and Mass Processing of Purchase Orders

Figure 7.4 illustrates, through the transaction ME22N, the purchase order that is created.

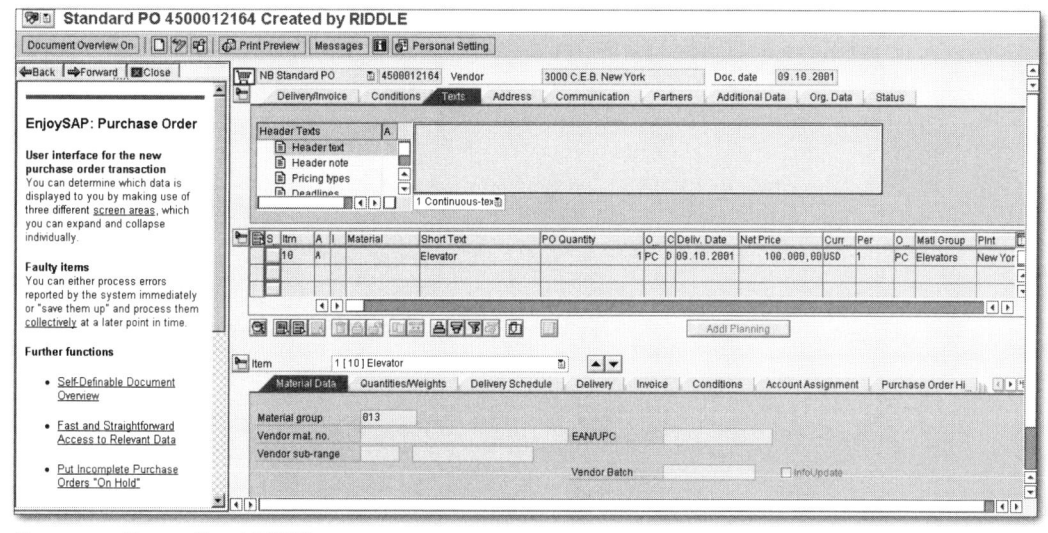

Figure 7.4 Transaction ME22N

Although this information will most likely be provided by your sales administrators, it is useful to know where to find it.

Just as with the other target modules, it is crucial that the purchase order has the right system status, so that time activities can be booked.

151

From practical experience, we have identified two showstoppers while working with purchase orders in the CATS Environment: the allocated deadline and the allocated quantity or budget. These are discussed below.

- **The allocated deadline**
  The time period allocated during the purchase order creation, for allocating time entries, is too narrow. This may cause additional tracking efforts for the time and purchase administrators.

> **Hint**
> Instead of setting the time period from February 1 to the end of February 2005, allow a buffer for the time allocation, i.e. from February 1 until the middle of March 2005. Late time allocation will still be possible. This will save valuable time for the time and purchase administrators since they won't have to manually extend purchase orders.

It is, highly desirable to set a buffer around these two important pieces of information. You can ask your purchase administrators to observe this flexibility criterion.

- **The allocated quantity or budget**
  The initial budget allocated to the purchase order is set according to the designated plan. However, since no warning is issued, external providers cannot suddenly allocate time entries through CATS. This might increase the flow of time activities but it can also harm the cash flow process already in place.

7.1.2 Integration with Human Resources

Once the purchase order has been created, it may be assigned to the external services provider. To achieve this user creation, the hiring process must occur so that the company's personnel database is updated per the requirements. The following actions must be taken. Through the transaction PERSONNEL ACTIONS (PA40), hire the External Provider with the Mini Master Data.

Figure 7.5 illustrates the master data created for a service provider. The master data is reduced for the service providers, since they only require a mini master data. All the information collected is similar to that collected for regular employees, e.g.

identity, organizational assignment, etc. In Figure 7.5 pay special attention to the provider's personnel number, which starts with the number 9.

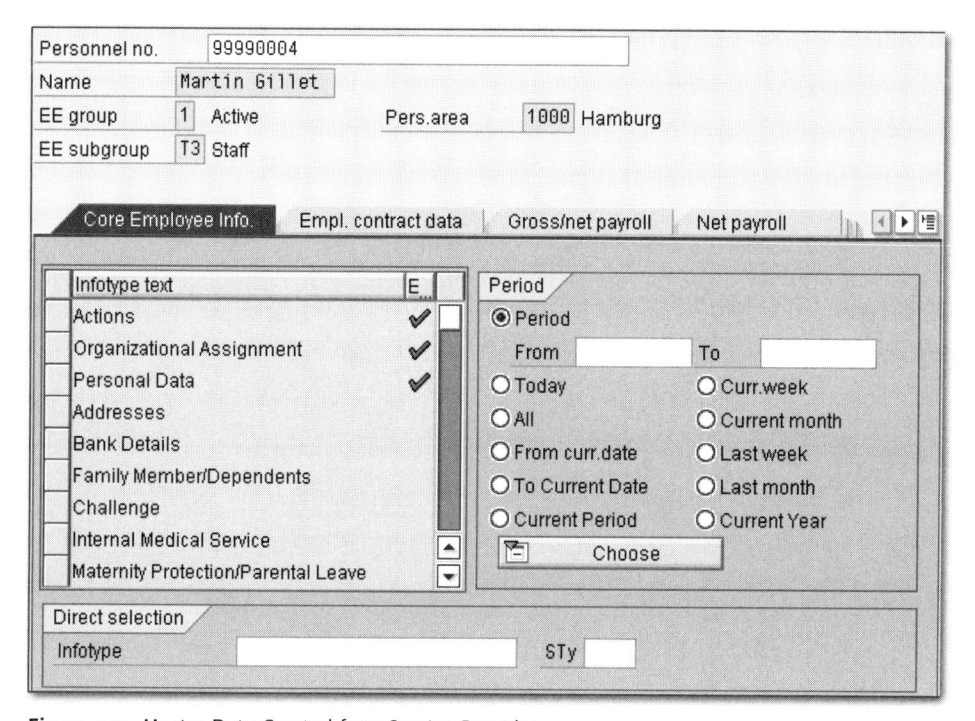

Figure 7.5 Master Data Created for a Service Provider

To speed up the time collection process, and to support the external provider, the purchase order has to be allocated to the Infotype 0315 — *CATS Time Sheet Defaults*.

Figure 7.6 highlights the fields available in the Infotype 0315 — *CATS Time Sheet Defaults*. Although this information is not mandatory, we recommended you add it so that the resource provider will not have to search for his or her purchase-order number. The risk of mistyping is also reduced.

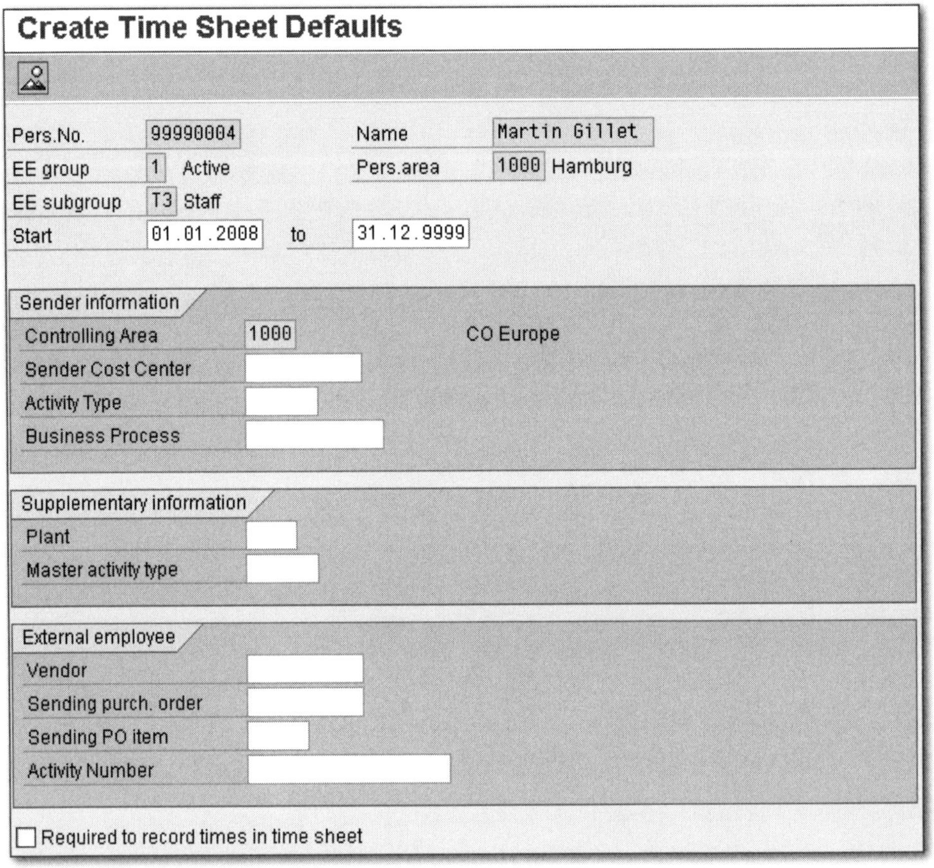

7 | Integration with External Services Management

Figure 7.6 Fields Available in Infotype 0315

Look carefully at the sub-screen section EXTERNAL EMPLOYEE. Along with the purchase order number, it helps to provide the following information.

- The vendor identity that identifies the vendor's details
- The (sending) purchase order that identifies the purchase order number
- The sending purchase order item that identifies the step within the purchase order
- The activity number that identifies the activity within the purchase order

This information will be useful because it will be defaulted in the service provider's time sheet. As a result we address two major objectives:

- Preventing service providers from having to search for the master data
- Reducing incorrect data collection to its lowest level

To clearly identify external staff in your structure, SAP advises using an internal numbering range for these resources. It will also be useful to clearly exclude external personnel from the company's core processes (e.g., Time Evaluation, Payroll, etc.). It will be useful to set the first digit of their personnel ID's as 9. This will ensure that this personnel range is left out of any process. Of the eight-digit personnel number, 9 is assigned as the first digit.

As an example we can take Martin Gillet: Service Provider 90000001. This step can be easily customized through the transaction PA04. Make sure that the range is internal, so that SAP can automatically index the numbers.

Figure 7.7 illustrates the different ranges provided in the system. Internal numbering means that SAP takes the lead in indexing the numbering. External numbering means that the end user has the lead in assigning the personnel number.

> **Caution**
> Be very careful in a productive environment since you could jeopardize the personnel master data. Work in conjunction with the HR Department. To assign the ranges created, you must also adapt the feature, NUMKR. This feature can be accessed through the Transaction PE03.

Let's take the analogy of a train entering a station. This feature will determine at which platform the train will stop. In our case, based on the decision criteria (i.e. Active External Service Provider), it will return the proper range. Do bear in mind that this is a program. Therefore, a backup plan is required, if no decision criteria succeeds. Think of our train again, which must stop at any platform even if none has been assigned to it.

Maintain Number Range Intervals

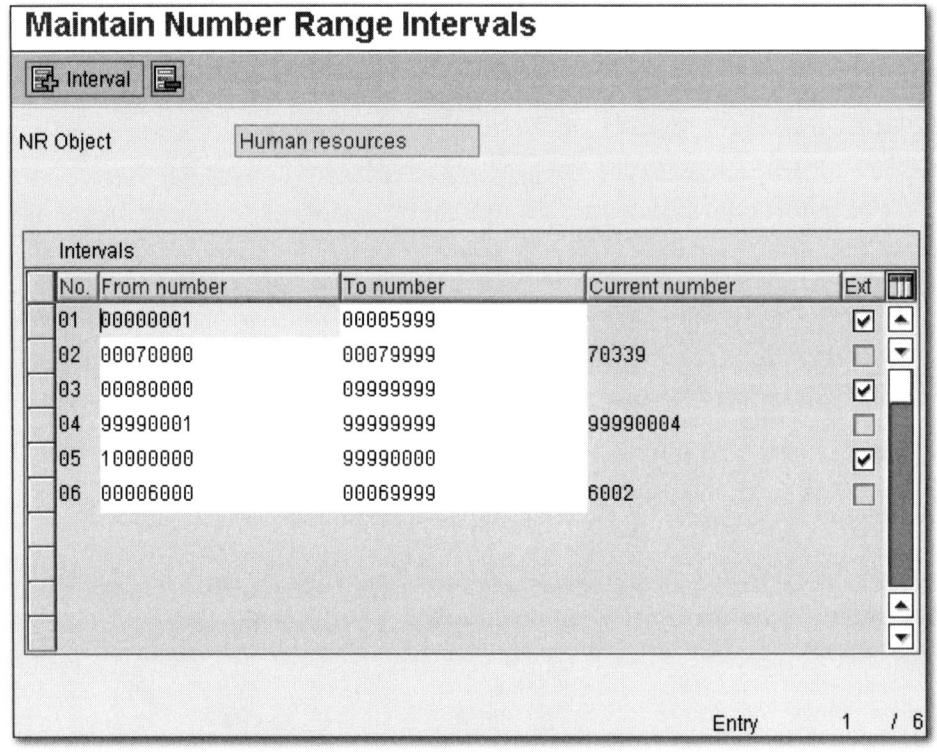

NR Object: Human resources

Intervals

No.	From number	To number	Current number	Ext
01	00000001	00005999		✓
02	00070000	00079999	70339	
03	00080000	09999999		✓
04	99990001	99999999	99990004	
05	10000000	99990000		✓
06	00006000	00069999	6002	

Entry 1 / 6

Figure 7.7 Different Ranges Provided in the System

Figure 7.8 illustrates the process of the decision tree, based on decision criteria, such as the employee group and subgroup, finally returning to the numbering range 04. Once this is done, please notify all relevant parties to exclude those resources whose IDs start with the number 9, from the Time Evaluation and Payroll processes.

During CATS project implementations there are frequent requests to assign the relevant purchase orders to the employees working on them through the SAP standard infotype.

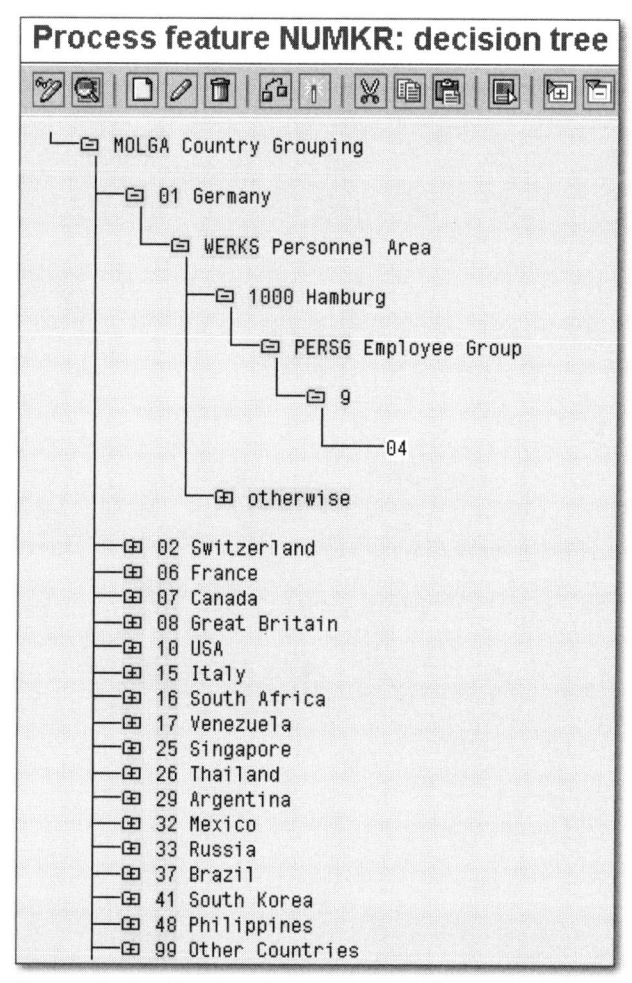

Background Information for External Services Management | 7.1

```
Process feature NUMKR: decision tree

└── MOLGA Country Grouping
    ├── 01 Germany
    │   └── WERKS Personnel Area
    │       ├── 1000 Hamburg
    │       │   └── PERSG Employee Group
    │       │       └── 9
    │       │           └── 04
    │       └── otherwise
    ├── 02 Switzerland
    ├── 06 France
    ├── 07 Canada
    ├── 08 Great Britain
    ├── 10 USA
    ├── 15 Italy
    ├── 16 South Africa
    ├── 17 Venezuela
    ├── 25 Singapore
    ├── 26 Thailand
    ├── 29 Argentina
    ├── 32 Mexico
    ├── 33 Russia
    ├── 37 Brazil
    ├── 41 South Korea
    ├── 48 Philippines
    └── 99 Other Countries
```

Figure 7.8 Decision Tree (Feature) NUMKR for Numbering Ranges Assignment

Let us assume that that the Purchase Order has been created though this is not mandatory for storing information in the Infotype 0315 — *CATS Time Sheet Defaults*. This will greatly enhance productivity since nobody will have to chase an account manager for the correct Purchase Order.

If the transactions seen in this chapter are not included in your user profile, ask your authorization system administrator to assign the display transaction codes to your profile. They could be added in a CATS basic display authorization profile. Alternatively, standard reporting can also be used to report on the Purchase Order assigned in the *CATS Time Sheet defaults* Infotype.

157

7 | Integration with External Services Management

7.2 CATS Integration Aspects for Materials Management

7.2.1 Focusing on the Available Fields for Materials Management

As we have seen in the customizing of the CATS interface, a wide range of fields are available. These fields can be set up under the CATS customizing or by simply calling the transaction code CAC2.

With regard to Project System module (PS), several fields are available for integration with the CATS. Table 7.1 provides a short list of the fields available for customizing the user interface (CATS data-entry sheet and worklist).

Technical Field	Field Description
CATSD-UNIT	Internal Unit of Measure
CATSDB-LTXA1	Short Text
CATSD-LSTNR	Service Number
CATSFIELDS-PERNR	Employee Number
CATSD-SEBELP	Sending PO Item
CATSD-SEBELN	Sending Purchase Order
CATSFIELDS-DISPTEXT1	(Order) Description
CATSFIELDS-DISPTEXT2	(Order) Description

Table 7.1 List of Available Fields for Customizing User Interface

7.2.2 CATS and Materials Management Transfer

Once you have complied with the business processes in CATS, (book, release, approve time entries), you can run the transfer for MM. Unlike the other SAP modules which use their own program transfer or use the mass transfer using the program RCATSTAL (transaction CATA), the transfer to MM can be exclusively done through its own transaction, as shown in Figure 7.9.

> **Hint**
> Parallel to the planned background job for the program RCATSTAL, add this MM Program in the batch chain. The transaction code called for the transfer to MM is CATM.

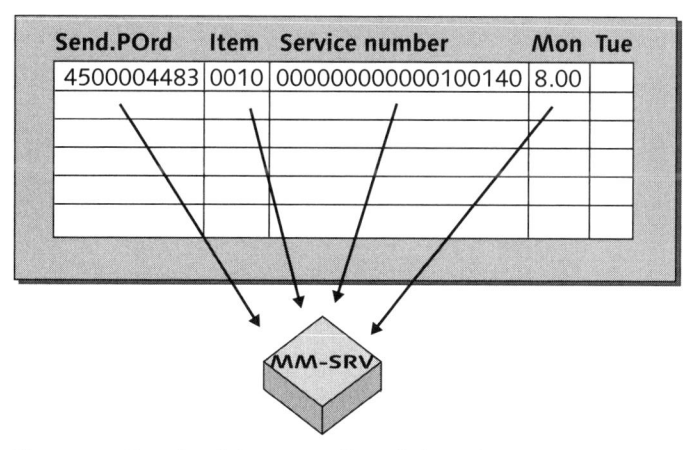

CATS Integration Aspects for Materials Management | 7.2

Figure 7.9 Transfer of the Data Collected Through CATS to MM

In previous SAP releases, MM time entries could not be deleted after approval. However, this is now possible. For more information, see Returns for Service Entry Sheets in the Time Sheet.

Controlling is most often fed indirectly by the surrounding SAP modules. To avoid double cost-posting, time entries collected in CATS can only be directly transferred to CO if you are working with HR and CO. Other combinations will feed PS and other target modules. Table 7.2 illustrates the authorized combinations for MM.

CO	HR	MM-SRV	PM/CS	PS
X	X			
	X	X		
	X		X	
	X			X
	X	X	X	
	X	X		X
		X	X	
		X		X

Table 7.2 Allowed Transfer Combinations for MM

159

7.3 Lessons Learned

In this chapter you learned of the key elements in the concept of MM for external services providers, with special attention given to the receiver object and the purchase order. We have carefully checked the available fields that are aimed towards MM.

With regard to CATS data transfer, special attention has been paid to the fact that unlike other modules MM is not part of a mass transfer program. A manual reception (good receipt) must be triggered in the target module.

Now that we have seen the available target modules and their respective integration with CATS, let's secure the use and the master data access. To secure data accuracy and to prevent any misuse of the system, we have to set up the appropriate authorizations.

Chapter 8 will highlight tips for setting up the correct authorizations for CATS.

8 Authorizations for CATS

Although this Essentials guide does not cover the SAP authorization setup in detail, this chapter will help you to understand the CATS authorization concept. This information will be valuable for the system administrator while setting up end-user access rights. It will also be useful for the users setting up CATS to know how to restrict the use of the CATS data-entry profiles.

Authorization objects as such do not exist for CATS. The CATS authorization concept is handled by standard HR objects such as, P_ORGIN (HR Master Data) and P_PERNR (Personnel number check). This chapter will show you how to fulfill the goals of authorization.

8.1 Setting Up the Authorization Group

In this customizing step, you need to define a four-character alphanumeric value to identify an authorization group to be used with CATS. Figure 8.1 shows customizing access for maintaining authorization groups among the CATS data-entry profiles.

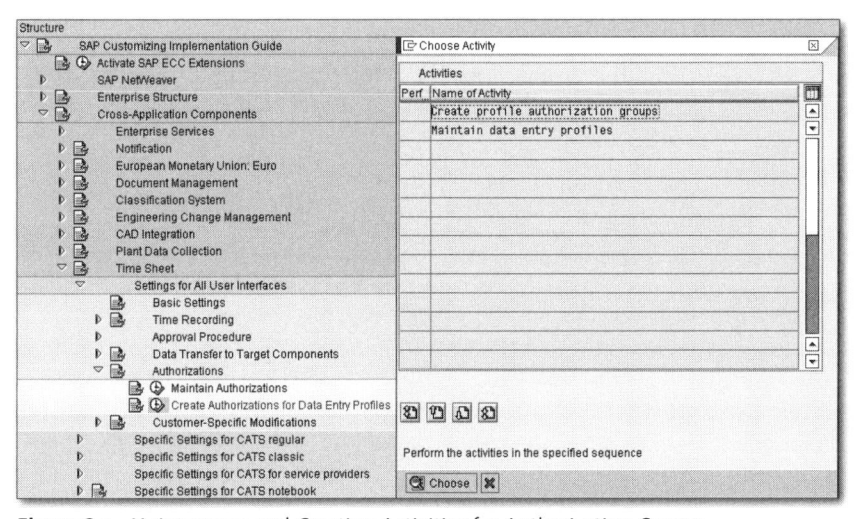

Figure 8.1 Maintenance and Creation Activities for Authorization Groups

161

Figure 8.2 illustrates a sample of three authorization groups created for CATS.

- Group 1: e.g., for regular end users
- Group 2: e.g., for managers
- Group 3: e.g., for time administrators or super-users

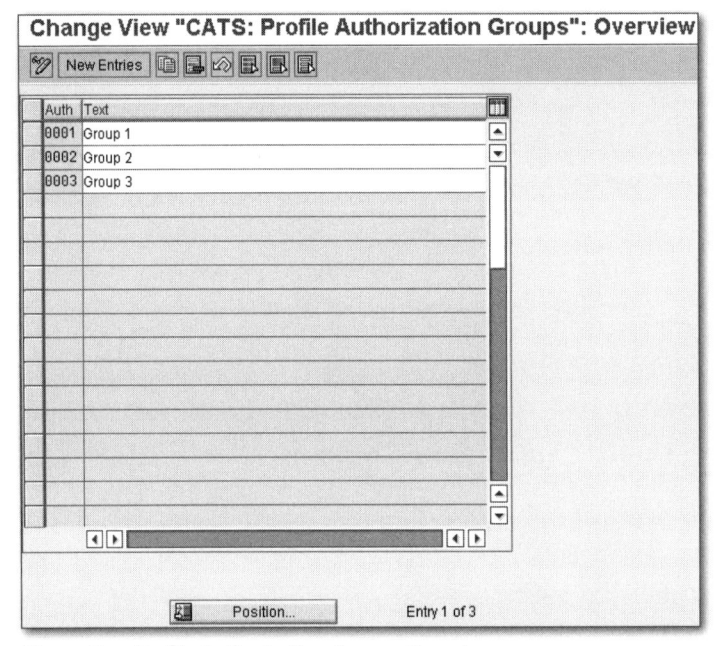

Figure 8.2 Profile Authorization Groups Overview

> **Hint**
> This customizing table can also be directly accessed through the transaction code CAC4.

8.2 Assigning the Authorization Group to the Data-Entry Profile

In this step, simply review the data-entry profile and, in the field AUTHORIZATION, assign the relevant authorization group according to your business requirement. Figure 8.3 illustrates assignment of the authorization group 0001 to data-entry profile US-EMPL (regular US employees).

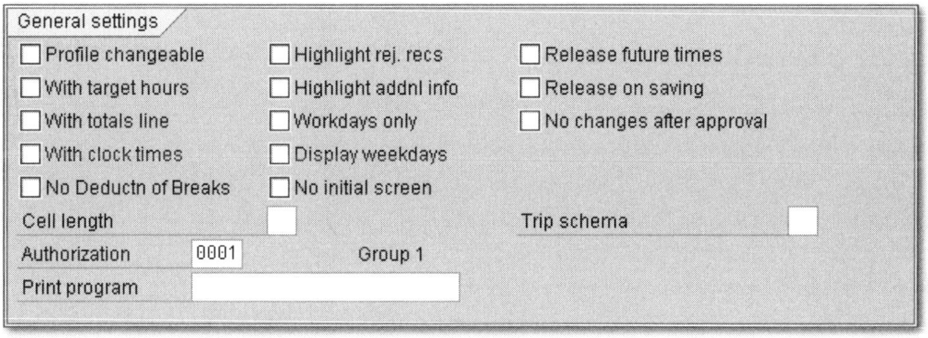

```
General settings
☐ Profile changeable      ☐ Highlight rej. recs      ☐ Release future times
☐ With target hours       ☐ Highlight addnl info     ☐ Release on saving
☐ With totals line        ☐ Workdays only            ☐ No changes after approval
☐ With clock times        ☐ Display weekdays
☐ No Deductn of Breaks    ☐ No initial screen
Cell length      [    ]                              Trip schema    [   ]
Authorization    [0001]           Group 1
Print program    [          ]
```

Figure 8.3 Assigning Authorization Group to Data-Entry Profile

The CATS authorization setup is now ready to be activated in the common authorization setup.

> **Hint**
> To access the SAP Profiles Configurator, use the transaction code PFCG.

8.3 Restricting Access to a Determined Data-Entry Profile and/or for Personnel

In the example illustrated by Figure 8.3, the system has been set up to allow only time entries using the data-entry profile US-EMPL with authorization group 0001. Authorization levels read-only (R for Read) and maintain (E for Edit) have been enabled.

To set up the system to allow time collection for the employer's personnel only, the field interpretation of assigned personnel number must be switched to `I` for individual.

To make this authorization check successful, Infotype 0105—*Communication*, sub-type 0001—*System user ID* must be declared for each employee.

> **Hint**
> To report on missing Infotype 0105—Communication, you can consider using the transaction code HRUSER.

Alternatively, for time administrators or managers, the value must be switch to E for all personnel numbers. The value *—which stands for full access—is not relevant in this authorization object.

Please note that a CATS virtual Infotype—0316—is enabled to achieve that authorization check. A virtual infotype exists only for technical reasons and therefore cannot be maintained through the standard functional transactions (i.e. PA30). The authorization group will be assigned in the field subtype.

Figure 8.4 shows the sample P_PERNR authorization object handled for CATS.

```
 Manually    HR: Master Data - Personnel Number Check              P_PERNR
   Manually  HR: Master Data - Personnel Number Check              T-T655046900
     Authorization level       E, R                                AUTHC
     Infotype                  316                                 INFTY
     Interpretation of assigned per  I                             PSIGN
     Subtype                   0001                                SUBTY
```

Figure 8.4 CATS Authorization Object P_PERNR

In this demo concept, access to HR has not been managed. In a real business scenario, you would have to narrow down the entries according to the enterprise and personnel structure defined in Customizing. The value * (All access) must be avoided to prevent unpleasant authorization surprises.

Figure 8.5 illustrates a sample of the P_ORGIN authorization object handled for Infotypes 0001 and 0002 with full read-only access.

```
 Manually    HR: Master Data                                       P_ORGIN
   Manually  HR: Master Data                                       T-T655046900
     Authorization level       R                                   AUTHC
     Infotype                  0001, 0002                          INFTY
     Personnel Area            *                                   PERSA
     Employee Group            *                                   PERSG
     Employee Subgroup         *                                   PERSK
     Subtype                   *                                   SUBTY
     Organizational Key        *                                   VDSK1
```

Figure 8.5 Authorization Object with Read-Only Access for Infotypes

8.4 Authorization for Reporting in CATS

To enable reporting access in CATS, the second CATS virtual Infotype—0328—must be used in the objectP_ORGIN.

Figure 8.6 shows the sample authorization object P_ORGIN Object handled for CATS Reporting with full read-only access.

```
⊟ ○○○ ▦ ⚲ Manually    HR: Master Data                    P_ORGIN
    ⊟ ○○○ ▦ Manually   HR: Master Data                    T-T655046901
         ─── ∗ ⚯ Authorization level      R                   AUTHC
         ─── ∗ ⚯ Infotype                 0328                INFTY
         ─── ∗ ⚯ Personnel Area           *                   PERSA
         ─── ∗ ⚯ Employee Group           *                   PERSG
         ─── ∗ ⚯ Employee Subgroup        *                   PERSK
         ─── ∗ ⚯ Subtype                  *                   SUBTY
         ─── ∗ ⚯ Organizational Key       *                   VDSK1
```

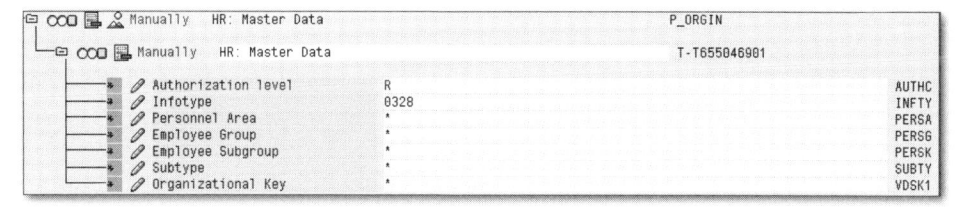

Figure 8.6 Authorization Object with Read-Only Access for Reporting

To help build the authorization profiles, you can use the authorization reporting tree, using the transaction code SUIM.

Additional objects such as the transaction codes (S_TCODE, P_TCODE) must also be managed. Please refer to your system administrator to narrow down the required authorization objects.

To allow managers flexible reporting, you can set the parameter ADAYS to 15 in the table T77S0. The tolerance for authorization will then become 15 days. This will be good for managers while reporting on master data, even if their staff members have recently changed positions.

8.5 Lessons Learned

Although ideally authorization should be an exact science, checking the authorization allocated to the end users almost always brings surprises. This chapter provided the basic authorization objects, virtual infotypes, and the customizing steps to start securing the system.

The best authorization concept always involves all parties in the setting up of the authorizations. In other words, communicate with the system administrator about what has been set up for CATS.

Apart from the additional standard classes available from SAP, for authorization concepts, we recommend the following books:

▸ *IBM Business Consulting GmbH*, 2003: This book has information about authorization concepts and also provides some guidelines for applying these concepts.

- *SAP Labs*, 2000: Though based on release 4.6 A/B, this book gives sound background information on the SAP standard authorization concept. It is especially useful for new members of the authorization team.

All these authorization concepts will probably be updated as business requirements continue to change. Therefore, we recommend using the standard authorization reporting tree to follow up on authorizations.

9 Reporting for CATS

After setting up CATS and working with the time entries, let's focus on reporting. Indeed, any functionality is useless if no efficient tool is provided to handle daily queries for the working times.

This chapter will give you a thorough look into the standard reporting available within the time sheet. Additional standard reporting is also useful while implementing CATS.

9.1 Employee Listing

End users usually need a short list of personnel during the time collection process. No fancy query needs to be built since a simple report is available within SAP. The employee listing report, RPLMIT00 can be accessed through the transaction code PAR2. This report provides a list with different pieces of information coming from HR.

Figure 9.1 shows the selection screen of the employee listing that provides a wide range of selection fields, including the personnel area, the personnel subarea, the cost center, etc. Figure 9.1 also shows the access to the Employee Listing Report selection screen. Once the report has been run, the outcome can easily be downloaded into third-party applications, such as Microsoft Excel, Microsoft Notepad, etc.

9.2 Master Data Export

Thanks to the number of its user-exits, CATS can be interfaced with third-party applications. These interfaces can be incoming or outgoing. In most cases, the flat files must provide basic information from the personnel master data. This master data can be the personnel number, the last and first name, the assignment, and the cost center.

9 | Reporting for CATS

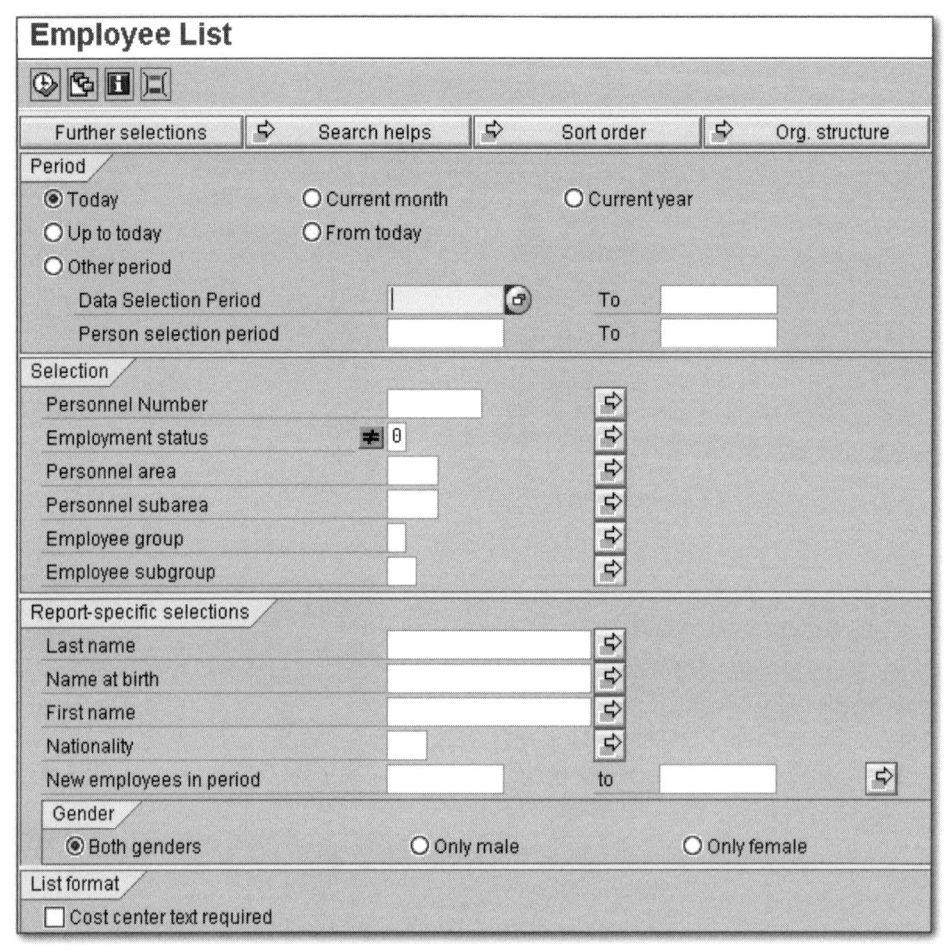

Figure 9.1 Selection Screen of the Employee Listing

Rather than create a specific program, up to release 4.6C, you can use the standard program RPLICO30, which can be accessed through the transaction code PAZZ. This report provides a direct download path to Microsoft Word or Microsoft Excel. Alternatively, a flat file can be generated directly and downloaded to the chosen directory. Figure 9.2 shows the many selection fields that can be used to narrow the personnel selection. It also illustrates the fields used to refine the personnel selection, using a standard report. Unfortunately, this transaction and report is no longer provided in releases ERP 5.0 and ERP 6.0.

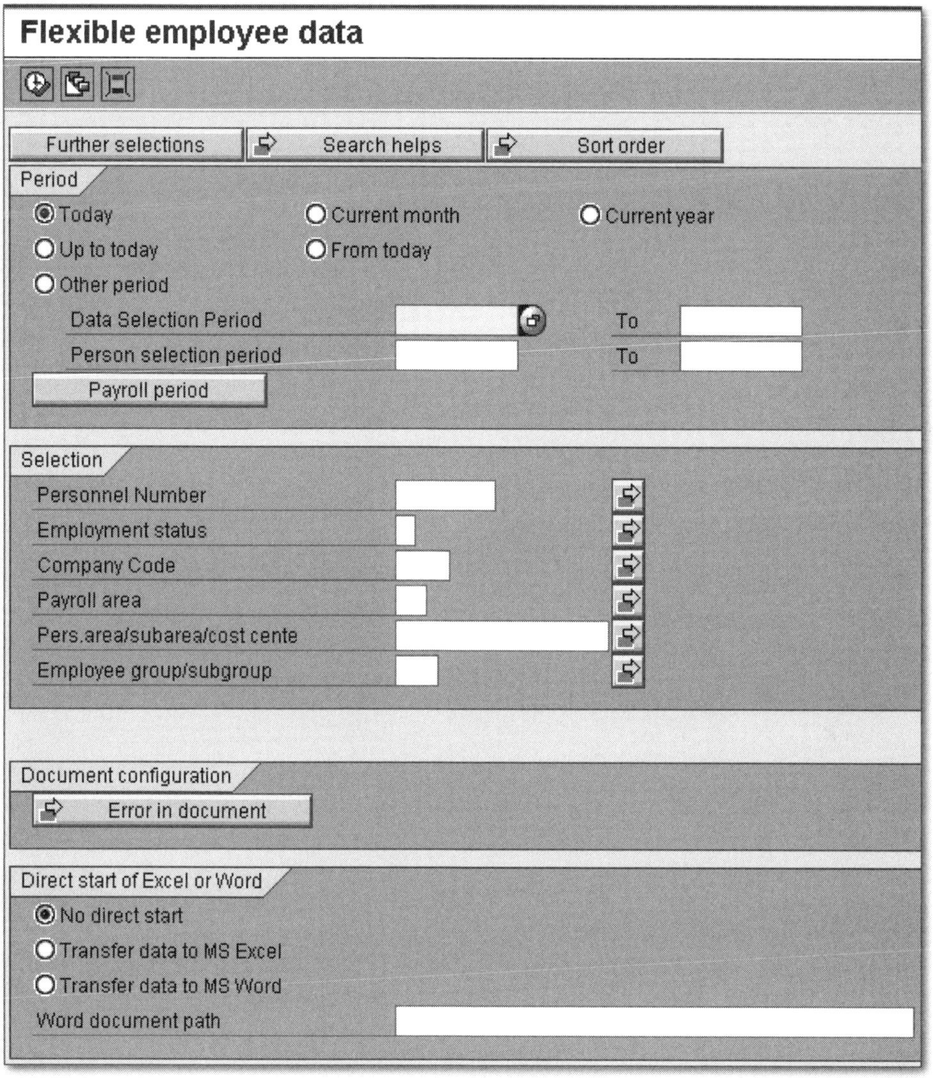

Flexible employee data

[Further selections] [Search helps] [Sort order]

Period
- ⦿ Today
- ○ Current month
- ○ Current year
- ○ Up to today
- ○ From today
- ○ Other period
  - Data Selection Period [   ] To [   ]
  - Person selection period [   ] To [   ]
  - [Payroll period]

Selection
- Personnel Number
- Employment status
- Company Code
- Payroll area
- Pers.area/subarea/cost cente
- Employee group/subgroup

Document configuration
- Error in document

Direct start of Excel or Word
- ⦿ No direct start
- ○ Transfer data to MS Excel
- ○ Transfer data to MS Word
- Word document path

Figure 9.2 Selection Fields for Narrowing Personnel Selection

In most SAP HR reporting, using the logical database PNP, can be tailored to the selection screen. With a mouse click you can remove or add fields to the selection screen.

If Organization Management is not set up or if there is no authorized access, you can hide the selection icon for Organizational Management. To achieve this, simply create the selection screen under REPORT CATEGORIES, which can be found under the customizing tree:

PERSONNEL MANAGEMENT • HUMAN RESOURCES INFORMATION SYSTEM • REPORTING • ADJUSTING THE STANDARD SELECTION SCREEN.

Once the report categories have been created, assign them to the reports you wish to adjust. Please be aware that unless a dedicated report category has been created and assigned to a dedicated report, SAP uses a default report category for all HR programs. SAP strongly advises you not to make any changes since it is used as a default value.

9.3 Display Working Times

In the standard CATS classic format, the report RCATS_DISPLAY_ACTIVITIES—which can be accessed through the transaction code CATS_DA—can be used to provide an exhaustive list of the activities collected. This report is based on a wide range of selection items, including:

- Basic selection criteria
- Further basic data
- Receiver account assignment
- Sender account assignment
- Data sources

Figure 9.3 shows the initial standard screen, giving a snapshot of the available selection criteria.

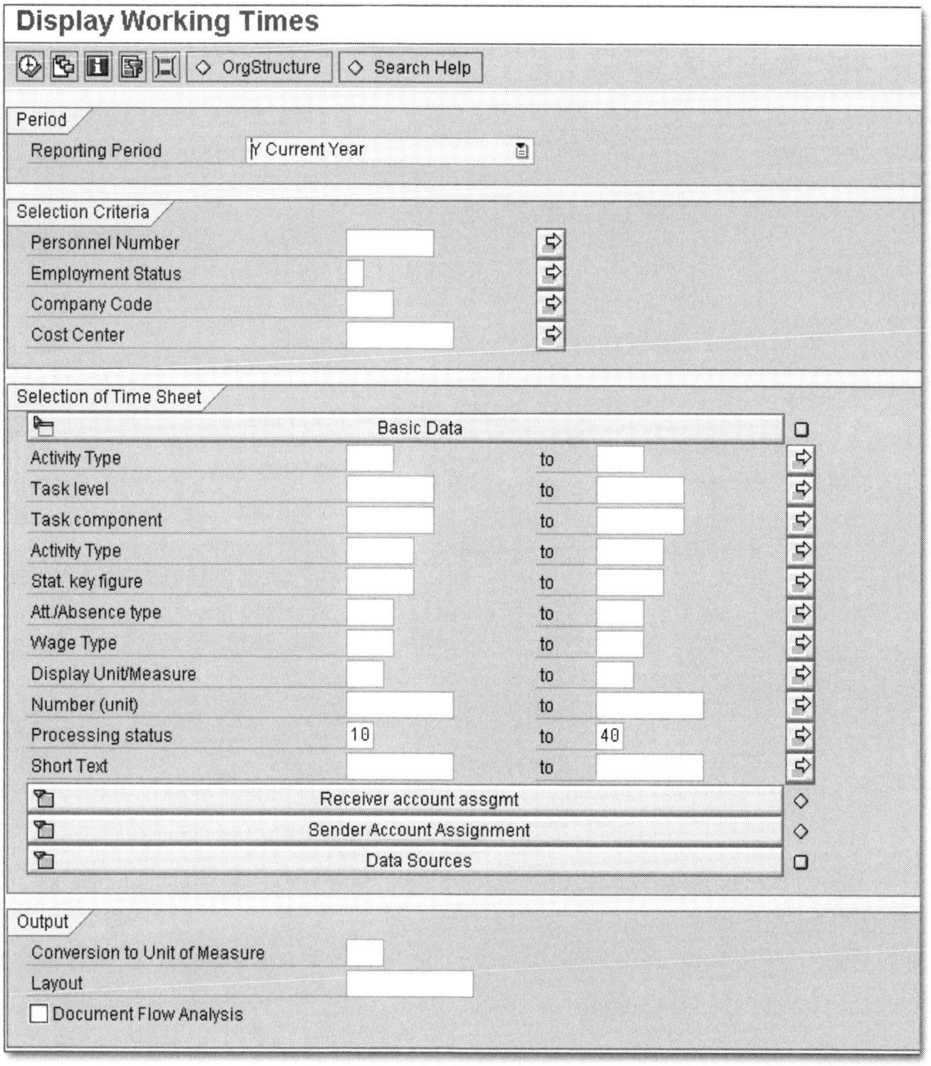

Display Working Times | 9.3

Figure 9.3 Available Selection Criteria

9.3.1 Data Sources

By choosing the option DATA SOURCES in the selection screen, you can select the CATS interface to be used for the report:

- CATS for Service Providers
- All other CATS interfaces

- All CATS interfaces
- From the archive

9.3.2 Document Flow Analysis

If you use Controlling and the Billing target components during the time-collection process, you can require the document number to be shown. This should only be done with small amounts of data, since it is time-consuming.

9.3.3 Display Work Times, Tasks, and Activities

In today's business environment, all processes are required to report on time entries. Several reports are available to the end user to provide information on the time entries collected through CATS. Although these reports are easy to use, it is useful to review their respective names so that you can select the best report to match your requirements.

- **Display working times**
  The report RCATS_DISPLAY_ACTIVITIES (transaction code CATS_DA) allows regular users to investigate time entries collected through CATS, by using the selection interface. Figure 9.3 shows the selection screen for this report.

- **Display work times and tasks for services providers**
  The report RCATSXT_DISPLAY_ACTIVITIES (transaction code CATSXT_DA) allows the regular user to investigate the data collected through CATS, from the service providers, by using the standard selection interface. Figure 9.4 displays the selection screen for this report.

- **Display work times and tasks for services providers: Display details**
  If you have service providers within the company, an additional report, RCATSXT_DISPLAY_ACTIVITY_DTL (transaction code CATSXT_DTL) allows the regular user to investigate in detail the data collected through CATS from the service providers. This report is useful as it provides a clear detailed view of the time entries booked by the service providers. Figure 9.5 illustrates the selection screen for this report.

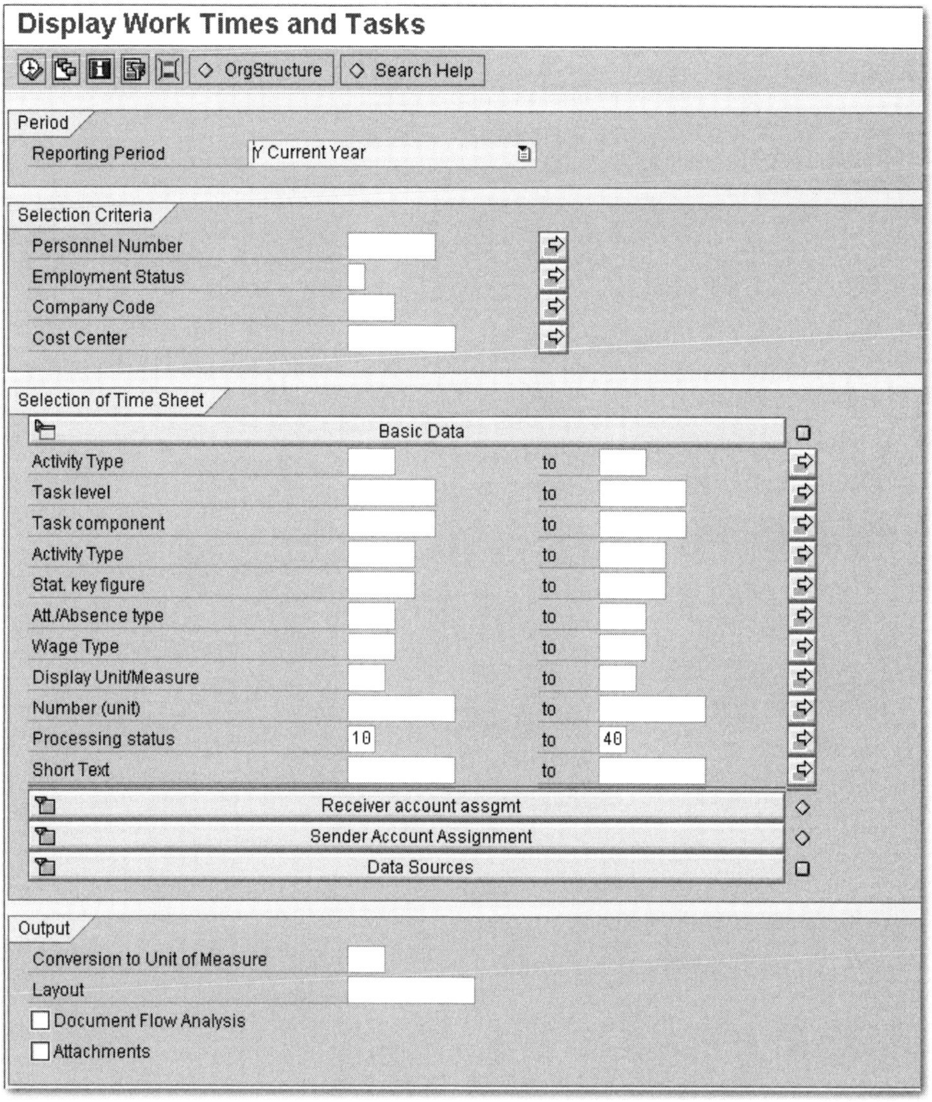

Display Working Times | 9.3

Display Work Times and Tasks

Period
Reporting Period: Y Current Year

Selection Criteria
Personnel Number
Employment Status
Company Code
Cost Center

Selection of Time Sheet

Basic Data

Field	From	to	To
Activity Type		to	
Task level		to	
Task component		to	
Activity Type		to	
Stat. key figure		to	
Att./Absence type		to	
Wage Type		to	
Display Unit/Measure		to	
Number (unit)		to	
Processing status	10	to	40
Short Text		to	

Receiver account assgmt
Sender Account Assignment
Data Sources

Output
Conversion to Unit of Measure
Layout
☐ Document Flow Analysis
☐ Attachments

Figure 9.4 Standard Selection Screen for Report RCATSXT_DISPLAY_ACTIVITIES

9 | Reporting for CATS

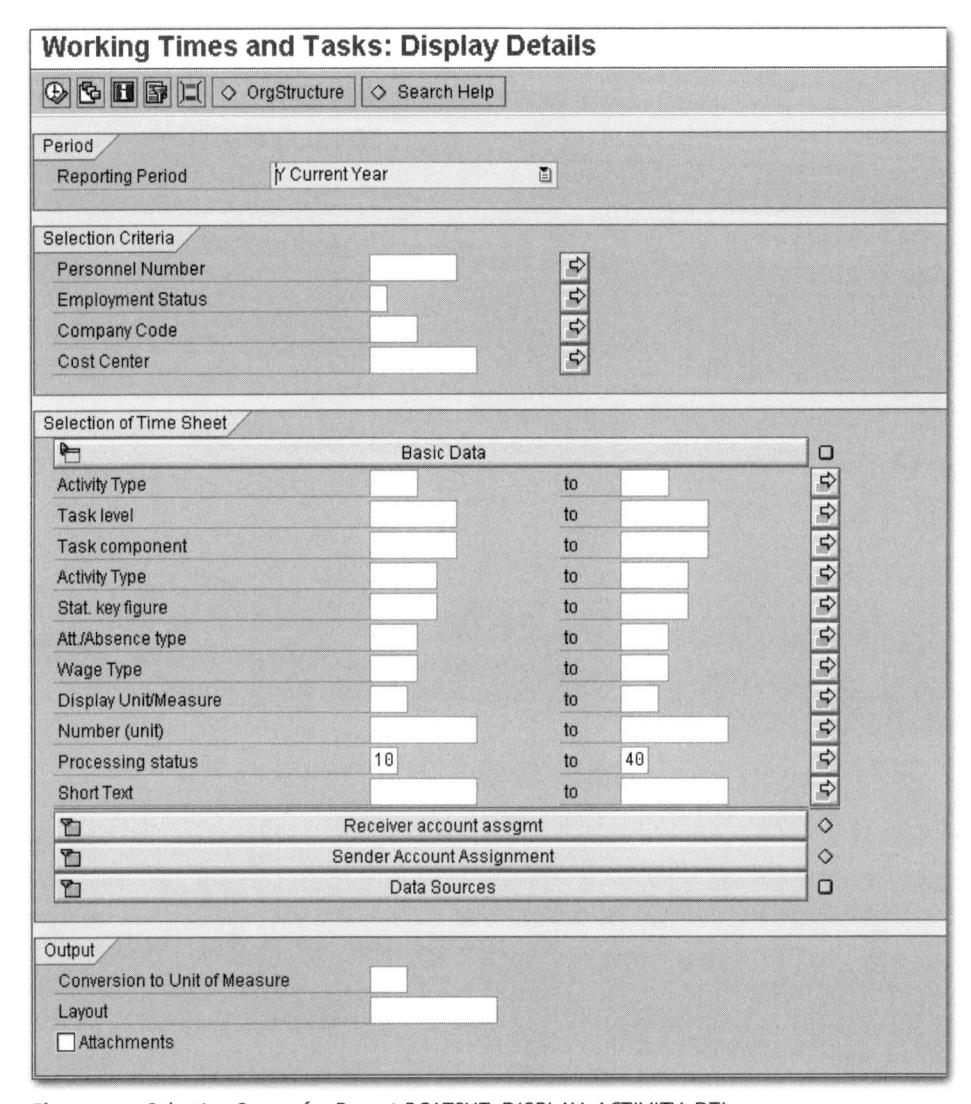

Figure 9.5 Selection Screen for Report RCATSXT_DISPLAY_ACTIVITY_DTL

9.4 Time Leveling CATC

To support the time administrators or the line managers, a standard program can be used to monitor the time entries. Indeed, time tracking can be a long lasting process throughout the week. SAP provides a flexible and useful tool that allows time administrators to manage and quickly select the missing time entries for the current period. Figures 9.6 and 9.7 show you the fields that can be selected to run the program.

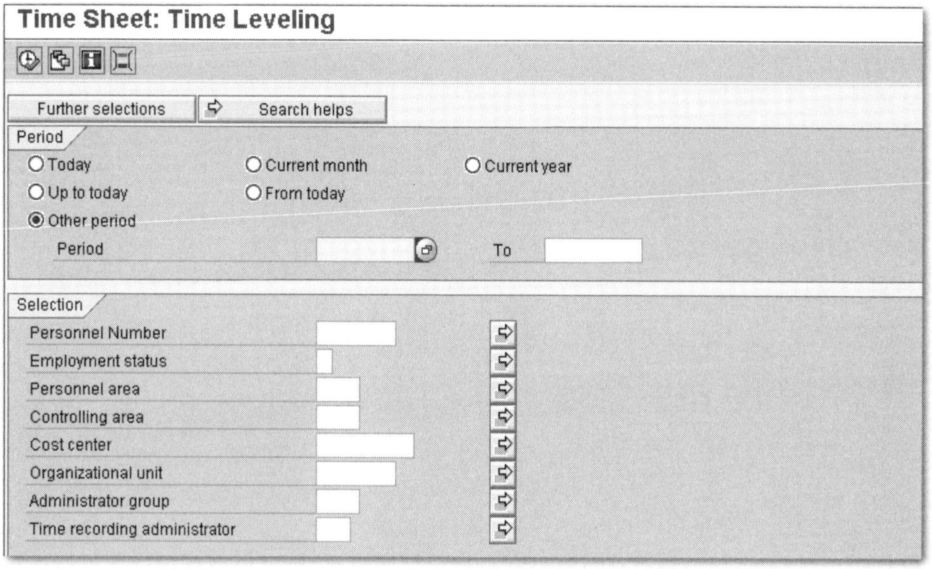

Figure 9.6 Fields that can be Selected to Run the Program (1)

Apart from the standard selection criteria, several other options are available which are examined below.

- Report specific selection of employees:
  We saw in Chapter 3, section 3.1, that the option REQUIRED TO RECORD TIMES IN TIME SHEET can be enabled for each individual. This option can then be used when running the program, by retrieving all the users who are supposed to collect their time entries through CATS

- Time Sheet Selection:
  Depending on your time investigation, you can choose from the following options in the Time Sheet Selection:

  - Time Sheet for which no time or quantities are recorded
  - Time Sheet with no time recorded
  - Selection according to specified number of hours
  - Selection according to the target hours stored in the Infotype 0007

9 | Reporting for CATS

- The criteria must be applied to each day or to each period
- Time settings must be according to your requirements
- Calculation of non-working days
- Target hours with an upward or downward tolerances
- Output options

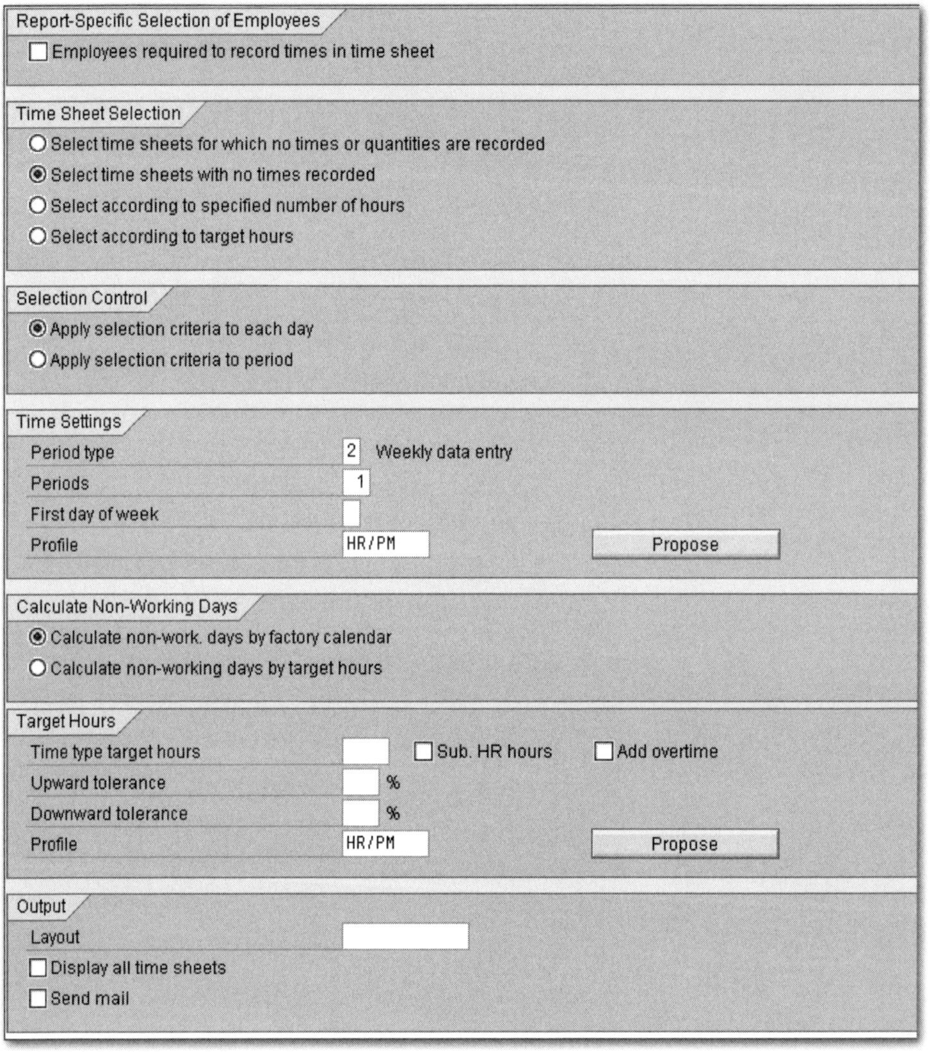

Figure 9.7 Fields that can be Selected to Run the Program (2)

To remind employees in a timely manner, e. g., each Friday morning, this program should be run on a periodic basis. To do so, schedule this program by defining a background job in transaction code SM36.

> **Hint**
> To optimize the reminders to the end users, check the box Send mail in the output options. This will trigger an email to the end user in his or her SAP Business Workplace. This email can also be forwarded to your email application by using the SAP Connect functionality. To view the SAP Connect process, use the transaction code SCOT.

9.5 Display Single Document

Each record in the CATS database is stored under a unique reference number. Although this number is not to be used by the end users, it can be displayed under the details of the entry. The support team or the help desk can then use the number provided. To enable a smooth and direct access to the piece of information being investigated, use the transaction code CAT8 (program RCATSBEL).

Though used by the help desk or the support team, this report is not likely to be used by end users. Figure 9.8 is a snapshot of the standard selection screen. Please note that the document number is required prior to accessing the report.

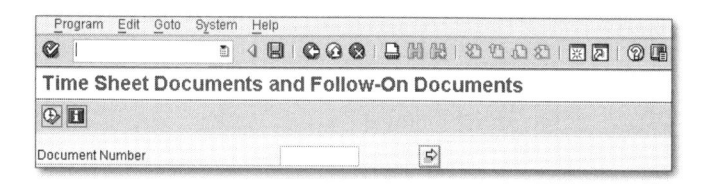

Figure 9.8 Standard Selection Screen

9.6 Approve Working Times from R/3 backend

9.6.1 Approve Working Times (Selection by Master Data)

As we saw in chapter 2, when dealing with customizing the CATS data-entry profile, an approval process can be enabled under the general settings. To provide team leaders, line managers, or project managers with an approval-reporting tool, several options are available.

9 | Reporting for CATS

If you have enabled the approval process in your customizing steps and the data has been collected, there are several ways to approve the time entries from the backend system.

The most commonly used program is RCATSC01, which can be used by calling the transaction code CAPS. This is the most suitable and user-friendly report as it uses the master data as a selection criterion, which provides a wide range of selection items to the end user. Figure 9.9 shows the selection screen for approving the times, using master data as the root-selection items.

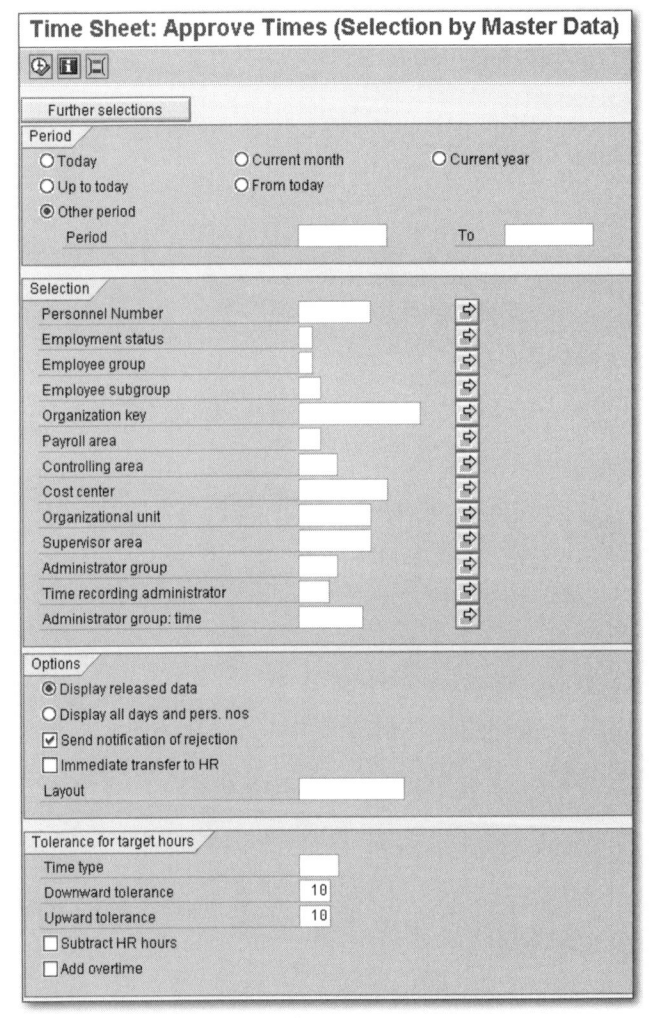

Figure 9.9 Selection Screen for Approving Times

178

Once you have run the report and approved or rejected the relevant time entries, the traffic light assigned to each time entry will move from orange to green for approved, and to red for rejected.

Please bear in mind that you must save these changes, otherwise the approved or rejected data will not be written to the interface tables, and you will lose your work.

9.6.2 Approve Working Times

In addition to the standard transaction CAPS, a more detailed approval program can also be used. The report RCATS_APPROVE_ACTIVITIES can support the end user to manage the processing statutes of the time sheet. It can be called by the transaction code CATS_APPR_LITE.

Figure 9.10 shows an exhaustive list of the available options for this transaction code. These available options are grouped into the following categories:

- Basic data
- Receiver Account assignment
- Sender Account assignment
- Data Sources

The selection screen also depicts the possibility of sending a rejection notification to the end user.

> **Hint**
> Recent studies among end users have shown that these rejection notifications can increase the number of emails, thereby acting like spam. Since the rejection will appear in the CATS screen, end users can find it in their collection screens or they can run standard reports, e. g., the transaction CADO.

Under certain restrictions (e. g., running the time sheet on the same system as the target modules) and depending on the customizing settings relevant to the target modules to be used, you can select the automatic transfer to the Human Resources module. This will ensure that the Time Evaluation is getting the information as it comes.

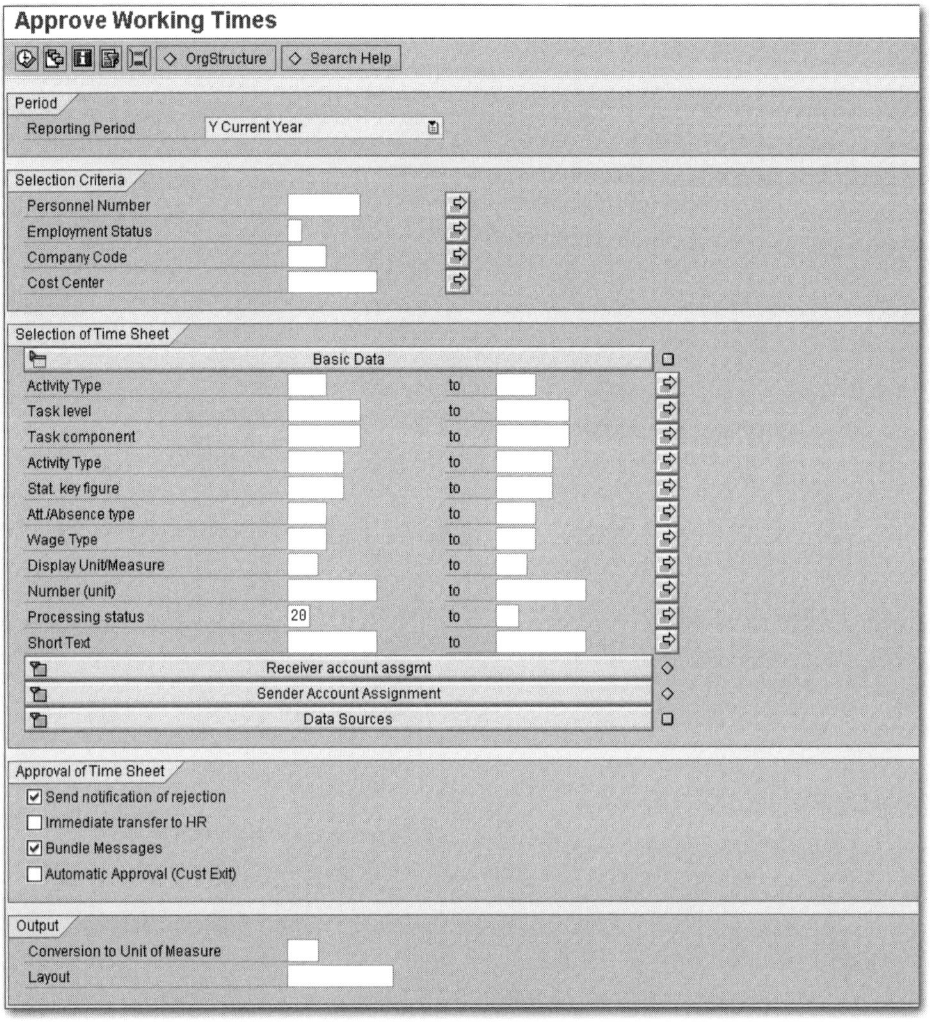

9 | Reporting for CATS

Figure 9.10 Working-Time Approval Options Under Basic Data

> **Hint**
>
> Set this transfer in background mode, overnight. This will secure the response time of your SAP system.

In some cases, basic time entries can be automatically approved by the system. For instance, some Line Managers demand that all overtime of less than two hours be automatically approved. To enable this option, the method APPROVE_CATS_CLASSIC can be used from the Business Add-In.

9.6.3 Approve Working Times and Travel Expenses

In addition to the standard approval programs, your company is likely to use the travel and expenses component. To approve the time entries and the travel expenses immediately, you can use the program R_APPROVE_ACTIVITIES_EXPENSES, which can be called using the transaction code ACTEXP_APPR_LITE.

Figures 9.11 and 9.12 illustrate the standard selection screen for approving the time entries and travel expenses. The following options are available for the trip selection:

- Basic data
- Cost Assignment
- Status
- Data Sources

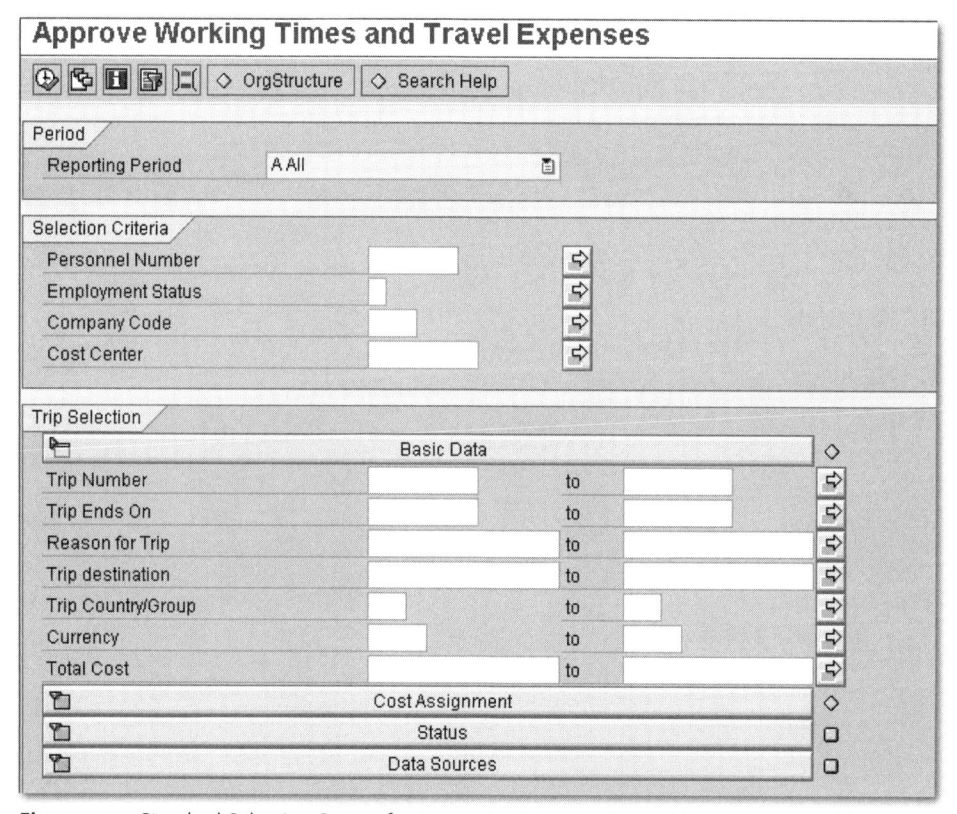

Figure 9.11 Standard Selection Screen for Approving Time Entries and Travel Expenses (1)

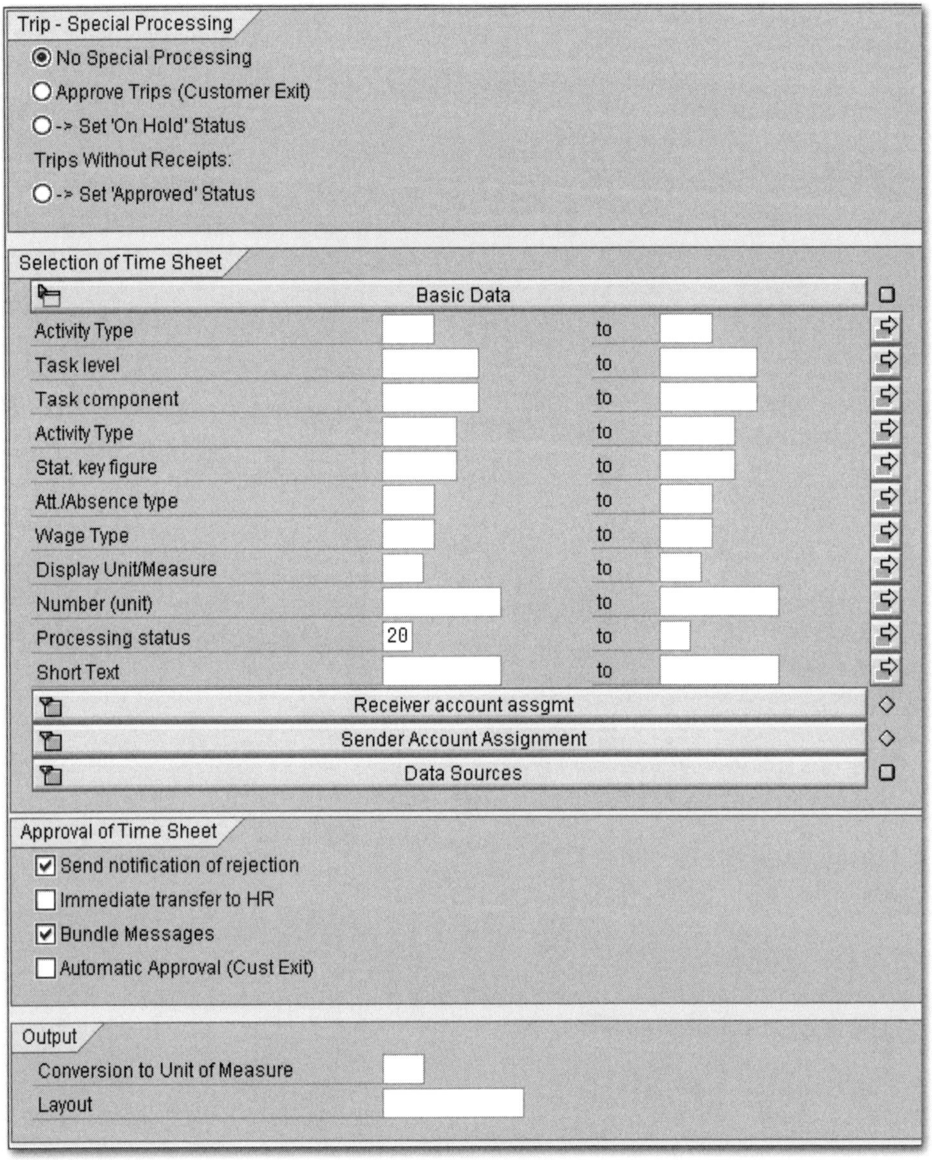

9 | Reporting for CATS

Figure 9.12 Standard Selection Screen for Approving Time Entries and Travel Expenses (2)

Please note that the retrieval of employees can also be done by using the Organizational Structure.

9.7 Approve Working Times from the Portal

9.7.1 Introducing a New Functionality

As we have seen up to now, approval processes could theoretically only be achieved through the backend system. There were, up to release ERP 6.0, two alternatives:

- (a) Web enable one of the R/3 transactions illustrated above, through the common web service WebGui
- (b) Develop your own screen, likely in Java or ABAP Web Dynpro

Option (a) is the quickest workaround, but unfortunately it triggers two major issues regarding the layout and the authorizations. Indeed, the layout rendering is similar to the R/3 layout, which is rather ugly in a portal. From the authorization point of view, as this is a web enabled transaction, users could directly run another transaction from the upper left corner, in the command box. System administrators I've worked with were not too thrilled about that.

Option (b) is of course the best way to meet the end user requirements, but would trigger a change request and budget to deliver such a development.

As of release ERP 6.0, SAP now delivers an approval screen that is now fully web enabled in Java. This screen provides in standard two views:

- The Line Manager View
- The Project Manager View

Runtime Technology	Java/Web Dynpro
Technical Name of iView	com.sap.pct.erp.mss.approve_time_manager
Technical Name of Web Dynpro Application	sap.com/mss~cat~approval/CatManagerApprove sap.com/mss~cat~approval/CatProjectApprove
Available as of	SAP NetWeaver 2004s
Data Origin	SAP ECC 6.0 and higher RFC function module called: • HRMSS_CAT_WD_APPROVAL
Software Component	EA-HR
Support	CA-TS-IA-XS

Figure 9.13 The New Approval Web Dynpro Properties

This new Web Dynpro can be located in the Portal Content Directory, under the Line Manager → Manager Self Services folder.

Figure 1.14 illustrates the new Web Dynpro localization in the Portal.

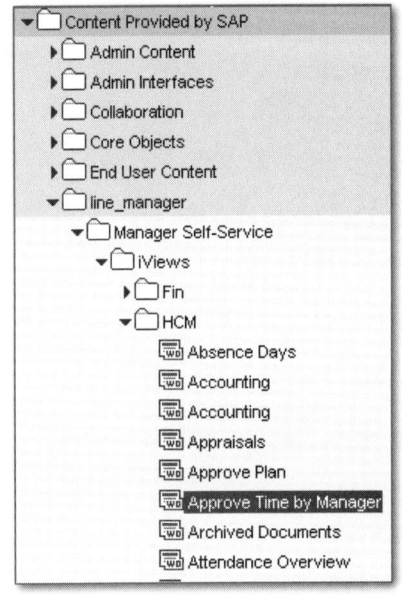

Figure 9.14 Web Dynpro Localization in the Portal

This Web Dynpro is a standard java application, as illustrated in Figure 9.15.

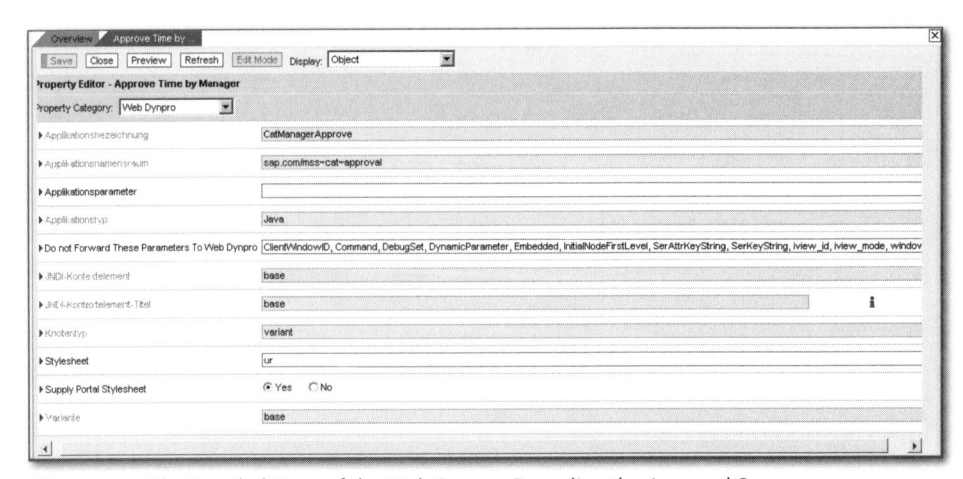

Figure 9.15 The Detailed View of the Web Dynpro Regarding the Approval Screen

9.7.2 Customizing the New Web Dynpro Approval Screen

Cherry on the pie, the Web Dynpro screen's functionalities can be adjusted using the standard customizing functionalities.

Figure 9.16 illustrates the different customizing steps available in the customizing tree regarding the Approval of Working Times.

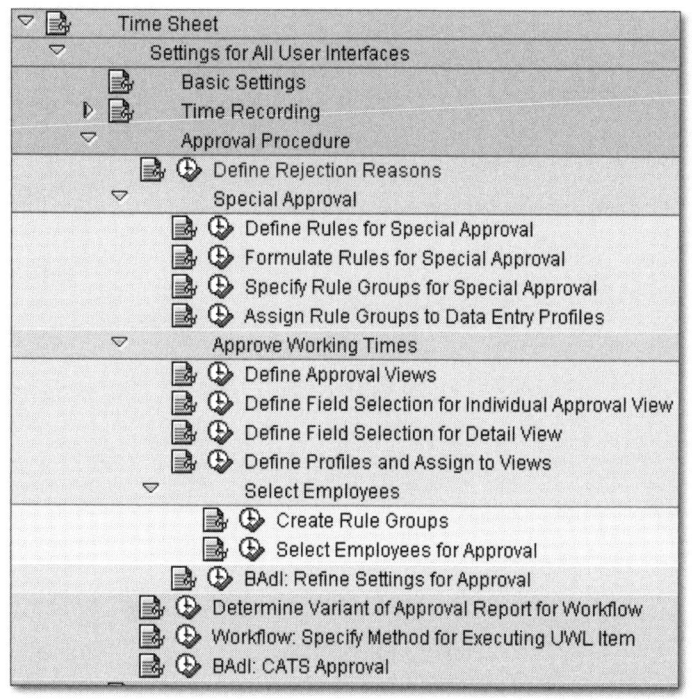

```
▽ Time Sheet
  ▽ Settings for All User Interfaces
       Basic Settings
    ▷ Time Recording
    ▽ Approval Procedure
         Define Rejection Reasons
      ▽ Special Approval
           Define Rules for Special Approval
           Formulate Rules for Special Approval
           Specify Rule Groups for Special Approval
           Assign Rule Groups to Data Entry Profiles
      ▽ Approve Working Times
           Define Approval Views
           Define Field Selection for Individual Approval View
           Define Field Selection for Detail View
           Define Profiles and Assign to Views
        ▽ Select Employees
             Create Rule Groups
             Select Employees for Approval
           BAdI: Refine Settings for Approval
           Determine Variant of Approval Report for Workflow
           Workflow: Specify Method for Executing UWL Item
           BAdI: CATS Approval
```

Figure 9.16 Customizing Access for the Approval Procedure

The customizing steps are the following:

▸ **Define approval views (table CATS_APPR_PERSPT)**
In standard, the system provides two views, Line and Project Manager; according to your business requirements, you could add one or more view, like an administrator view for example.

9 | Reporting for CATS

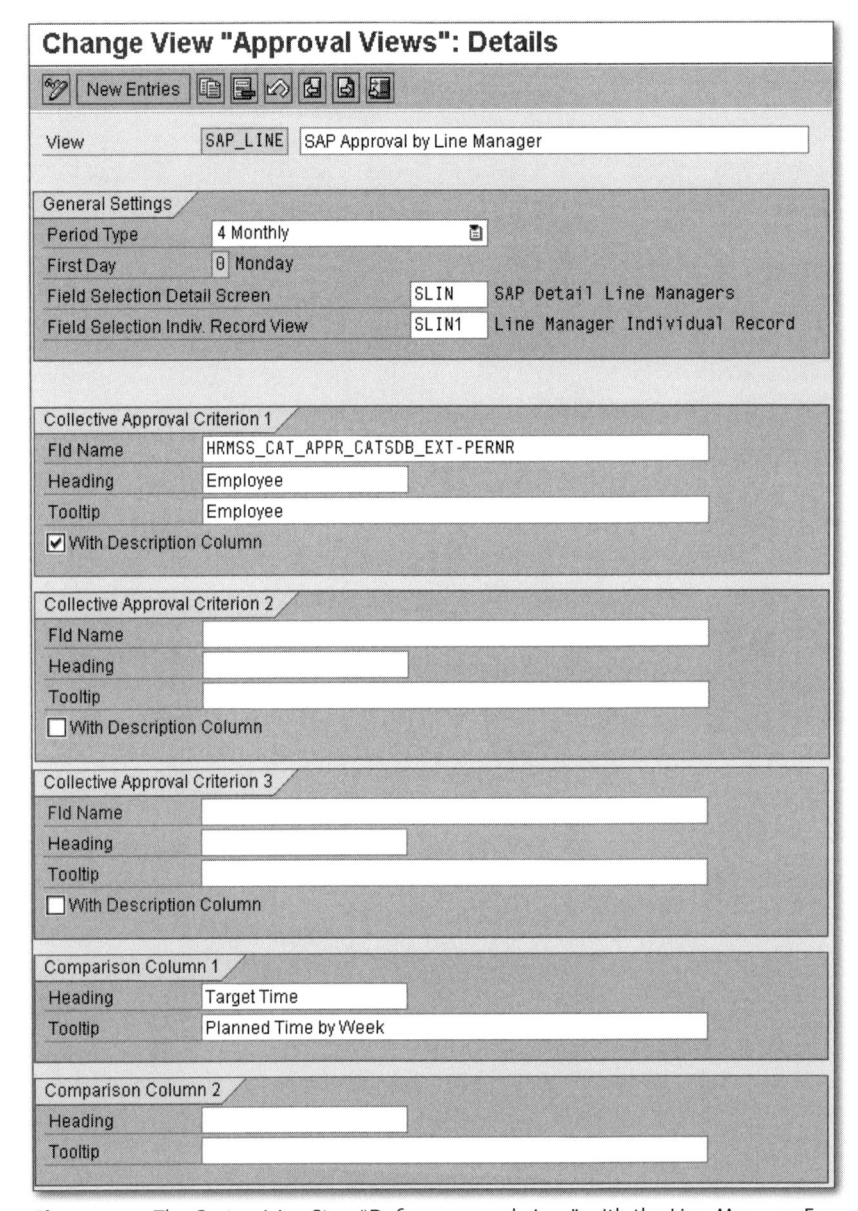

Figure 9.17 The Customizing Step "Define approval view," with the Line Manager Example

- **Define field selection for individual approval view (table V_PT_FIELD_SEL)**
  In this step, you are defining and assigning the fields you would like to see in the individual approval view.

Figures 9.18 and 9.19 are illustrating the customizing step 'Define Field Selection for Individual Approval View' with the Line Manager as an example.

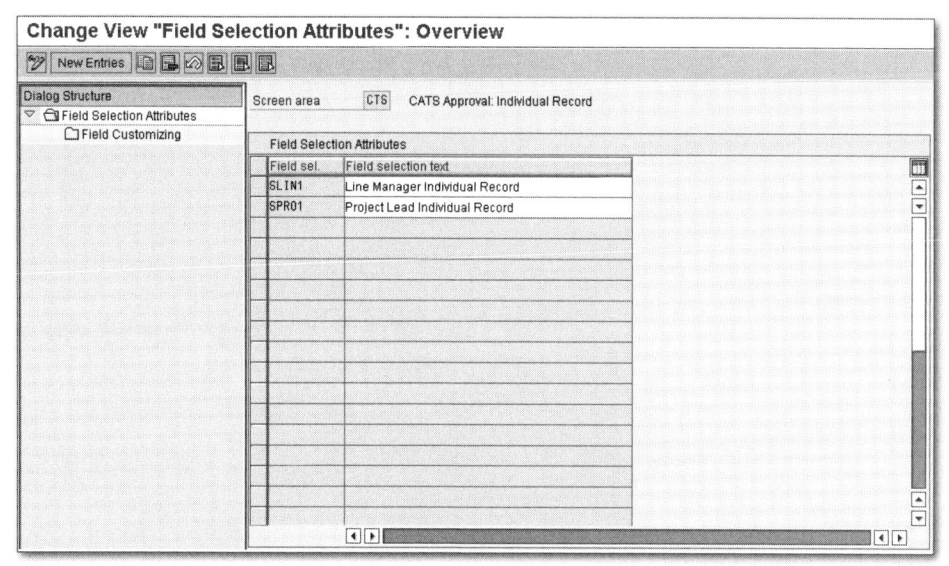

Figure 9.18 The Customizing Step "Define Field Selection for Individual View" (1)

Figure 9.19 The Customizing Step "Define Field Selection for Individual View" (2)

- **Define field selection for detail view (table V_PT_FIELD_SEL)**
  In this step, you are defining and assigning the fields you would like to see in the detail approval view.

  Figure 9.20 illustrates this customizing step with the Line Manager as an example.

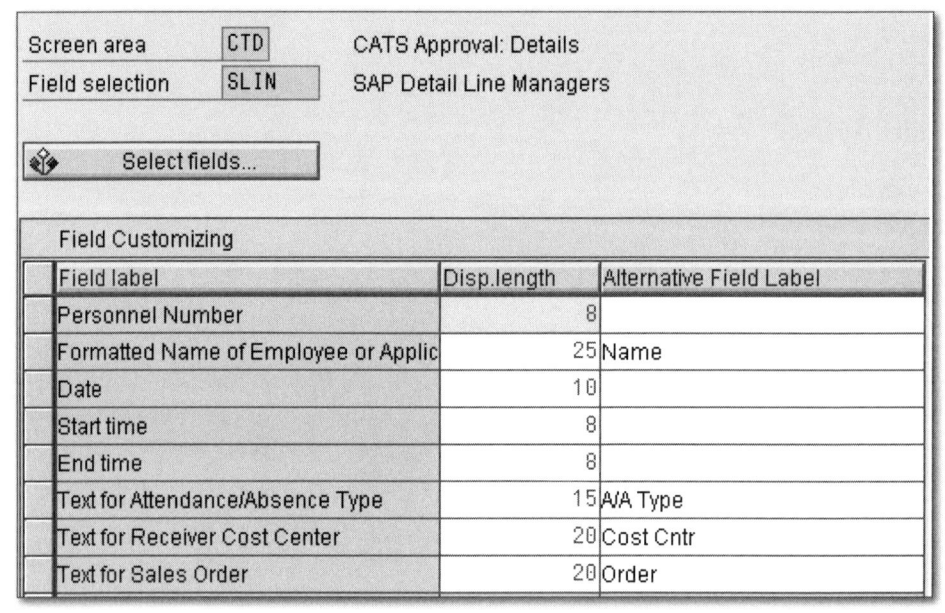

  Figure 9.20 The Customizing Step "Define Field Selection for Detail View

- **Define profile and assign to view (table V_CATS_APPR_CUST)**
  In this step, illustrated in Figure 9.21, you are binding the profile to the views.

  Figure 9.21 Define Profile and Assign to View

In regards to the employee selection, the system also provides two customizing steps to define the employee list:

▶ **Create rule groups (table V_HRWEB_RULE_GRP)**
In this step, you are defining the different groupings that will apply when dealing with the approval process. The groupings are then determined thanks to the feature WEBMO — Define Rule Group for Customizing Tables in Web Environment — that most of us already know very well as this is the feature already in use when dealing with the Leave Request, another web enabled service in the Employee Self Services (ESS).

Figure 9.22 shows the different rule groups. Carefully notice the Manager's Approval group.

Figure 9.22 The Different Rule Groups

Figure 9.23 shows the decision tree (feature) WEBMO, which still requires our configuration shall we need a special approval process.

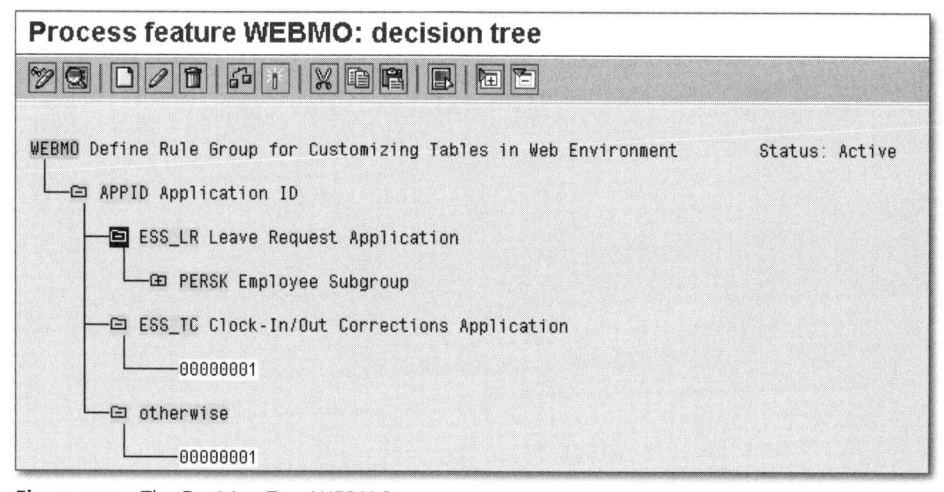

Figure 9.23 The Decision Tree WEBMO

Do not forget to activate the feature once it has been updated. Failing to activate will result in process failure.

- **Select Employee for approval (table V_PTREQ_TEAM)**
  In this step, you are binding the rule groups created previously with the view and groups as well as the group of the organization. This step is illustrated in Figure 9.24.

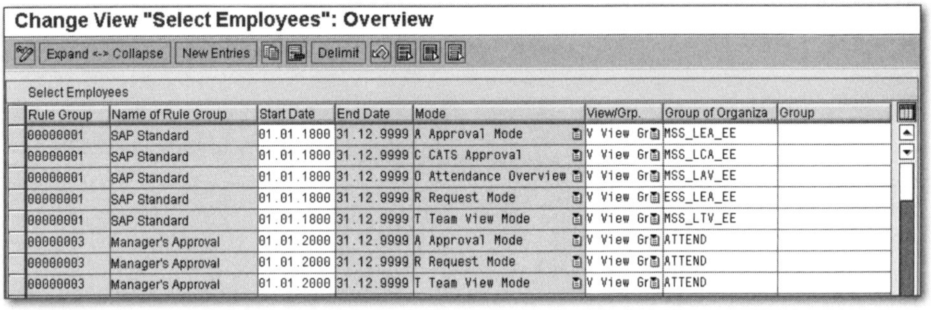
Change View "Select Employees": Overview

Expand <-> Collapse | New Entries | Delimit

Select Employees

Rule Group	Name of Rule Group	Start Date	End Date	Mode	View/Grp.	Group of Organiza	Group
00000001	SAP Standard	01.01.1800	31.12.9999	A Approval Mode	V View Gr	MSS_LEA_EE	
00000001	SAP Standard	01.01.1800	31.12.9999	C CATS Approval	V View Gr	MSS_LCA_EE	
00000001	SAP Standard	01.01.1800	31.12.9999	O Attendance Overview	V View Gr	MSS_LAV_EE	
00000001	SAP Standard	01.01.1800	31.12.9999	R Request Mode	V View Gr	ESS_LEA_EE	
00000001	SAP Standard	01.01.1800	31.12.9999	T Team View Mode	V View Gr	MSS_LTV_EE	
00000003	Manager's Approval	01.01.2000	31.12.9999	A Approval Mode	V View Gr	ATTEND	
00000003	Manager's Approval	01.01.2000	31.12.9999	R Request Mode	V View Gr	ATTEND	
00000003	Manager's Approval	01.01.2000	31.12.9999	T Team View Mode	V View Gr	ATTEND	

Figure 9.24 Select Employee for Approval

Carefully notice that SAP has reused here a standard table, already provided in earlier releases, for the Leave Request.

These customizing steps are not mandatory as the standard system already provides a clean online approval process. However, we do appreciate SAP's position to provide a flexible mean to adapt the Web Dynpro where appropriate. We just wish they had done the same with the Employee Self-Services (ESS) Web Dynpro. You will find in the resource guide (Appendix A) the web resources where you can find and read the whole SAP standard documentation regarding this new CATS functionalities.

Shall you still have specific requirements, you could always take advantage of the Business Add In (BAdI) BADI_CATS_APPROVAL(CATS-Genehmigung), with the Method CHECK_APPROVAL_BY_EXCEPTION.

9.7.3 Working with the New Approval Screen

The new screen "Approve Time Sheet Data" takes you to the collective approval screen.

9.7.4 Collective Approval

The collective approval screen provides to the managers a summary of the time activities requiring an approval. This screen is provided in standard, through the Manager Self Services role, in the workset "My Team."

This screen is taking full advantage of the standard Java Web Dynpro technology. Aside the astonishing layout, compared to R/3 transaction web enabled, you can see the roadmap provided to the end user, which clearly identifies the step the end user is currently working on. Figure 9.25 is illustrating the main collective approval screen with sample master data.

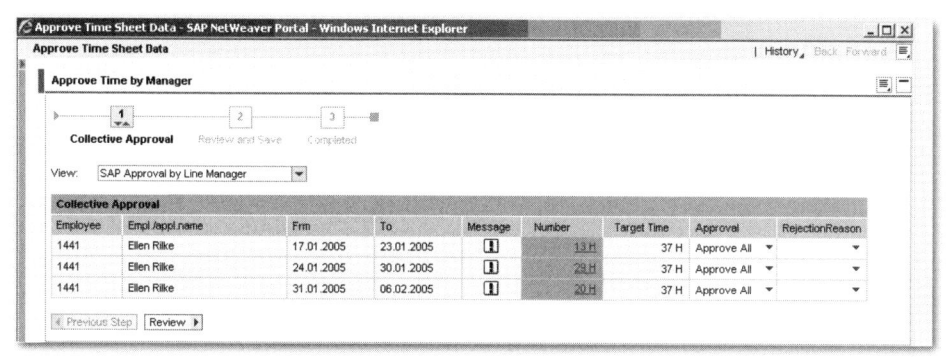

Figure 9.25 Main Collective Approval Screen

As you can see in the figure, the screen is divided into different sections:

- Employee Personnel Number
- Employee First and Last name
- From (start date)
- To (end date)
- Warning sign, shall a system message be returned
- Number (of hours worked) (with background color according to the number of hours worked)
- Target time entries, which are checking the time entries as stored in the infotype 0007 — Planned Working Time
- Approval column with the following options : approve all, reject all, resubmit all
- Rejection reason, as defined in the customizing (transaction CAC3)

These fields can be adjusted, as we have seen previously in the customizing steps.

This screen also gets interactive! By clicking on the hyperlink provided in the column Number, the system leads you to the "Individual Approval Screen."

9.7.5 Individual Approval

This screen, shown in Figure 9.26, provides a focus on one particular employee reporting to the manager, which helps the manager to isolate data from the overall summary.

It provides data already approved, and the new entries requiring approval now.

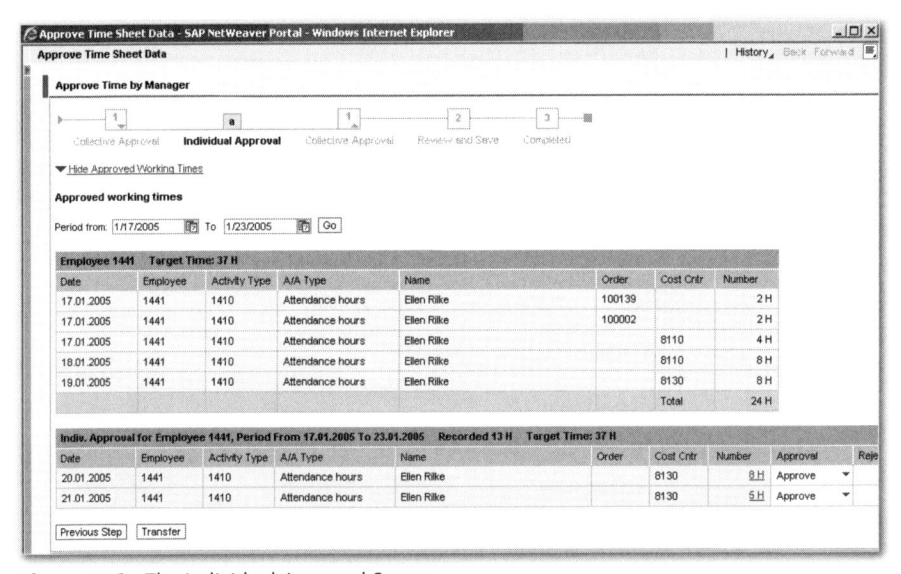

Figure 9.26 The Individual Approval Screen

If the manager wants to hide the approved hours, the screen provides the option 'Hide approve working times'. This will be very helpful, depending on the number of entries your manager is looking at.

In this screen, as illustrated in the figure, the manager can deal individually with the time entries from his/her teammate. This screen provides a myriad of handy information too, depending on the information collected during the time collection, in order for the manager to make a decision to either approve or reject (or resubmit) the time entries.

Just like the collective approval screen, the columns and fields provided in this individual screen can be customized as illustrated earlier in the chapter.

The standard approval column provides the same three entries as in the collective approval screen: approve all, reject all, resubmit all.

Once the manager is done with the approval process, the transfer icon must be clicked on so that you can move to the last step: the review and save step.

9.7.6 Review and Save

As a standard functionality in most SAP Web Dynpro, there is a review step that the end user must go through, just like if we were reading once more a form before mailing it. Figure 9.27 illustrates the review and save step.

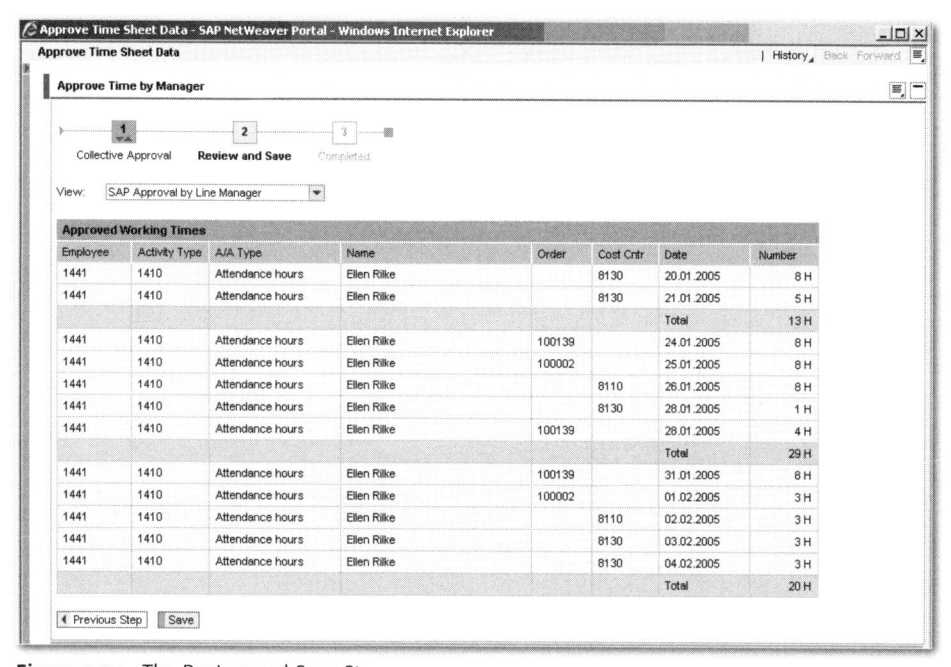

Figure 9.27 The Review and Save Step

The review screen provides a summary of all actions taken by the managers, regarding the time activities of his/her team mates. If the manager has forgotten something or just needs to make another correction, the icon "previous step" can always be hit in order to return to the previous step.

Once the manager is satisfied with the time entries, the icon "save" must be clicked on in order to save the data and allocate the CATS appropriate status to the time entries as explained earlier.

In conclusion, we would all agree that SAP has taken the time to listen to our demands in order to provide an online screen for CATS approval. This clearly fills a crucial functionality that all managers were missing ever since the beginning of Manager Self-Services in release R/3 enterprise (4.70).

Managers will benefit from a straightforward screen providing all the required information.

9.8 CATS General Reporting

Once we have collected time entries in CATS, all the information stored can be used to run reports. The program CATSSHOW, which can be accessed by calling the transaction code CADO, provides the selection fields for accessing the data. Figure 9.28 provides a snapshot of the standard selection screen.

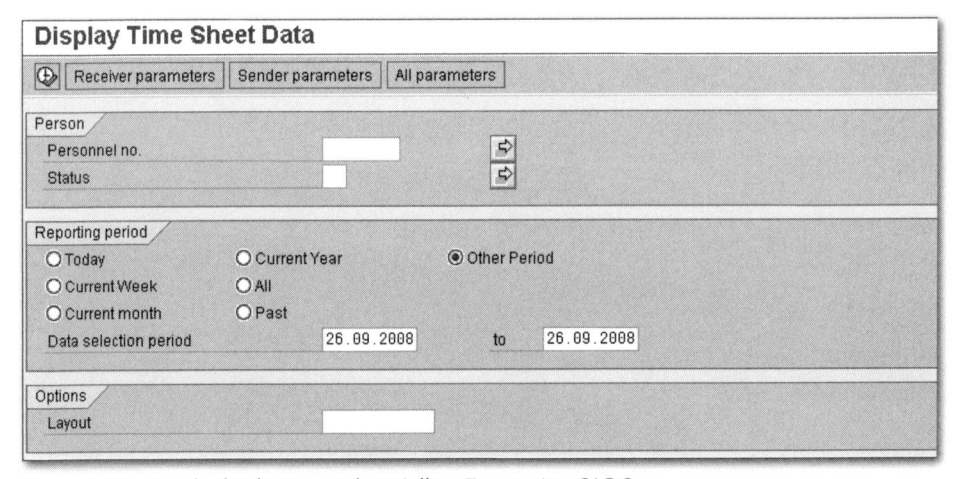

Figure 9.28 Standard Selections When Calling Transaction CADO

In addition to the standard selection criteria, additional selection items can be used:

- **Receiver parameters** (i. e. the cost center): Figure 9.29 illustrates these options.

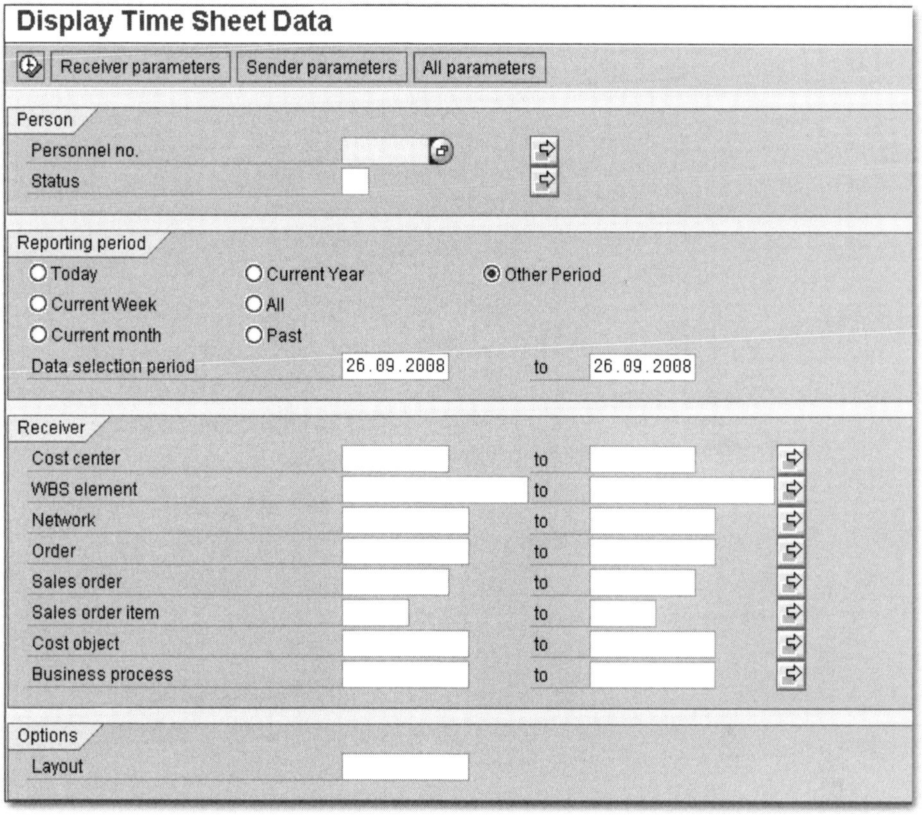

CATS General Reporting | **9.8**

Display Time Sheet Data

Receiver parameters | Sender parameters | All parameters

Person
Personnel no.
Status

Reporting period
○ Today   ○ Current Year   ● Other Period
○ Current Week ○ All
○ Current month ○ Past
Data selection period   26.09.2008   to   26.09.2008

Receiver
Cost center   to
WBS element   to
Network   to
Order   to
Sales order   to
Sales order item   to
Cost object   to
Business process   to

Options
Layout

Figure 9.29 Receiver Parameters

These parameters identify all the receiver parameters onto the user who has collected his/her time entries. The receiver parameters are:

▶ Cost Center

▶ WBS Element

▶ Network

▶ Order

▶ Sales Order / Sales Order item

▶ Cost object

▶ Business Process

9 | Reporting for CATS

- **Sender parameters** (i. e. the purchase order): See Figure 9.30 for this option. These parameters identify all the sender parameters used while collecting the time entries. The sender parameters are :
    - Cost Center
    - Activity Type
    - Sender Business Process
    - Purchase Order/Purchase Order Item
    - Service Number

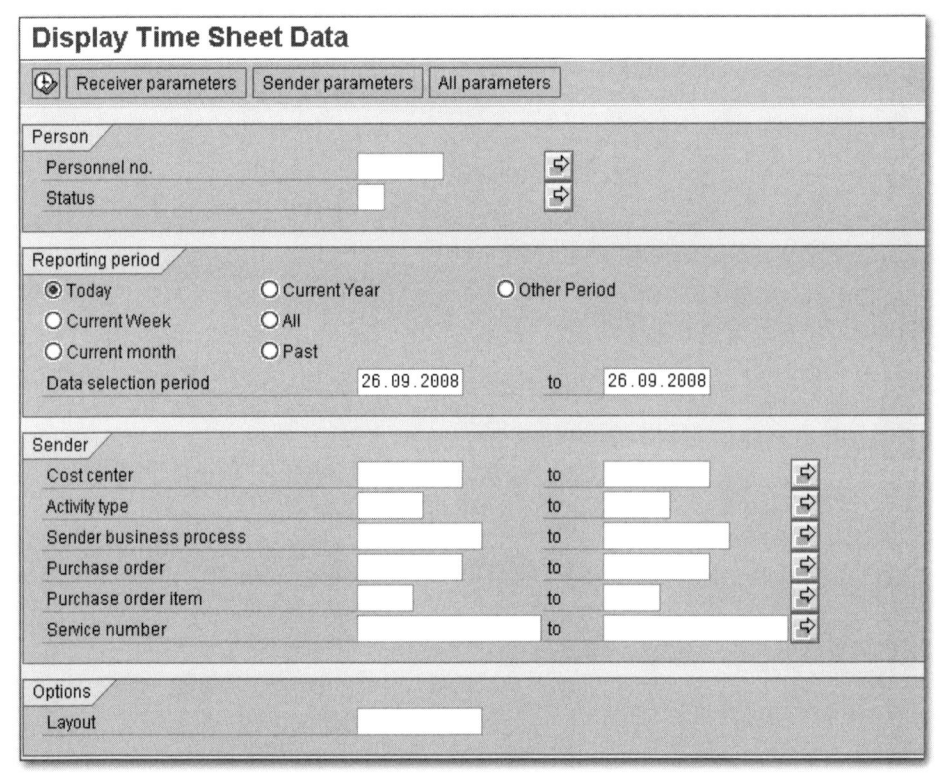

Figure 9.30 Sender Parameters

- **All parameters:** Figure 9.31 illustrates the full scenario. This option provides a combination of all the receiver and the sender parameters, thus making it easier for the end user to run the report.

196

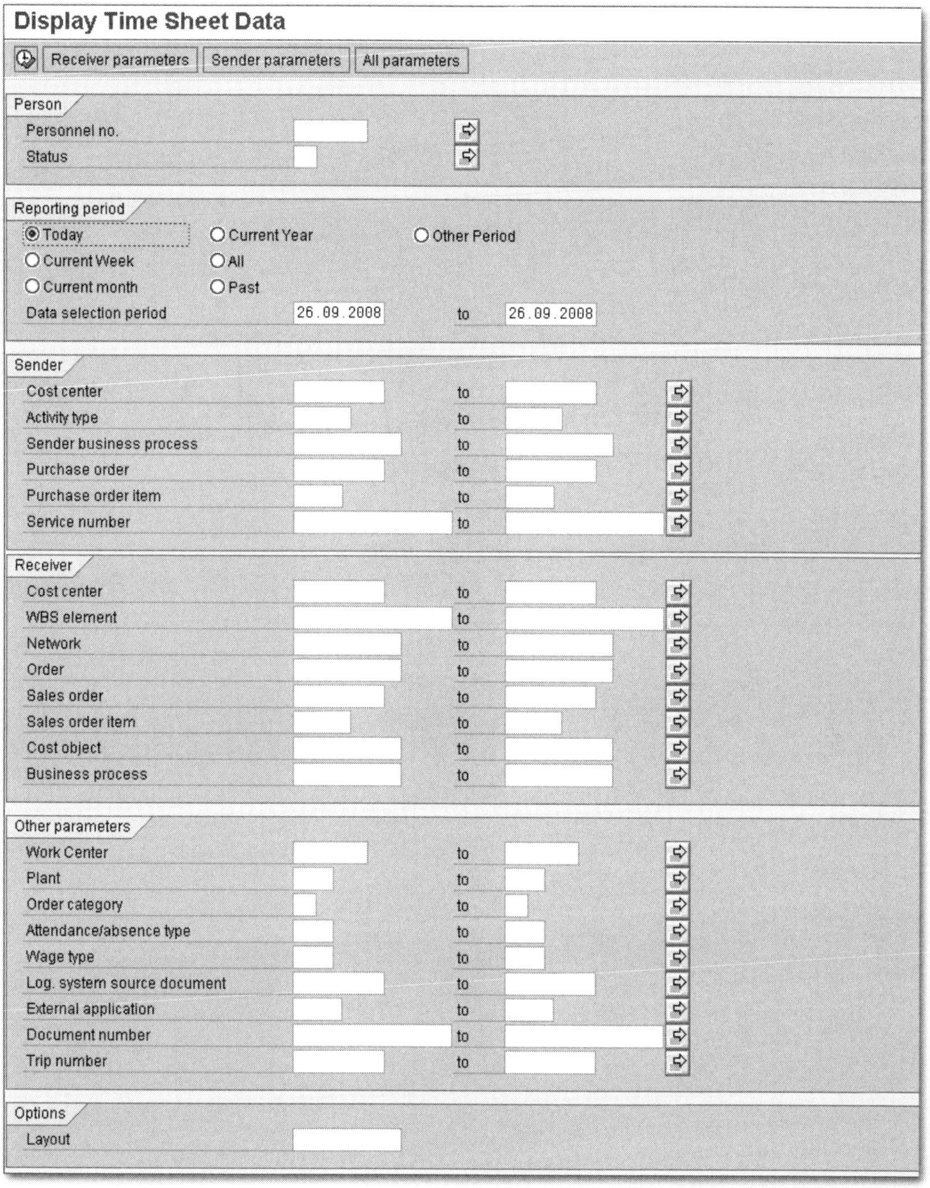

CATS General Reporting | 9.8

Display Time Sheet Data

[Receiver parameters] [Sender parameters] [All parameters]

Person
- Personnel no.
- Status

Reporting period
- ⦿ Today
- ○ Current Week
- ○ Current month
- ○ Current Year
- ○ All
- ○ Past
- ○ Other Period
- Data selection period 26.09.2008 to 26.09.2008

Sender
- Cost center ... to
- Activity type ... to
- Sender business process ... to
- Purchase order ... to
- Purchase order item ... to
- Service number ... to

Receiver
- Cost center ... to
- WBS element ... to
- Network ... to
- Order ... to
- Sales order ... to
- Sales order item ... to
- Cost object ... to
- Business process ... to

Other parameters
- Work Center ... to
- Plant ... to
- Order category ... to
- Attendance/absence type ... to
- Wage type ... to
- Log. system source document ... to
- External application ... to
- Document number ... to
- Trip number ... to

Options
- Layout

Figure 9.31 General Reporting with All Parameters Shown

> **Hint**
> The field layout, located at the bottom of the screen allows the end user to choose a convenient layout format. When running the report for the first time, you can save the layout used on the screen and then call it back while running the report, saving yourself some time.

9.9 Archiving

Although outside our current scope, the archiving process must be looked at early in the CATS implementation, because the time entries will generate many lines of code in the system. This may result in insufficient space in the standard tables and a slower response time, while approving the hours.

Check with the Office Automation team about the current archiving strategy, and find out how the CATS component can be added to the procedure. The transaction code SARA (report SAPMAADM) allows you to access the standard archiving tool.

The object CATS_DATA can be used to store CATS time entries. Ideally, online access to the main CATS database (CATSDB) will be available for the current year and the previous year. All older data will be archived. Figure 9.32 shows the initial screen for accessing the archiving tool. Be sure to set the object CATS_DATA in the required field.

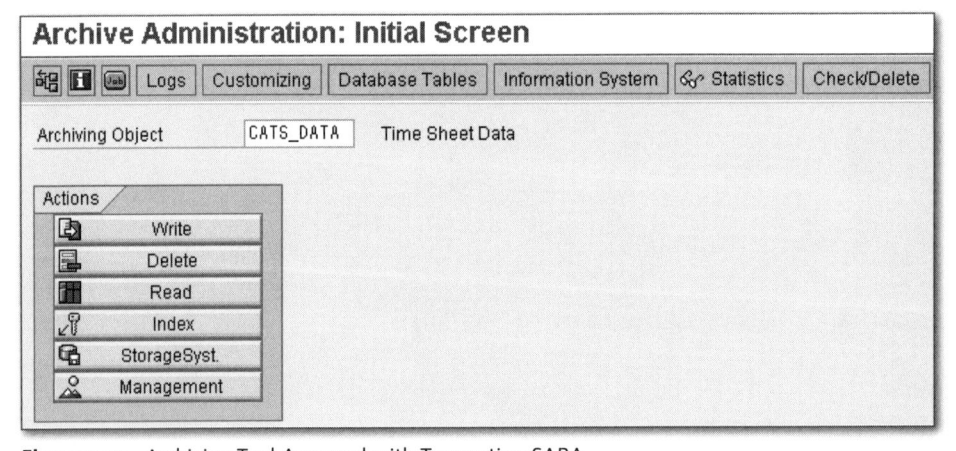

Figure 9.32 Archiving Tool Accessed with Transaction SARA

Once the data archiving process is set up, the report RCATS_ARCH_READING will be used to read the data already archived.

The programs provided here above are meant for the SAP R/3 backend system. If you run BW, you can store this out-of-date information as a flat file on the Data Warehouse server. It will be a smoother reporting technique, since the end user can use Business Explorer (BEx) through Microsoft Excel.

9.10 Reorganizing the Time Sheet

All through the CATS process, data is collected through a single point of entry. This data then moves from the central CATS database (CATSDB) to the target modules once it has been approved. This approval can be automatically done by the system or by a designated approver.

The technical layer between the main CATS database and the respective target modules is made of interface tables. These interface tables are meant to ensure a viable technical process. They should not be managed directly nor used directly for reporting.

As SAP is a living system, in some circumstances, the interface tables can lose their alignment with the target module. Administrators must, therefore, use a tool report for these inconsistencies.

To solve basic inconsistencies, a standard program has been provided to check and see if any problem has arisen or simply to correct a wrong alignment. The report RCATSRIF, which can be accessed through the transaction code CATR, can fulfill this requirement. Figure 9.33 shows the initial screen of reorganization table.

Note the following options:

- **Log** will provide an exhaustive index of the actions performed
- **Test run** will run the program in test mode, without any changes

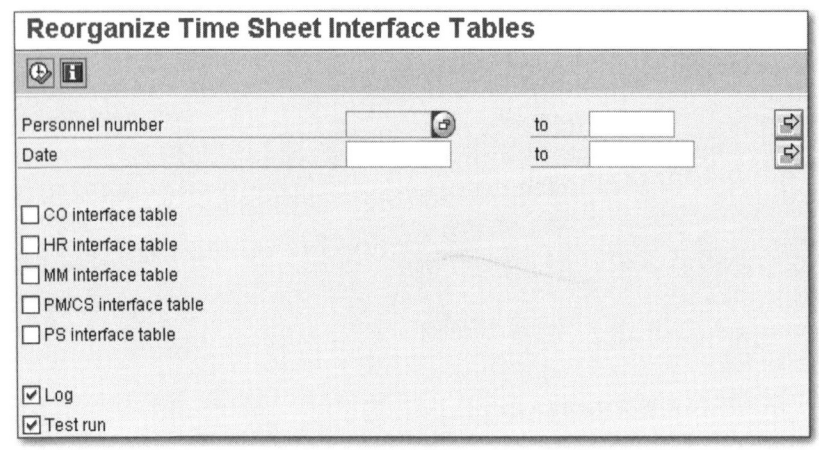

Figure 9.33 Reorganization Screen Accessed with Transaction CATR

9.11 User-Linking to Employees

CATS can be Web-enabled. To do this, assuming that all the required customizing has been taken care of, the system administrator must set up the SAP users. Remember that each personnel number must have a dedicated SAP User ID in Infotype 0105—*Communication*, subtype 0001—*System User Name*.

What can easily become a nightmare for the system administrators can be easily managed by using the transaction code HRUSER.

Figure 9.34 shows the standard initial screen, highlighting its different possibilities, which are:

- Preparation
- User and authorization assignment
- User attributes
- Corrections

The preparation allows you to assign the employees to the existing SAP user ids if these have already been created by the system administrator.

User-Linking to Employees | **9.11**

```
Set Up and Maintain ESS Users (Start)
 Log   Log(s)   Log(s)   User Attributes   Job Overview
 Preparation
   Assignment of employees to existing users
   Copy SAP role -> customer namespace

 User/authorization assignment
   Change user attributes/key date
   Select employees using employee master
   Preselect employees using org. assignment
   Key date:            26.09.2008  O Other date
   User attributes
     User group         ESSUSER
     Role Assignment
       O Local role assignment
       ⦿ No role assignment

 Correction
   Delete ESS users
```

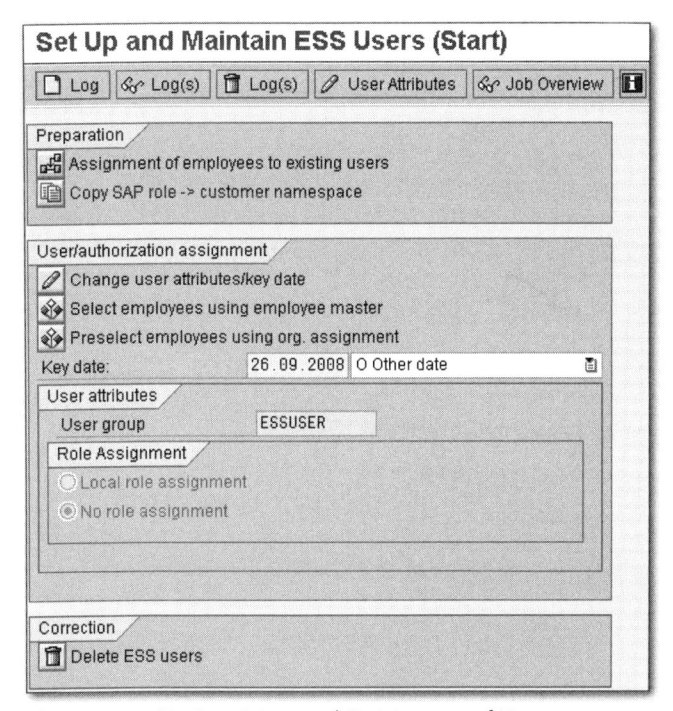

Figure 9.34 Starting, Setup, and Maintenance of Users

The user and authorization assignment allows you to set up the following user attributes:

- Key date
- Password assignment
- Role assignment
- Logon data

A simple icon also provides the possibility to delete old and/or obsolete user IDs.

> **Hint**
>
> A random password assignment can be enabled by setting up the user-exit HRESSW4 (function module EXIT_SAPLEHUS_001). This will ensure a more secure access. Although you might not have administrator rights in the productive system, you can use the transaction SU01D to display a system user name.

201

9.12 Common Authorization Reporting

While setting up the roles and profiles you can use the standard reporting tree to monitor the use of the standard authorization objects, the transactions used by users, etc. The transaction code SUIM can be used to access this standard reporting tree.

Figure 9.35 shows the programs that are most likely to be used while setting up the authorization. You can read the SAP Labs (2000) book for additional support on authorization management.

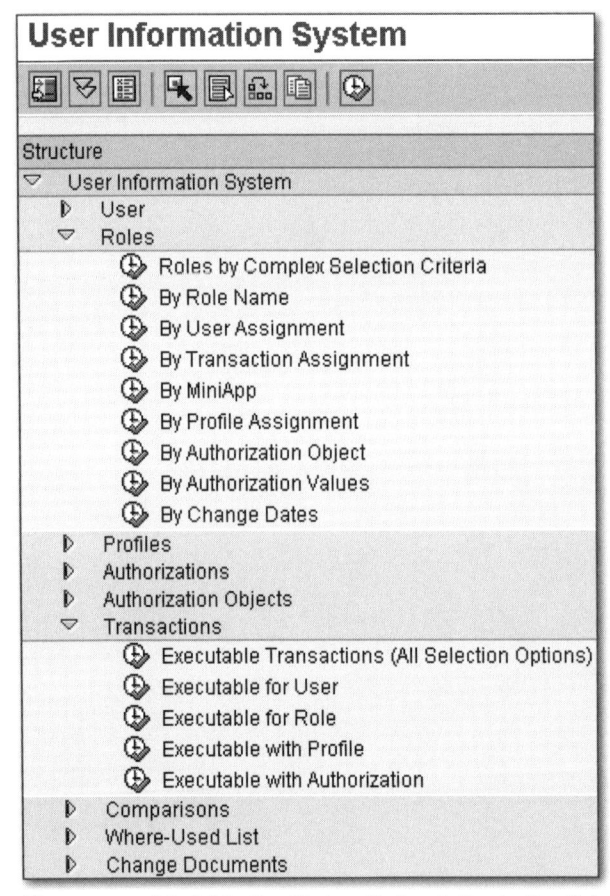

Figure 9.35 Administrative Choices During Authorization Setup

9.13 Reporting per Target Component

In addition to the reporting that is dedicated to functionalities and utilities, this section will provide, as a reminder, the standard reporting available in each target module. The reporting provided is used only to report on the time activities.

Bear in mind that once CATS has been set up, to secure the main reporting within CATS, all modifications must be done through CATS and not through the confirmation transaction codes in each target component. Failure to do so compromises the consistency of the main report CATSSHOW (transaction CADO).

9.13.1 Human Resources

With regard to the employee time and labor, the following reports can be directly used within HR:

- Transaction PT_QTAL allows the display of employee's labor and time
- Transaction PT_QATT allows the display of attendances list
- Transaction PT_QABS allows the display of absences list
- Transaction PT_QREM allows the display of employee remuneration information
- Transaction PT65 allows the display of attendances and absences in a graphical mode

9.13.2 Finance & Controlling

According to the setup achieved in your system, several report groups have been created.

To select the relevant report group, call the transaction code GR55.

9.13.3 Plant Maintenance & Customer Service

In the Plant Maintenance and Customer Service module, the transaction code IW47 (program RIAFRU20) allows display of the Plant Maintenance and Customer Service confirmations.

9.13.4 Project System

With regard to the Network Component selection, the transaction code COMPXPD can be used. The transaction code CNE2 can also be used to monitor the project progress.

9.13.5 Materials Management

For Materials Management, the following functionalities are available.

- For the service entry sheets, the transaction code ML84 can be used to monitor the service entry sheets
- Depending on the selection chosen from the purchase requisition — the RFQ/Quotation, the Purchase Order, the contract, or the entry sheet — the transaction code MSRV6 can be used to report on these services.

9.14 Lessons Learned

This chapter described the standard programs used to manage the time sheet before, during, and after time collection. These reports can be used daily to monitor all activities.

We also saw that managers have choices when dealing with time approval. They can first request which time entries have to be approved, then they can choose which interface they would rather use: R/3 screens or the web enabled screens. All of this thanks to the approval procedure provided as of release ERP 6.0.

In addition to these reports, additional useful reporting possibilities were introduced with regard to the personnel master data and the authorization setup.

Special attention was paid to the technical transactions used to reorganize the interfaces tables from the time sheet database (the table CATSDB) and its interface tables to the different target modules.

Once the time entries are collected through CATS, the standard reporting that most users are using in their respective field or competences can still be used to report on these activities. If these reports are not enough to provide the desired information, you can create ABAP or ad hoc queries. This can easily be done by the end user.

As a last resort, specific reports can also be created. A careful check of the available Business Application Program Interfaces (BAPIs) should be done to reduce the amount of work and, most important, the maintenance.

Appendices

A	Resource Guide	207
B	Frequently Asked Questions	221
C	Bibliography	227

A   Resource Guide

This resource guide will facilitate quick browsing for specific information.

A.1   List of Transaction Codes

Figures A.1 and A.2 display the customizing and functional transaction codes that are useful while implementing CATS.

CAC1	Time Sheet: Maintain Profiles
CAC2	Time Sheet: Field Selection
CAC3	Time Sheet: Rejection Reasons
CAC4	CATS: Profile Authorization Groups
CAC5	Define Customer Fields
CAC6	Allowed Print Reports
CAC7	Number Range Maintenance: CATS
CAC8	Number Range Maintenance: CATS_INTRN

Figure A.1   Customizing Transaction Codes

CAT2	Time Sheet: Maintain Times
CAT2_ISCR	CATS: Maintain Times (Init. Screen)
CAT3	Time Sheet: Display Times
CAT3_ISCR	CATS: Display Times (Initial Screen)
CAT4	CATS: Approve Data
CAT5	Data Transfer CATS -> PS
CAT6	Transfer External -> Time Management
CAT7	CATS: Transfer Data to CO
CAT8	Time Sheet: Document Display
CAT9	Data Transfer CATS -> PM/CS
CATM	Selection From Time Recording

Figure A.2   Functional Transaction Codes

A.2   Message Class HRTIM00CATS

To find the different messages that appear while using CATS, remember that—as with all standard messages—the CATS messages are stored in Table T100. All relevant CATS message are stored under the message class HRTIM00CATS.

A.3 List Tables and Structures

Tables A.1 and A.2 provide snapshots of the CATS structures and tables.

Technical Name	Description
TCATS	CATS: Data entry profile
TCATSA	CATS: Profile Authorization Groups
TCATSAT	CATS: Text for Profile Authorization Groups
TCATSD	CATS: Rejection reasons
TCATSDLIST	CATS: Profile for reporting (List Display)
TCATSDT	CATS: Text table for rejection reasons
TCATST	CATS: Text for table variants
TCATS_ITS	Time Sheet: Data Entry Profile ESS scenario
TCATS_SHLP_ITS	Time Sheet: Possible entries help in Internet
TCATP	CATS: Allowed reports
TCATPT	CATS: Allowed reports: Texts
TCATR	Dynamic function module call from tree structure
CATSDB	Central Database for the Cross Application Time Sheet
CI_CATSDB	Customer included in the CATS database (Structure)
CATSDEL	Table with deletion time of deleted CATS records
CATSCO	Controlling transfer table for CATS
CATSCOSUM	Summarization Controlling transfer table for CATS
CATSHR	Human Resources transfer table for CATS
CATSMM	Materials Management transfer table for CATS
CATSPM	Plant Maintenance / Customer Service transfer table for CATS
CATSPS	Project System transfer table for CATS
CATS_ARCH_IDX	Index Table for Data Object selection
CATS_BIW_DELTA	Transfer CATS data to BW: Document numbers
CATS_BIW_SELOPT	Selection criteria for Delta management (CATS to BW)
CATS_BW_TIME	Transfer Time Sheet into BW: Time Stamp
CATS_MY_DATES	CATS notebook: Periods for target hours and data storage

Table A.1 CATS Structure List

Technical Name	Description
CATS_MY_DOCU	CATS notebook: Create and distribute HTML
CATS_MY_FIELDSEL	CATS notebook: Field selection
CATS_MY_FIXTEXT2	CATS notebook: Fixed texts
CATS_MY_FIXTEXTS	>Obsolete<

Table A.1 CATS Structure List (Cont.)

Technical Name	Description
CATS_MY_PICKLIST	Additional field names for which there can be picklists
CATS_MY_PUSH	CATS notebook: Synchronize Static Objects
CATS_MY_TEXTS	>Obsolete<
CATS_MY_TEXTS2	CATS notebook: References to data elements for fields texts
CATS_MY_TEXTS_C	CATS notebook: Customer specific fields
CATS_MY_UNITS	Units used in CATS notebook
CATS_TEMP	Database for templates
CATSOFFTRANSEY	CATS Offline Transaction keys
CATS_GUID_KEY	Link: GUID and external CATS key
PA0315	CATS Sender information (Table)
P0315	CATS Sender information (Structure)
T526	HR administrators

Table A.2 CATS Tables with Descriptions

A.4 Summary of Fields Used in CATS and Target Components

This information can be found in CA500 — Cross Application Time Sheet (CATS) training material. Many fields are available for CATS setup. Tables A.3, A.4, and A.5 provide a reference list of the fields available and their respective usability in the target components. Please note that in the first column A indicates the sender of an activity allocation and B the controlling receiver object.

A | Resource Guide

	Field Name	Technical Name	Target Components	Notes
	Att./Absence type	CATSD_AWART	HR	
	Work Center	CATSD-ARBPL	PM/PS/CS	
	Extra pay indicator	CATSD-AUFKZ	HR	
	Accounting indicator	CATSD-BEMOT	PM/PS/CS	
	Description	CATSFIELDS-KOSTLLXT	None	
	Valuation basis	CATSD-BWGRL	HR	
	Name	CATSFIELDS-DISPTEXT1	None	
	Name	CATSFIELDS-DISPTEXT2	None	
B	Receiver order	CATSD-RAUFNR	PM/CS/CO	1 & 3
B	Rec. Business Process	CATSD-RPRZNR	CO	
B	Rec. Cost Center	CATS-KOSTL	CO	
B	Receiver Cost object	CATSD-RKSTR	CO	
B	Rec. Sales Order Item	CATS-RKDPOS	CO	
B	Rec. Sales Order	CATSD-RKDAUF	CO	
B	Rec. WBS element	CATS-RPROJ	CO	
	Final Confirmation	CATSDB-AUERU	PM/PS/CS	
	Full day	CATSDB-ALLDF	HR	
	Internal unit of measure	CATSD-UNIT	CO/MM/HR	
	Capacity Category	CATSD-KAPAR	PM/CS/PS	
	Controlling area	CATSD-KOKRS	CO/PM/PS/CS	
	Cost Center	CATSFIELDS-HDRKOSTL	None	
	Short Text	CATSDB-LTXA1	All	
A	Activity type	CATSD-LSTAR	CO	
	Service number	CATSD-LSTNR	MM	
	Wage type	CATSD-LGART	HR	
	Overtime comp. type	CATSD-VERSL	HR	
	Name Employee / Appl.	CATSFIELDS-LISTNAME	None	
	Name Employee / Appl.	CATSFIELDS-ENAME	None	
	Network	CATSD-RNPLNR	PS	3
	Object type	CATSD-OTYPE	HR	
	Personnel Number	CATSFIELDS-PERNR	All	
	Position	CATSD-PLANS	HR	

Table A.3 CATS Setup Fields (1)

Summary of Fields Used in CATS and Target Components | **A.4**

	Field Name	Technical Name	Target Components	Notes
	Premium indicator	CATSD-PRAKZ	HR	
	Premium number	CATSD-PRAKN	HR	
	Forecast finish (date)	CATSD-PEDD	PM/CS/PS	
	Trip number	CATSD-REINR	None	
	Remaining Work	CATSDB-OFMNW	PM/CS/PS	
	Sending PO item	CATSD-SEBELP	MM-SRV	
	Sending purch. Order	CATSD-SEBELN	MM-SRV	
A	Sender Cost Center	CATSD-SKOSTL	CO	
A	Sender Bus. Process	CATSD-SPRZNR	CO	
	Split number	CATSD-SPLIT	PM/CS/PS	
	Statistical key Figure	CATSD-STATKEYFIG	CO	
	Det. Status auto.	CATSFIELDS-AUSTAT	PM/CS/PS	
	Tax area	CATSD-WTART	HR	
	Price	CATSD-PRICE	CO	
	Pay scale group	CATSD-TRFGR	HR	
	Pay scale level	CATSD-TRFST	HR	
	Partial Confirmation	CATSDB-ERUZU	PM/CS/PS	
	Transaction currency	CATSD-TCURR	CO	2
	Suboperation	CATSD-UVORN	PM/CS/PS	
	Operation	CATSD-VORNR	PM/CS/PS	
	Previous day indicator	VTKEN	HR	
	Currency	CATSD-WAERS	HR	
	Plant	CATSD-WERKS	PM/CS/PS	

Table A.4 CATS Setup Fields (2)

A | Resource Guide

Field Name	Technical Name	Target Components	Notes
Additional Field1	CATS_ADDFI-FIELD1	None	
Additional Field2	CATS_ADDFI-FIELD2	None	
Additional Field3	CATS_ADDFI-FIELD3	None	
Additional Field4	CATS_ADDFI-FIELD4	None	
Additional Field5	CATS_ADDFI-FIELD5	None	
Additional Field6	CATS_ADDFI-FIELD6	None	
Additional Field7	CATS_ADDFI-FIELD7	None	
Additional Field8	CATS_ADDFI-FIELD8	None	
Additional Field9	CATS_ADDFI-FIELD9	None	
Additional Field10	CATS_ADDFI-FIELD10	None	

Table A.5 CATS Setup Fields (3)

> **Note**
>
> The configuration of the order determines to which target component the data is transferred. Time Sheet data is transferred to Plant Maintenance (PM) or Customer Service (CS) only if the order permits these confirmations.

> **Note**
>
> Currency for Price field is only used in conjunction with an activity type.

> **Note**
>
> If you enter objects in combination with a wage type, the target component is selected based on the characteristics of the wage type. If the bonus indicator for time leveling and Time-Sheet fields is left blank in table T511, Time-Sheet data is transferred to Controlling.

A.5 CATS Configuration Assistant

This tool provides a quick reference checklist for deploying CATS in regards to the customizing steps. Figures A.3, A.4, A.5, and A.6 illustrate the basic profile scenarios, showing settings for the employee, the time administrator and the manager. They provide an overview of the following steps:

- General settings
- Time settings
- Person selection
- Accounting variant
- Default values
- Worklist
- General data-entry checks
- Data-entry checks for users of HR
- Authorizations
- Print entry sheet data
- Workflow

Thanks to my colleague Dieter Flack for providing us with this useful tool.

CATS Configuration Assistant	Profile 1	Profile 2	Profile 3	Comment
	EMPLOYEE	TIMEADM	MGR	Key can be up to 8 characters long. First character must be a letter.
	Employee Profile	Time Administrator Profile	Manager Profile	
GENERAL SETTINGS				
1. Will the user be allowed to make nonessential setting changes to the profile?	No	No	No	
2. Will this profile display the employees' daily work schedule?	Yes	Yes	Yes	
3. Will this profile display a row with a sum of all the hours entered for each day?	Yes	Yes	Yes	
4. Will this profile display clock-in and clock-out times?	Yes	Yes	Yes	
5. Should unpaid breaks be taken into account when calculating the total number of hours?	Yes	Yes	Yes	
6. Should rejected records be highlighted?	Yes	Yes	Yes	
7. Should fields containing additional information (e.g. short and/or long text) be highlighted?	Yes	Yes	Yes	
8. Should users be allowed to enter times on non-working days?	Yes	Yes	Yes	
9. Should weekdays (Mo, Tu, We, etc.) be displayed in addition to dates?	Yes	Yes	Yes	
10. Should the system skip the CATS selection screen?	Yes	No	No	You must default the Employee Personnel Number (via parameter ID 'PER' or Infotype 0105 Subtype 0001) and the CATS Data Entry Profile (via parameter ID 'CVR')
11. Can data entered for future dates be released?	Yes	Yes	Yes	
12. Should the data be released on saving?	Yes	Yes	Yes	
13. Is approval required?	Yes	Yes	Yes	
14. Will the user be allowed to edit approved times?	No	No	Yes	CATS will require that the employee be assigned a plant (which in turn should have a factory calendar assigned to it) in HR Infotype '0315 - CATS: Sender information'.
15. Will data be transferred directly to HR upon save?	No	No	No	
16. Will the user be recording objects other than hours (e.g.	Yes	Yes	Yes	
17. You may specify a trip schema if your users will be jumping from CATS to the Travel Management Module.				

Figure A.3 CATS Configuration Assistant—General Settings

A | Resource Guide

	TIME SETTINGS				
17	What data entry period will the profile use?	Weekly	Weekly	Weekly	
18	What day of the week should be displayed first?	Monday	Monday	Monday	This selection only works with periods weekly and bi-weekly
19	The initial entry screen should display ___ periods back in relation to today's date.	1	1	1	The symbol must be placed to the right of the number
20	How many screens can the user scroll back?	8	8	8	Do not enter a symbol with the number
21	How many screens can the user scroll forward?	8	8	8	Do not enter a symbol with the number
	PERSON SELECTION				
22	Will this profile be used for entering data for a *single* or *multiple* employees at a time?	Single	Multiple	Multiple	
23	Will the 'Personnel Number' field in the CATS Initial Entry screen be *open* for entry or should the profile provide a *list* of employees?	Open	List	List	
24	If you have chosen *List* in Q23, the Employee selection can be done either by: (a) Time Administrator, (b) Organizational Unit, (c) Cost Center, or (d) report.		Time Administrator	Report	
25	Enter the name of your report here ONLY if you wish to use your own program to build the list. Otherwise, the list will be built using SAP's standard report.				
	ACCOUNTING VARIANT				
26	Which accounting scenario would you like to use?	Scenario #2	Scenario #2	Scenario #2	
	#1 Send all charges go against Master CCtr. This is the same variant used by the system prior to release 4.6a.				
	#2 Transfer all data to HR and calculate Personnel costs using payroll. Charge costs to the Receiver object. Do not trigger an Activity Allocation.				
	#3 Transfer all data to HR and calculate Personnel costs using payroll. Charge costs to the Sender object. Then, trigger an Activity allocation between the Sender and the Receiver objects.				
	#4 Transfer all data to HR and calculate Personnel costs using payroll. Charge costs to the employee's master cost center. Then trigger an activity allocation between the Master Cost center and the Sender object and then a second activity allocation between the Sender and the Receiver objects.				
27	For scenarios #3 and 4: would you like to document the link between the cost assignment and the activity allocations in Controlling?	No	No		

Figure A.4 Settings in CATS Configuration Assistant

	DEFAULT VALUES				
28	Should the profile default the employee's controlling area?	Yes	Yes	Yes	
29	If the profile is to default the Receiver Cost Center, should it be the employee's home CCtr. (from Infotype 0001) or an alternate CCtr. (Infotype 0315)?	0001	0001	0001	
30	Should the profile default the Activity Type set for the employee in Infotype 0315?	No	No	No	
31	Should the profile default the Purchase Order set for the employee in Infotype 0315?	No	No	No	
32	Should the profile default the Service Master set for the employee in Infotype 0315?	No	No	No	
33	Do you wish to default an Attendance Type or a Wage Type	Attendance	Attendance	Attendance	
34	Specify the Attendance/Absence or Wage type number	0800	0800	0800	
35	Should the profile default the *Sender Business Process* set for the employee in Infotype 0315?	No	No	No	
	WORK LIST				
	NOTE: *If you are not using a work list you can skip this section*				The Work list can't be used if the profile uses selection for several employees
36	Should the worklist contain a list of previously charged objects for the employee? If yes, please specify the maximum number of days in process for the object.				
37	Should Resource Planning data be contained in the work list?				
38	Should operations and sub-operations, or activity elements which are assigned to the user via the *work center*, be displayed in the work list?				
39	Should data from the Pool of Confirmations be contained in the work list?				
40	Should the values contained in the work list be determined via user exit/enhancement CATS0001?				
41	Should the user be allowed to copy hours from the work list into the entry list?				This can only work if another setting from the work list has been selected as well.
42	Should the hours displayed in the Worklist be distributed on workdays only?				

Figure A.5 Default Values and Work List in CATS Configuration Assistant

	GENERAL DATA ENTRY CHECKS				
43 -	What type of message should the profile use when clock-in/out times between two records collide?	Error message	Error message	Error message	
44 -	What type of message should the profile use if the user attempts to enter more than 24 hours in one day?	Error message	Error message	Error message	
45 -	Do you wish to subtract Attendances/Absences entered in the HR module from the time type displayed in CATS?	No	No	No	
46 -	What is the minimum percentage by which the entered hours may fall below target hours? (Enter in format ##)				
47 -	What type of message should the profile use if the target hours fall below the minimum percentage variation specified above?	Error message	Error message	Error message	
48 -	What is the maximum percentage by which the entered hours may exceed target hours? (Enter in format ##)				
49 -	What type of message should the profile use if the target hours exceed the maximum percentage variation specified above?	Warning	Warning	Warning	
50 -	Specify a *technical time* type if you wish to overwrite the daily work schedule displayed on the screen with a technical time type (Enter in format ####).				
51 -	Should the system add overtime hours specified in Infotype 2005 to the number of planned hours?	No	No		
	DATA ENTRY CHECKS FOR USERS OF HR				
51 -	What type of message should the profile use when conflicts occur with available absence/ attendance quotas in the HR module?	Warning	Warning	Warning	
52 -	What type of message should the profile use whenever CATS records collide with HR records?	Warning	Warning	Warning	
	AUTHORIZATIONS				
53 -	What authorizations number will you use for this profile? (Enter in format ####)	0001	0002	0003	These authorizations codes must be set up in step 'Profile Authorization Groups' (Table TCATSAT)
	PRINT ENTRY SHEET DATA				
54 -	Specify a custom program if you want to use your own program for printing time sheet contents.	RCATSP01	RCATSP01	RCATSP01	Program must be contained in table TCATP: 'Customer Programs'
	WORKFLOW				
55 -	Specify a workflow task ID if you wish to use workflow with this profile	Manager TS 20000460	Manager TS 20000460	Manager TS 20000460	The system delivers the following sample tasks in 4.6c: 40007901, 20000460, 20000459, 20000450, and 20000459. For standard functions 20000450 and 20000459 the recipient determination can take place automatically.
56 -	Do you wish for the Workflow recipient to be determined automatically by the system?	Yes	Yes	Yes	

Figure A.6 Data-Entry Checks in CATS Configuration Assistant

A.6 CATS BAPIs

Figures A.7, A.8 and A.9 display the BAPIs that ABAP programmers and developers can use to further enhance CATS.

A | Resource Guide

Object	
Object Name	CATimeSheetManager
Short description	Time sheet manager
Object type	BUS7024
Pack.	CATS
Component	CA-TS
Person responsible	SAP
Created on	16.02.1999
Release	46A

Status	
Release status	Released
Last changed by	SAP
Changed on	25.01.2000

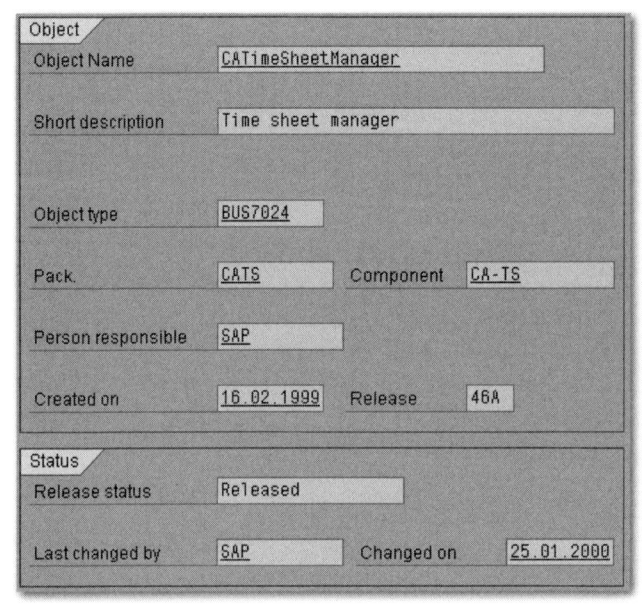

Figure A.7 Business Application Programming Interface for CATS (1)

Object	
Object Name	EmployeeCATimeSheet
Short description	Employee time sheet
Object type	BUS7025
Pack.	CATS
Component	CA-TS
Person responsible	SAP
Created on	16.02.1999
Release	46A

Status	
Release status	Released
Last changed by	SAP
Changed on	11.05.1999

Figure A.8 Business Application Programming Interface for CATS (2)

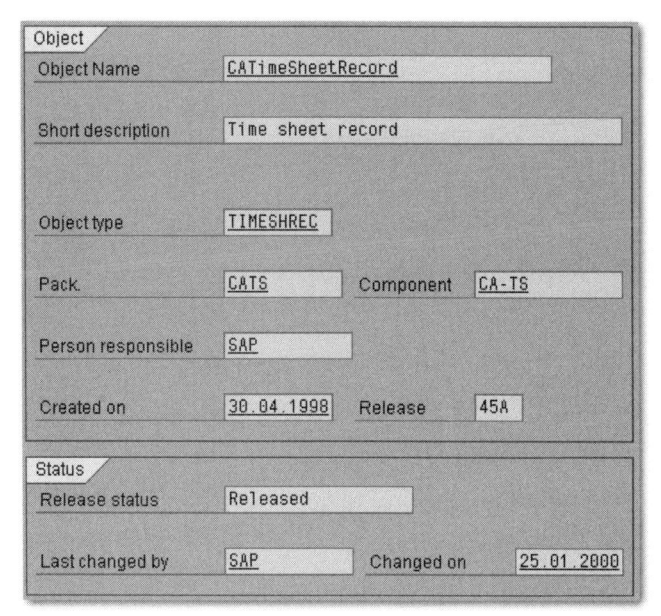

Figure A.9 Business Application Programming Interface for CATS (3)

A.7 CATS BAdIS

Figure A.10 shows the standard BAdIs available for CATS up to release ERP 6.0.

CATS_DERIVATIVES	Change of Derivation Values
CATS_REPORTING	CATS Reporting and Approval
CATS_WORKLIST_ADDIN	CATS: Structure Worklist Using BAdi
CATSBW_CUST_ISOURCE	Transfer Control of Time Sheet Data into BW
CATSXT_EVENT	CATSXT: Customer Fields and Data Checks
OFFLINE_APPL	Customer Exit for Offline Application with WAF Com

Figure A.10 Business Add-Ins for CATS up to Release ERP 6.0

A.8 Some Useful OSS Notes

The acronym for the Cross Application Time Sheet in SAP is CATS. Please ensure that the note you use is pertinent for the current SAP release.

▸ Note 570471: FAQ 2, Confirmations in the Project System

- Note 653209: FAQ, CATS/CATM—Transfer to MM
- Note 721799: Mobile Time Sheet 1.6 for Laptop—Composite Note
- Note 126129: Adding customer fields to CATS ITS
- Note 376188: Supported user exits from CATS in CATW service
- Note 814830: Notes containing correction reports for CA-TS-PS issues.
- Note 333884: Which default values are used when
- Note 808293: CATS Support Workshop
- Note 861689: CATS Approval with CAPS—Performance Problem
- Note 555947: PS/PM: Confirmation by CATS (Consulting note)
- Note 737423: Multiple work items created in CATS approval workflow
- Note 875790: RCATS_DISPLAY_ACTIVITIES - Memory Overflow
- Note 887925: CATS Reporting—Document flow analysis
- Note 304647: Purpose of transactions CATSXT and CATSXC
- Note 1019376: ESS CATS: worklist becomes un-protected
- Note 871197: CATS Web Dynpro: Search help fields are not filled
- Note 858985: Deleting F4 help for operation number field on CATS
- Note 951708: CATS: Agent Determination with CATS Workflow tasks
- Note 953722: CATS Approval: Special approval in Web Dynpro
- Note 951884: CAPS: Workitem gets terminated after approval
- Note 1155422: Package:PAOC_FACE_ESS_CATS does not exist ECC 600
- Note 1054953: CATS Web Dynpro:Deactivated absense types remain editable
- Note 1002270: CATS Web Dynpro: Date format error in Details screen
- Note 505134: Analysis report for confirmation
- Note 380282: Confirmation: Analysis for interface with CO
- Note 1142234: CATS_CHECK_INPUT fails for OLC order
- Note 212705: Missing CO docs in confirmation: Correction program
- Note 155282: CO docs for confirmation: Correction program

A.9 Websites

Additional information and the latest news can be found at:

- *http://service.sap.com/cats*
  SAP official website for accessing information regarding CATS
- *http://service.sap.com/erp-hcm*
  SAP official website for accesing information regarding SAP HCM
- *https://www.sdn.sap.com/irj/sdn*
  Access to SAP Developer Network to seek and share information
- *http://help.sap.com/printdocu/core/Print46c/en/data/pdf/CATS/CATS.pdf*
  Standard documentation, providing the CATS basis (release 4.6C) for newbies
- *http://help.sap.com/saphelp_erp60_sp/helpdata/ en/64/400b2b470211d189720000e8322d00/frameset.htm*
  Online official help for CATS (ERP 6.0)
- *http://help.sap.com/saphelp_erp2004/helpdata/ en/64/400b2b470211d189720000e8322d00/frameset.htm*
  Online official help for CATS (ERP 5.0)
- *http://help.sap.com/saphelp_470/helpdata/ en/64/400b2b470211d189720000e8322d00/frameset.htm*
  Online official help for CATS (R/3 Enterprise 4.70)
- *http://it.toolbox.com/wiki/index. php/Setup_the_CATS_-_Cross_Application_Time_Sheet*
  I have compiled a blog where we can all add and share CATS knowledge
- *http://www.hrexpertonline.com/downloads/Manuel% 20Gallardo%20Sample%20CATS%20user%20exit%20code.txt*
  Further to Manuel Gallardo's article in HR Expert, download free sample ABAP code for CATS user exits CATS0002, CATS0003, CATS0004, CATS0006, CATS0009, and CATS0010
- *http://www.workflowbook.com/*
  It provides insight information regarding Workflow
- *http://www.workflowbook.com/TransactionIndex.pdf*
  It provides a free guide of Workflow transactions and reports

A.10 Recommended Readings

A.10.1 Recommended Articles

- "Always Land on Your Feet with This Introduction to CATS" by Martin Gillet
  http://www.hrexpertonline.com/archive/Volume_05_(2007)/Issue_02_(March)/V5I2A1.cfm?session=

- "Improve Data Entry Efficiency with CATS User Exits" by Manuel Gallardo
  http://www.hrexpertonline.com/archive/Volume_05_(2007)/Issue_03_(April)/V5I3A2.cfm?session=

- "Load Time Data from an External System Into CATS with Ease" by Manuel Gallardo
  http://www.hrexpertonline.com/archive/Volume_06_(2008)/Issue_02_(March)/V6I2A2.cfm?session=

- "Use Standard SAP to Restrict Access in a CATS Implementation" by Deepankar Maitra
  http://www.hrexpertonline.com/archive/Volume_02_(2004)/Issue_08_(October)/V2I8A4.cfm?session=

A.10.2 Recommended Books

- *Configure and Use CATS* by Manuel Gallardo
  http://www.sap-press.com/product.cfm?account=&product=H2990
  Provides more information for tuning CATS closer to business requirements

- *Practical Workflow for SAP* by Alan Rickayzen et al
  http://www.sap-press.com/product.cfm?account=&product=H950
  Provides insight information on how to setup workflow

B   Frequently Asked Questions

Here are answers to some of the most common questions regarding CATS integration.

Q: *What is CATS?*
A: CATS stands for the Cross Application Time Sheet. It allows time collection for labor times among all SAP components except the Production Planning (PP), which deals with machine times.

Q: *What should I remember when upgrading a system to a newer release?*
A: Be sure to transfer all time entries to avoid inconsistencies once the new release is live. This will save time otherwise spent in fixing inconsistencies.

Q: *How can I delete data from CATS that has been already transferred into target module(s)?*
A: For all the target modules (HR, PS, CS, PM, CO), except MM, cancel in CATS the time entries that you want to cancel. For MM, the time entries have to be canceled directly in the target component.

Q: *How do I restrict the content of the table containing the CATS profiles?*
A: Maintain a view on the table, using the TCATS-VARIANT. This will ensure that all the users won't see the entire table content.

Q: *How can I enable CATS through the company intranet?*
A: There are two options:

- You can use the CATS ESS service CATW (this requires an Internet Transaction Server — ITS).
- You can use the latest Web Application Server (WAS) and integrate the ESS service CATW into the SAP Enterprise Portal (EP).

Q: *How do I enable CATS through the Internet?*
A: Set the ESS service CATW and update the R/3 backend accordingly. Since this will be Web-enabled, clearance from the security department will be required to allow access from outside the company's premises.

Q: *How do I check the relevant time status for my time entries?*
A: In the R/3 system, check the field status. On the intranet/Internet, check the traffic light (orange = ending for action, red = rejected, green = approved).

B | Frequently Asked Questions

Q: *How do I identify the lack of authorization for a manager wanting to approve data?*
A: Use the standard transaction SU53 to identify the authorization missing from your profile. Ask your system administrators to update your profile.

> **Tip**
>
> Once an employee changes from one position to another, set the parameter ADAYS in table T77S0 to 15. This will allow a 15-day tolerance so that both the sending and receiving managers can still see the employee in their reporting structure.

Q: *How do I change the CATS field name in the system: e. g., Jean-Marie Dupont to Dupont Jean-Marie (useful for Microsoft Excel downloading)?*
A: Use the customizing option NAME FORMAT provided in the customizing tree. Apply it in the employee's Infotype 0002 — Personal Details.

Q: *What are the CATS infotypes?*
A: On top of the SAP Human Resources Mini Master, SAP provides the Infotype 0315 – CATS default. This infotype stores the default values when dealing with time collection.

Virtual Infotypes 0316 and 0328 are also delivered for authorization purposes only. The fact that these two infotypes are virtual means that they exist for technical reasons and can therefore not be maintained through functional transactions such as PA30 – Maintain Data.

Q: *What are the most used user parameters for CATS?*
A: CVR for defaulting the CATS profile, PER for defaulting the Personnel Number, SAZ for defaulting the time administrator, SGR for defaulting the time administrator group.

Q: *Is it possible to add more than 10 additional fields in CATS?*
A: Even if it is possible to add more than 10 fields in the Customer Include (CI) of the CATSDB Structure, the 10 additional fields are hard coded by SAP when assigning the fields to the CATS data entry profile. It is therefore not possible in SAP to add more than 10 additional fields.

Q: *Does CATS provide an online version?*
A: Yes, depending on the SAP release you are using, you can consider the web service CATW for time collection up to release 4.70 (R/3 enterprise) and the Web Dynpro for time collection as of release ERP 5.0. As of ERP 6.0, SAP also provides the Web Dynpro for the approval screen.

Frequently Asked Questions | B

Q: *When accessing CATS in the Employee Self-Services (ESS) or the Manager Self-Services (MSS), we get the critical error message "User SAMPLE does not exist in this period." What's wrong?*
A: No matter who is connecting in the SAP system through the portal — the Employee or the Manager — each SAP userid must be mapped with a personnel number. This is achieved through the infotype – 0105 – Communication, subtype 0001 – SAP Userid. Check that this infotype exists for the relevant time period.

You can use the transaction HRUSER to view in mass the infotype 0105 and the user mappings.

For the managers, you must also be sure that in the Organizational Management, they are also assigned as managers (relationship A/B 012 in the Organizational Structure).

Q: *In the new Web Dynpro for the time collection for the Employee, we can only see a weekly and daily view, even if in customizing we have set up different time periods.*
A: Unfortunately, regarding the Employee Time collection Web Dynpro, customizing settings have no impact as SAP only provides in standard the weekly and daily view.

Q: *In CATS R/3, we can book time on behalf of several persons, for example, based on the cost center of the time administrators. How do we enable this for the online version?*
A: Unfortunately, SAP does not provide an online version for multiple time entries. It seems logical as CATS time entries are booked through the Employee Self Services (ESS), which only allows one personnel number against a SAP userid. The workarounds are (from favorite option to least favorite option):

- Enable Employee Self-Services (ESS) through Manager Self-Services (MSS). Managers can then book time on behalf of their teammates.
- Develop your own ABAP or Java Web Dynpro to meet this requirement.
- If you have enabled the Adobe Server (ADS), develop your own pdf-based file for time entries.
- Web enable, through webgui, the CATS multiple time entries screen in the portal.
- Web enable, through webgui, the Time Manager Workplace functionality in the portal.

Q: *We are planning to upgrade our SAP core component. Any side impact you would know about?*
A: No side impact is reported. Nonetheless, to be on the safe side, always approve and transfer all time activities from the CATSDB.

Q: *Our development team found out that there are additional CATS infotypes, such as HRP5587. What are these used for?*
A: When Customer Relationship Management (CRM) is in use, it needs to compile this HR information. The CRM system must be prepared for this new information! SAP made available in standard the following HR-PA infotypes in the CRM system: 0000, 0001, 0002, 0006, 0009, 0105, 0315. The HR-infotype 0000 corresponds to the CRM-infotype 5580, 0001 corresponds to 5581, 0002 corresponds to 5582, 0006 corresponds to 5583, 0009 corresponds to 5584, 0105 corresponds to 5585, 0315 corresponds to 5587.

More information can be read in the cookbook (OSS note 758426 - HR-ALX: Enhancement of the ALE value distribution), section 4.2.2.

Q: *We have upgraded to ERP 6.0. All our workflows are down when it used to work just fine in ERP 5.0 and under. What's wrong?*
A: As of SAP release ERP 6.0, SAP has released new workflow tasks, which replace the 'old' ones. Kindly read the online documentation provided by SAP as well as the OSS note 951708 - CATS: Agent Determination with CATS Workflow tasks (ERP 6.0).

Q: *CATS Tasks won't start, what's wrong. What do I start to check?*
A: Here are a few checks to start with. First, check that the user is correctly mapped to a personnel number through infotype 0105 – Communication, subtype 0001 – SAP Userid. Then, as illustrated in Chapter 2, check if the tasks is the correct one, against the SAP release used. Check then if the tasks is active. Check also if the buffer of the Organizational Structure has been refreshed (transaction code SWU_OBUF).

Q: *When using CATS Web Dynpro, the time entries are displayed with the unit of measurement in the internal format. What do we do?*
A: Excellent question, this is a bug. Currently, there is no released OSS note regarding this issue. The class CL_XSS_CAT_OUTPUT_CONVERTER must be corrected by SAP. Stand by for SAP correction delivery. Also, monitor the availability of these OSS notes:

1225349 CATS WD:Unit of Measurement in the internal format
1163465 CATS WD:Unit of Measurement in the internal format

These OSS notes are still under pilot release, as of September 2008. This means that regular customers have no access to them until "pilot customers" have acknowledged the solution provided by SAP. It will then be available to regular customers.

Q: *Approval transactions are taking a very long time.*
A: Perhaps ask your development team to archive the CATSDB with old records (for example, from two years ago and more). Perhaps ask them as well to set indexes in the Database so that standard reports and transactions will go through the CATSDB faster.

C   Bibliography

- CA500 training material release 4.6C: Material Number 50043486, 2000.
- Cross Application Time Sheet (CATS): Release 4.6C, 4.70, ERP 5.0 and ERP 6.0 Online Help, 2001.
- SAP Labs Inc., *R/3 Authorization Made Easy 4.6A/B* (Johnson Printing Service, 2000).
- IBM Business Consulting GmbH, *SAP Authorization System* (SAP PRESS, 2003).
- Rickayzen, et al, *Practical Workflow for SAP* (SAP PRESS, 2002).
- "Always Land on Your Feet with This Introduction to CATS," by Martin Gillet *(http://www.hrexpertonline.com/archive/Volume_05_(2007)/Issue_02_(March)/V5I2A1.cfm?session=)*
- "Improve Data Entry Efficiency with CATS User Exits," by Manuel Gallardo *(http://www.hrexpertonline.com/archive/Volume_05_(2007)/Issue_03_(April)/V5I3A2.cfm?session=)*

Index

A

Absence Quotas, 93
Absences, 96
Accounting, 19
Accounting Variant, 30
Actions, 87
Administrator, 29, 88
approval, 177, 181
Archiving, 198
Attendances, 97
Authorization, 24, 27, 59, 161
Authorization Reporting, 202

B

BAdI, 78, 79, 81, 217
BAPI , 79, 81, 215
buffer the organizational structure, 42
Business Application Program Interface, 77
Business Information Warehouse, 15
BW, 77

C

CATC, 174
CATS profile, 25
CATW, 44, 221, 222
Communication, 26, 163
Configuration Assistant, 212
Controlling, 17, 63, 85, 106, 107, 121, 126, 147, 159
Controlling Transfer, 124
Cost accounting variant, 30
cost center, 30, 112, 167
Customer Fields Enhancements, 72
Customer Functions, 76
Customer Service, 17, 126, 127
Customer-Specific Text Fields in Data-Entry Profile, 75
Customer-Specific Text Fields in Worklist, 76
Customizing, 21

D

Data-Entry Section, 43
Deactivate Functions in the User Interface, 70
Determine the Target Hours, 66

E

Employee's Remuneration Statement, 98
Employee Listing, 167
enhancements, 65
Enterprise structure, 88
ESS, 44, 51, 54, 221
ESS Profile, 44
External Services, 17
External Services Management, 149, 150

F

Finance, 85, 106
Finance & Controlling, 203
Financial Accounting, 109, 118, 126
Financials, 19

H

help entries, 55
Hide Fields, 44
HR Master Data, 161
Human Resources, 16, 19, 83, 105, 109, 115, 126, 147, 152, 203

Index

I

Implementation Guide, 21
infotype, 83
Integration Overview, 16
interface tables, 16
Internet Transaction Server, 15, 221

M

maintenance order, 130, 132
Master Data, 168
Material Management, 19, 148, 149, 204
Material Management transfer, 158
messages, 69, 207
Mini Master Data, 152

O

Organizational, 30
Organizational Assignment, 111
Organizational Management, 99, 170
Organizational Plan, 88
Organizational Structure, 111

P

Payroll, 105, 109, 155, 156
Personal Data, 89
Personnel Actions, 152
Personnel Administration, 83, 85, 99, 111
personnel area, 85, 167
Personnel Development, 83, 99, 111
Personnel structure, 88
Personnel Time Management, 129, 141
Person Selection, 28
plan data for activity types, 115
Plan Maintenance Transfer, 137
Planned Working Time, 92
Plant Maintenance, 17, 19, 126
Plant Maintenance & Customer Service, 203

printing, 35
Project Builder, 142
Project Management, 141
Project System, 17, 19, 138, 140, 148, 158, 203
Purchase Order, 150

R

Rejection Reasons, 61
Reporting, 167

S

SAP Enterprise Portal, 11, 15, 221
Service Management, 19
Service Provider, 17
Settings, 43
Structures, 208
Subscreen on Data-Entry Screen, 77
Subscreen on the Initial Screen, 73
Supplement Recorded Data, 67
system status, 132

T

Tables, 208
target module, 221
Technical Overview, 15
The Company Code, 85
Time Evaluation, 105, 155, 156
time management, 105, 109
to create an infotype, 143
Travel Expenses, 181, 183, 185, 190
Travel Management, 18

U

user parameter, 26
Users ESS, 203

V

Validate Entire Time Sheet, 73
Validate Recorded Data, 68

W

WEB, 50
Web Application Server, 221

Websites, 218
Web Time Sheet, 44
Work Breakdown Structure, 138, 139, 143
Work Center, 127, 139
workflow, 35
Workflow Recipient for Approval, 74
Working Times, 181, 183
worklist, 32, 33, 43, 67

www.sap-press.com

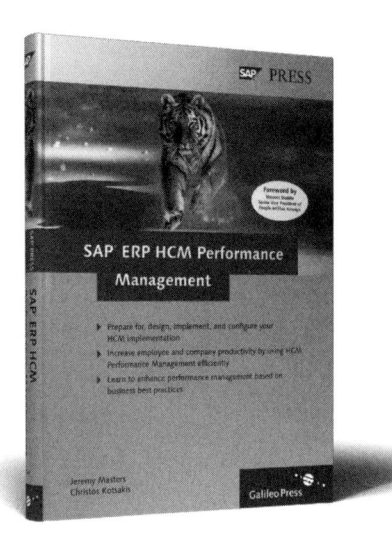

Prepare for, design, implement, and configure your HCM implementation

Increase employee and company productivity by using HCM Performance Management efficiently

Learn to enhance performance management based on business best practices

Jeremy Masters, Christos Kotsakis

SAP ERP HCM Performance Management

From Design to Implementation

This comprehensive book is an indispensable reference for HR professionals, analysts, and consultants learning how to implement SAP ERP HCM Performance Management. The book teaches you everything you need to know about the Objective Setting and Appraisal (OSA) module within SAP so that you can identify and retain key talent within your organization. You'll take a step-by-step journey through the design and implementation of your own performance management application that will help you improve your companies' performance and talent management processes. The book covers all the latest releases, including the R/3 Enterprise Release (4.7), SAP ERP 2004 (ECC 5.0) and SAP ERP 2005 (ECC 6.0).

302 pp., 2008, 69,95 Euro / US$ 69.95
ISBN 978-1-59229-124-3

>> www.sap-press.de/1421

SAP PRESS

www.sap-press.com

- Provides a complete guide to configuring CATS
- Covers all essential CATS enhancements and User-Exits
- Includes user-exit sample code, a sample program for loading external CATS data, and a configuration assistant tool on the website

Manuel Gallardo

Configuring and Using CATS

SAP PRESS Essentials 51

This Essentials is a complete guide to effectively configuring CATS to meet your business needs. It provides detailed explanations of items to consider before beginning an implementation, along with steps for setting up CATS to fulfill the many complex configuration requirements. It also includes details about each CATS user-exit and tips on what functionality can or cannot be accomplished with particular user-exits. In addition, explanations for how to prevent and correct performance problems, answers to frequently asked questions, and tips for audit report development are provided.

approx. 160 pp., 68,– Euro / US$ 85
ISBN 978-1-59229-232-5, Oct 2008

>> www.sap-press.de/1864

SAP PRESS

www.sap-press.com

Learn how to implement and configure the SAP US Benefits Module

Work through the entire employee life cycle from enrollment to COBRA

Explore practical scenarios and examples to guide your own benefits processes

Satish Badgi

Configuring US Benefits with SAP

SAP PRESS Essentials 40

Configuring SAP US Benefits is a comprehensive, hands-on approach to configuring SAP's US Benefits module. The book is written for payroll and benefits departments using SAP (power users), project teams, aspiring consultants, off-shore and outsourced benefit administrators, and benefit providers using or interacting with SAP customers. It provides the foundation for the entire benefits process of the employee lifecycle from enrollment, benefits changes, and FSA and Claims processing to termination and COBRA. In addition, the book details the US-specific benefits plans and teaches benefits managers how to configure them for their companies. Practical scenarios and examples are used throughout, including differentiating benefits by geography, unions, and employee groups; driving costs based on coverage and options; driving costs by groupings such as age and salary; enrollment changes and their impact within 30/60 days of life events; default plans vs. automatic plans; driving Infotype 0171 (defaults for groupings); and life events and benefit changes.

75 pp., 2008, 68,– Euro / US$ 85, ISBN 978-1-59229-164-9

>> www.sap-hefte.de/1608

www.sap-press.com

Provides an overview of ESS and MSS, what it is, how it has evolved over the years, and how it fits into an HR Service Delivery model

Covers the fundamentals of implementing SAP ESS/MSS, including the Homepage Framework and integration with the SAP NetWeaver Portal

Provides an overview of Duet™ focusing on key areas, and provides a roadmap of future releases/functionality.

Uses ECC 6.0 and SAP NetWeaver Portal 7.0

Jeremy Masters, Christos Kotsakis

Implementing Employee and Manager Self-Services in SAP ERP HCM

Written for HR managers, power users, IT professionals, and consultants, this is the first comprehensive guide to what Employee and Manager self services (ESS & MSS) are all about. Not only does it explain ESS & MSS, but it also teaches how to implement an effective strategy in SAP ERP HCM. The book details the baseline ESS/MSS functionality in SAP's latest release (ECC 6.0) using NetWeaver Portal (EP 7.0. It also covers more advanced topics like developing self-service applications with the Floor Plan Manager, authorization management (i.e., security), workflow, and delegation. In addition, Duet™ is used as the example of an intuitive (and familiar) user interface. The book concludes with real-world case studies as examples of effective ESS/MSS applications currently in use.

approx. 432 pp., 69,95 Euro / US$ 69.95
ISBN 978-1-59229-188-5, Nov 2008

>> www.sap-press.de/1682

SAP PRESS

www.sap-press.com

Provides a complete guide to Organizational Management (OM) with SAP ERP HCM

Teaches all functions of OM from a global perspective

Includes practical integration and customizing tips and techniques

Sylvia Chaudoir

Mastering SAP ERP HCM Organizational Management

This book teaches the HCM team how to maximize the organizational management (OM) component of SAP ERP HCM. It takes readers beyond the basics, by delving into all aspects of the component as well as the little-known concepts. It teaches all of the key OM functions, their purpose, and how to use and customize them. Numerous examples from customers are used to provide context for decisions and to explain the benefits of the choices that can be made. And in-depth explanations and practical examples are used to help readers leverage the many available organizational objects to get the most out of their SAP HR implementation.

348 pp., 2008, 69,95 Euro / US$ 69.95
ISBN 978-1-59229-208-0

>> www.sap-press.de/1796

SAP PRESS

www.sap-press.com

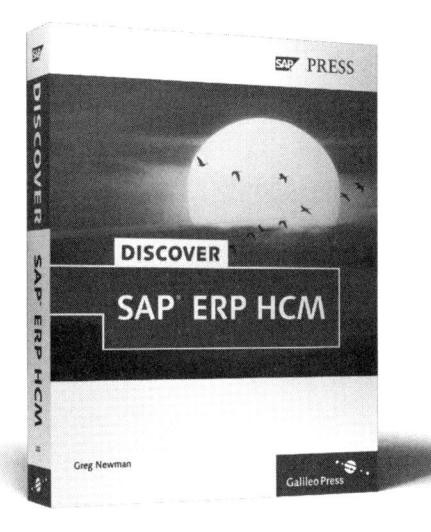

Teaches readers what SAP ERP HCM is and how it can benefit their company

Provides a detailed overview of all core functionality

Includes practical insights and real-world case studies to show HCM at work

Greg Newman

Discover SAP ERP HCM

This book is an insightful, detailed guide to what SAP ERP HCM is all about and how it can make companies more effective in managing their own HR processes. The book details all of the major components of SAP HCM, explaining the purpose of the components, how they work, their features and benefits and their integration with other components. It uses real-world examples throughout to demonstrate the uses, benefits, and issues encountered by existing SAP HCM users to ground the book in reality rather than just marketing hype. After reading this book, readers will have a broad understanding of SAP's HCM offering and insight into existing customer experiences with the product.

approx. 400 pp., 39,95 Euro / US$ 39.95
ISBN 978-1-59229-222-6, Dec 2008

>> www.sap-press.de/1846

SAP PRESS

www.sap-press.com

Learn how to set up the Time Management to meet your business needs

Explore configuration and customization options

Find out how to use Infotypes and BAdIs to streamline and integrate cost-intensive processes

Brian Schaer

Time Management with SAP ERP HCM

This book provides a detailed guide to understanding, implementing, and configuring the Time Management component of SAP ERP HCM. It teaches readers the core topics of Time Management and provides the foundational information they need for implementing and configuring the business requirements. It also provides insight into some of the more advanced topics, such as process flows.

approx. 500 pp., 69,95 Euro / US$ 69.95
ISBN 978-1-59229-229-5, Dec 2008

>> www.sap-press.de/1848

www.sap-press.com

Provides a complete guide to the functionality of E-Recruiting

Teaches how to configure and use E-Recruiting with other HCM components

Uses a real-world workflow approach

Ben Hayes

E-Recruiting with SAP ERP HCM

This book provides a practical guide to configuring and using SAP E-Recruitment effectively in the real-world. It is written to teach SAP ERP HCM users and the implementation team what the E-Recruiting tool is so that they can use it effectively in their recruitment process and integrate it easily with other HCM components. Beginning with an overview, the book progresses through the configuration process from a real workflow perspective. And all of the processes are covered in the order in which they are used in a real recruiting project. The book also details how to integrate E-Recruiting with other SAP components, and, as applicable, examples of companies using E-Recruiting successfully will be integrated throughout.

approx. 320 pp., 69,90 Euro / US$ 69.95
ISBN 978-1-59229-243-1, Jan 2009

>> www.sap-press.de/1957

SAP PRESS

ISBN 978-1-59229-260-8

© 2009 by Galileo Press Inc., Boston (MA)
2nd Edition, updated and revised

Galileo Press is named after the Italian physicist, mathematician and philosopher Galileo Galilei (1564–1642). He is known as one of the founders of modern science and an advocate of our contemporary, heliocentric worldview. His words *Eppur si muove* (And yet it moves) have become legendary. The Galileo Press logo depicts Jupiter orbited by the four Galilean moons, which were discovered by Galileo in 1610.

Editor   Justin Lowry
Copyeditor   Justin Lowry
Cover Design   Jill Winitzer
Photo Credit   Image Copyright TebNad, 2008. Used under license from Shutterstock.com.
Layout Design   Vera Brauner
Production   Kelly O'Callaghan
Typesetting   Publishers' Design and Production Services, Inc.
Printed and bound in Canada

All rights reserved. Neither this publication nor any part of it may be copied or reproduced in any form or by any means or translated into another language, without the prior consent of Galileo Press GmbH, Rheinwerkallee 4, 53227 Bonn, Germany.

Galileo Press makes no warranties or representations with respect to the content hereof and specifically disclaims any implied warranties of merchantability or fitness for any particular purpose. Galileo Press assumes no responsibility for any errors that may appear in this publication.

"Galileo Press" and the Galileo Press logo are registered trademarks of Galileo Press GmbH, Bonn, Germany. SAP PRESS is an imprint of Galileo Press.

All of the screenshots and graphics reproduced in this book are subject to copyright © SAP AG, Dietmar-Hopp-Allee 16, 69190 Walldorf, Germany.

SAP, the SAP-Logo, mySAP, mySAP.com, mySAP Business Suite, SAP NetWeaver, SAP R/3, SAP R/2, SAP B2B, SAPtronic, SAPscript, SAP BW, SAP CRM, SAP Early Watch, SAP ArchiveLink, SAP GUI, SAP Business Workflow, SAP Business Engineer, SAP Business Navigator, SAP Business Framework, SAP Business Information Warehouse, SAP inter-enterprise solutions, SAP APO, AcceleratedSAP, InterSAP, SAPoffice, SAPfind, SAPfile, SAPtime, SAPmail, SAP¬access, SAP-EDI, R/3 Retail, Accelerated HR, Accelerated HiTech, Accelerated Consumer Products, ABAP, ABAP/4, ALE/WEB, BAPI, Business Framework, BW Explorer, Enjoy-SAP, mySAP.com e-business platform, mySAP Enterprise Portals, RIVA, SAPPHIRE, TeamSAP, Webflow und SAP PRESS are registered or unregistered trademarks of SAP AG, Walldorf, Germany.

All other products mentioned in this book are registered or unregistered trademarks of their respective companies.

Interested in reading more?

Please visit our Web site for all
new book releases from SAP PRESS.

www.sap-press.com